Turkey Tracks

From Hatch to Harvest

by Ransom Jones

A complete textbook on
the wild turkey and its hunting

Copyright (c) 1995 by Ransom Jones

All rights reserved. No part of this book may be reproduced or transmitted in any form or by any means, electronic or mechanical, including photocopying, recording or by any information storage and retrieval system without permission in writing from the publisher.

ISBN 0-936513-08-X

Library of Congress 95-80183

Published by:
LARSEN'S OUTDOOR PUBLISHING

Distributed by:

BRELL MAR PRODUCTS, INC.
Manufacturer of
Hide um Hunter (R) Blinds and Safety Harness
Johnny Reb (R) Marine Products
Amacker (R) Tree Stands
Preston Pittman Game Calls
113 Boyce Drive, Brookhaven, MS 39601
(601)833-2050

PRINTED IN THE UNITED STATES OF AMERICA

1 2 3 4 5 6 7 8 9 10

HUNTING THE WILD TURKEY IN THE 1950'S

My first experience hunting the wild turkey with my Uncle Rodney in the 1950's was at a time when:

1) The only turkey call was a snuff can, wing bone, a homemade slate call with a corncob striker, and if you were lucky, you owned a box call;

2) No one had a four-wheel drive vehicle. You walked;

3) There were no ATV's. If you had a horse or a mule, you could ride it;

4) No one had a pump or semi-automatic shotgun. Everyone shot a single or double barrel shotgun;

5) There was no insect repellent known to us. We sprayed ourselves with DDT;

6) There was no commercial camouflage on the market;

7) Shotgun shells were made out of paper. If they got wet while they were in your gun, they would swell up and you could not get them out of your gun. If they got wet before you put them in your gun, they would swell up and you could not get the shell in your gun;

8) Many people used carbide lights rather than flashlights;

9) There were no turkey decoys; and,

10) Worst of all, there were not very many wild turkeys.

-- Ransom Jones

4   *Turkey Tracks*

DEDICATION

To Charles Rodney McMichael, my uncle, the best turkey hunter I ever knew and the person who taught me how to turkey hunt; to my brother, Charles Jones, who has been a lifetime hunting partner; and to my two children, Sali and Rance, whom I love more than life itself.

Charles Rodney McMichael, Deceased, my uncle, the best turkey hunter I ever knew, and the person who taught me how to turkey hunt.

CONTENTS

Hunting The Wild Turkey In The 1950's 3
Dedication 5
About The Author 9
Acknowledgments 13
Foreword 17

1. Introduction 19
2. About The Turkey 23
3. Safely Hunting The Turkey 37
4. Ethics 49
5. Turkey Hunting Equipment 67
6. Scouting And Preparation For The Hunt 89
7. Hunting The Wild Turkey 117
8. Turkey Responds On The Roost 135
9. Roosted Turkey That Will Not Gobble 161
10. The Morning You Do Not Hear A Turkey Gobble .. 165
11. Calling 193
12. After The Shot 203
13. Sub Species Of The Wild Turkey 205
14. The National Wild Turkey Federation 221
15. Conclusion 233

Appendices
A. Glossary of Terms 249
B. References 255
C. Don't Take A Jake 257
D. The Wild Turkey 265

ABOUT THE AUTHOR

The author has been involved in wild game hunting, conservation of wildlife and education of the public through various media outlets. He is the former anchor of the Escude Outdoor Show broadcast in the mid-1980's in the Jackson County, Mississippi viewing area and is a former outdoor columnist for The Mississippi Press serving the Mississippi Gulf Coast area. He has also authored articles for the Southern Whitetail Journal. Jones has over forty years experience as a hunter and has hunted the wild turkey in Mississippi, Florida, Alabama, Texas, Louisiana, Kansas, New Mexico, South Dakota, Wyoming, South Carolina and Oklahoma. He has also hunted in Tennessee, Colorado, Kentucky, Michigan and Montana. Jones has given lectures on hunting the whitetail deer, the wild turkey and bass fishing.

The author has been a professional turkey hunting guide. He has guided turkey hunts in Florida for the Osceola turkey, in Mississippi for the Eastern turkey, and in Texas and Oklahoma for the Rio Grande turkey. As a guide and pursuing the sport of turkey hunting on his own, the author has also been a video cameraman on many turkey hunts for all four of the subspecies of the wild turkey located in the United States, and has completed a Grand Slam of those four subspecies.

The author served two terms as the President of the Mississippi Still Hunters' Association and has served on the Board of Directors of the Mississippi Still Hunters' Association, the Mississippi Wild Turkey Federation and the Mississippi Wildlife Federation. He is a former President of the Singing River Bassmasters, the Jackson County Chapter of the Mississippi Still Hunters' Association and holds a lifetime membership with the National Wild Turkey Federation and the Mississippi Wildlife Federation. In 1978, he was the National Champion of the American Angler Team Fishing Tournament held on Toledo Bend.

The author is also the President and Chairman of the Board of Directors of Preston Pittman Game Calls, Inc. and is a practicing attorney having been admitted to the Bar of the State of Mississippi in 1966. He is also a member of the Board of Directors of Brell-Mar, Inc., manufacturers of Johnny Reb Marine Accessories, Hide-Um-Hunter Hunting Accessories and Amacker Tree Stands, and is also a member of the Board of Directors for Indian Archery Outfitting. He is listed in Who's Who in American Professional Excellence, Who's Who Among Mississippi Lawyers, and is a member of the Mississippi Trial Lawyers Association, the American Trial Lawyers Association and the Fifth Circuit Court of Appeals Bar Association.

The Author

The author with mounts of his Grand Slam. The bottom left is the Osceola, top left is the Merriam, bottom right is the Eastern, and top right is the Rio Grande.

ACKNOWLEDGMENTS

Dr. George Hurst
Dr. Hurst, in my opinion, is the leading wildlife biologist doing research on the wild turkey in the United States of America. His research at Mississippi State University is invaluable in conserving the wild turkey. Dr. Hurst assisted in writing the biology section of this book and made certain that the contents of that section are accurate.

David Godwin
David is a wildlife biologist with the Mississippi Department of Wildlife, Fisheries & Parks. He made some excellent suggestions included in this book concerning predation of the wild turkey, especially making the distinction between nest predators and brood hen predators.

Mike "Rainman" Lambeth
Mike wrote the foreword for this book and has been a hunting companion in the past, will be in the future and is a good friend.

Paul Rishel
Paul proposed several questions to me that had been asked of him about the wild turkey, and those questions

gave me many ideas about what turkey hunters want to know. As a result, much of what is in this book came from the questions asked by Paul.

Tommy Bourne

Tommy contributed two excellent stories that can be used as examples of different tactics employed in hunting the wild turkey. Tommy is a great hunter, a great turkey caller, and a very good friend.

Thomas Neuberger

Thomas Neuberger taught me a great deal about decoy placement. He is an excellent turkey hunter and a good hunting partner and an all-around good guy.

Troy Ruiz

Troy Ruiz - the best videographer I have ever met. He hunts a turkey with a camera better than most people can hunt them with a gun. You have to know Troy to appreciate his enthusiasm, desire, endurance and ability. Troy contributed the picture of the turkey nests in the book. He is one of the most dependable people I know.

Verona Inabinette

Verona helped get many of the photos used in this book and made some great suggestions that are included in the book, including the title. Although she is just learning to turkey hunt, she is becoming an excellent turkey hunter.

Walt Larsen

Walt did a great job in suggesting the design of the cover of this book. Walt also read the manuscript and made many suggestions that are incorporated, and for that I will be forever grateful.

David Rainer
David is an outdoor writer who took the time to read this manuscript and make some suggestions about how it should read. David also sent me a number of photographs and gave me permission to use any or all of them. I have had the privilege to be on the same hunt with David.

John Wood
John is an outdoor writer who contributed to the style of the book. I would like to thank John for taking the time to read this manuscript, and many of the suggestions he made are incorporated in this book. I have had the privilege to hunt with John.

Jennifer Pribanic
Jennifer is a paralegal on my staff who, while performing her duties as a paralegal in my law office, helped prepare the manuscript of this book. She has put as much effort into this book as I have. Without her, this book probably would not have been written.

Thanks to all of the above mentioned people for the valuable contributions they made to this book. All have been of great assistance to me.

Mike "Rainman" Lambeth. My thanks go to Mike for writing the Foreword to this book. Mike is one of my very good friends and one of my turkey hunting partners.

FOREWORD

The name *Meleagris Gallopavo* may remind some people of the scribbled Latin one would expect to find on a doctor's prescription. To scientists and biologists it represents the genus and species of a once diminishing, but now abundant, member of the Aviarian family; but to sportsman and naturalists alike it represents the wild turkey.

The wild turkey is considered by many people to be the grandest bird of all. Because the bird is strong, wary, intelligent - and to a certain extent adaptable - it is to Benjamin Franklin's credit that he thought the bird should be our national Emblem.

The wild turkey family is comprised of six subspecies: the Eastern strain, which inhabit the eastern half of the United States; the Rio Grande, which are primarily found on the plains of Kansas, Oklahoma and Texas; the Merriams, found in the mountain areas in the western half of the United States; the Osceola turkey, found exclusively in the palmetto swamps of Florida; the Goulds variety, which inhabit the deserts in southern Arizona and Mexico; and finally the Jungle Dwelling Oscellated, found in the Yucatan Peninsula of southern Mexico and in some parts of Central America.

In fact, wild turkeys inhabit 49 of the 50 states in the U.S.A. and have successfully been transplanted to inhabit several countries abroad. Whether you're a bird watcher or a hunter the sights and sounds of a wild turkey will stir your emotions and embrace the very essence of nature. Today, wild turkeys thrive thanks to the restocking efforts of the National Wild Turkey Federation and many other sportsmen and conservation groups. This book, though written with the turkey hunter in mind, serves as a complete text on the subject. Whether you are an expert hunter or a beginner, the insight gleaned from this book will improve your knowledge as you gain a perspective on one of God's finest creations.

The author, Ransom Jones, is a dedicated woodsman with a passion for the outdoors. He has spent extensive time researching turkeys for many years. Jones studies and films wild turkeys year round. He has dedicated his life to improve the habitat for turkeys and deer, as well as many nongame species in his home state of Mississippi. Ransom is the President of Preston Pittman Game Calls, as well as a personal friend of mine. Having spent time afield with Jones, and having had lengthy conversations with him over turkeys and turkey hunting, I feel qualified to write this foreword on his behalf.

Ransom Jones is a sportsman in the truest sense. His ethics and standards speak volumes and will be reflected throughout this book. Because of his efforts and groups like the N.W.T.F., future generations will have the privilege of hearing a big tom gobbler greet the morning with a resounding gobble, or perhaps be able to view the majesty of a boss long beard displaying for his hens. May the grandeur of this bird be esteemed highly, and may the legacy of the wild turkey live on forever.

Mike Lambeth

1

INTRODUCTION

Before undertaking to read this book, you need to know that this is nothing more than an accumulation of facts and opinions about the wild turkey and how to hunt the turkey. I believe that the facts contained within these pages are accurate and well documented in scientific data. The opinions contained within the pages of this book are solely mine, some with which you may agree and some with which you may not agree. However, everything in this book is designed to assist you in locating, hunting and harvesting the mature wild turkey gobbler.

In writing this book, I have been mindful of the fact that most hunters are very individualistic and are very opinionated in their approach and methods of hunting various game. Turkey hunters are probably the most dogmatic, opinionated and obstinate of any group of hunters, bar none. The opinions expressed in this book are opinions arrived at after 40 years of personal observations and direct encounters with various wildlife. In addition, I own approximately 4,000 acres of land, on which, the past eight to ten years, I have conducted an extensive management program for the Eastern wild turkey and the white tailed deer. On these 4,000 acres of land, there is no livestock and there is no farming. The only purpose for this land is to hunt the white-tailed deer and the wild turkey, and to manage those animals in the most efficient, biological way. The point is, that the opinions expressed in this book have some basis in my experience and my actual hands-on involvement in the management of wildlife. Those opinions are put here for you to evaluate and reach your own conclusions. You may accept them in <u>toto</u> or you may reject them in <u>toto</u>, or you may accept a portion of them or you may reject a portion of them. But the purpose of putting them on paper is to give you the advantage of the author's experience and what he has learned over many years of being involved with wildlife.

This introduction would be incomplete if I did not tell you that this book is written from the basis that hunting the wild turkey is an individual sport, and one in which, you as an individual, should participate in alone as much as possible. You should read as much as you can about the wild turkey and reach your own conclusions - without the influence of those who have had little or no experience in hunting the wild turkey. You should do all of your own scouting, and read the sign - without being influenced by what that sign means to others. In this way, you learn from your own mistakes and you are not likely to repeat them.

Hunting the wild turkey is the most difficult hunting sport known to humanity. The turkey is probably the most difficult game alive to hunt. He is unpredictable. He has the best eyesight of any critter of the woods and the best hearing. He is prey for a number of animals, which makes him very suspicious of anything he sees in the woods. He is virtually impossible to still hunt or stalk hunt; you must call the wild gobbler to you and that is difficult because that involves reversing nature (which will be treated extensively in this book.) All these factors and others make him the most difficult game to harvest that I have ever hunted.

For these reasons, you should learn to hunt the wild turkey alone. Hunting the wild turkey with a friend, or with other people, just increases your chance of not being able to kill the wild turkey. The more people in the woods, the more likely it is that someone will make a mistake which will prevent you from killing a turkey. The best advice that I can give you is to learn the wild turkey and to hunt alone, and that way you can make all of your own decisions about how you want to hunt without having to accommodate the opinions of anyone else on what you should and should not do in a given circumstance. This book is written for you, as an individual, to teach you, as an individual, what you need to do to become a more proficient turkey hunter. This book is not designed to teach you and your friends how to hunt wild turkeys as a group, and should not be read from that perspective. Once again, if you are going to become a good turkey hunter, it is a sport you have to pursue on your own without the assistance of anyone else. You start learning to hunt the wild turkey on your own by doing all of your own scouting, and by learning to recognize and read turkey sign when you see it.

This book is a textbook on hunting the wild turkey; it is also designed as a storybook to, hopefully, entertain you as well. It deals with the basics and intricacies of turkey hunting. Within the pages of this book there is a discussion of the basic biology of the wild turkey - from the date the turkey hen lays her first egg to the date the poults become mature turkeys. It deals with safety factors you must know in hunting the wild turkey. There is an indepth discussion on each of the following: the ethics of hunting the wild turkey, the equipment you are going to need and how to use that equipment, how to scout for the wild turkey and what to look for while scouting, and how to hunt turkey gobblers of all kinds, whether they gobble or do not gobble; whether they are with or without hens; whether it is morning or afternoon, and whether it is cold, hot, wet, dry, foggy, still, or windy. Finally, there is a discussion of the sub-species of the American wild turkey, with particular emphasis on the four major sub-species located within the continental United States.

If you will read this book as a teaching manual, you will come out a much better turkey hunter and therefore much better prepared to go into the woods. I hope this book will kindle some interest in you for not only hunting the wild turkey, but also for the conservation and preservation of this magnificent bird.

2

ABOUT THE TURKEY

If you are going to hunt the wild turkey, it is absolutely necessary that you know something about him before you hunt him. To completely understand the wild turkey and how he behaves cannot be done without complete knowledge of his existence, from the time he is in the egg until he is an adult gobbler. A complete background on the wild turkey begins with nesting and follows through with the first year of a turkey's life.

Two types of predators have an impact on turkey populations during the nesting season. There are the nest predators, such as the raccoon, opossum, skunk, snakes, and the domestic dog, all of which eat the eggs and destroy the nest. There are also the predators of the brood hen, which include the coyote, fox, bobcat, great horned owl and the domestic dog. Although these predators primarily prey on the hen, they will occasionally eat the eggs. During the first two weeks of a turkey poult's life, these animals can have a significant impact on the survival rate of the poults.

Turkey hens will generally nest in thick areas such as old fields or thickets in forests, where the eggs are concealed. Nests are concealed from the many predators that eat turkey eggs. The raccoon is by far the most destructive animal, while the opossum is probably the second worst enemy of the nesting wild turkey.

The raccoon and the opossum find turkey nests in two ways. Both of these animals roam around the woods at night. In many cases, these animals just happen upon a turkey nest, and help themselves to the eggs. The nest is destroyed before the hen starts to incubate the eggs. After the hen starts to incubate the eggs, sometimes the raccoon and the opossum pick up the scent of the hen on the nest and follow it to the nest. They will flush the hen off the nest and destroy the eggs.

The only natural enemy of the raccoon is the human being, but because there is no longer a demand for raccoon hides, there has been a proliferation of the raccoon population. More raccoons searching for food means more turkey nests are getting destroyed.

The crow is also high on the list of enemies of the wild turkey. A crow will sometimes follow a hen turkey to her nesting area and when she leaves the nest, the crow will attack it. A crow pecks a hole in an egg even though it may not eat it. A crow will eat many eggs when it breaks them open, but the eggs that it does not break open will have holes pecked in the shell, thereby assuring they will not hatch.

Much like the raccoon, opossums and skunks will break many eggs before they have an opportunity to hatch. However, the skunk does not do nearly the amount of damage as the opossum and the raccoon. I have found nests destroyed by raccoons and every egg in the nest would be broken. I have also found nests with eggs intact except for holes pecked in them. Crows had merely pecked one or two holes through the shell of the egg, thereby killing the small turkey inside.

The domestic dog is another enemy of the nesting wild turkey. The dog will generally not break every egg in the nest, but, it does sometimes catch and kill wild turkey hens

A nest of turkey eggs which have been laid in a cutover.

while they are incubating their eggs. Obviously, when this happens, the eggs will not hatch.

Turkeys will lay their eggs in areas where the nest cannot be easily found by these predators, such as cutovers and pine plantations where there is a large amount of undergrowth. Nests are also built in the woods against old logs or at the base of large trees, but many times these nests will not survive predation. Other problems include severe floods in river bottom areas where turkeys have built their nests.

Another factor that affects turkey populations - in conjunction with brood hen predators - is rainfall. When a brood hen gets wet, she has a distinct odor about her (if you have ever smelled wet feathers you are familiar with the smell). Of course, the brood hen predators all have very sensitive noses and can pick up the scent of a wet hen much

About The Turkey 25

easier than that of a dry hen. During nesting seasons with above-average rainfall, predation on the brood hen by fox, bobcat, coyotes and domestic dogs will be greater.

Another important factor is the amount of harassment a turkey hen has while she is incubating her eggs. The more times she is flushed from her nest, the more likely she will abandon it. If predators continually harass a hen while she is nesting, of course she is going to abandon her eggs and the nest will not hatch.

Sometimes, a human being flushing the turkey from her nest once is sufficient to cause the hen to abandon it. If you happen to flush a hen from the nest, do not stop to count the eggs or in any way disturb it because that may cause the hen to abandon it. You certainly do not want to continue to return to that nest and take the chance of continuously flushing the hen off the nest.

If, when you find a nest, the hen is not on it, that does not mean you did not flush the hen off the nest. She probably saw you coming long before you got to the nest and ran off without you even knowing it. So, even under these circumstances, do not spend any time around the nest, and certainly do not disturb the nest in any way.

The mating period for turkeys varies throughout the United States. In the southeast, where the weather gets warm earlier in the spring, the breeding season will sometimes start during the last part of February, and will extend through late April or early May. However, in the southeast, turkeys lay their eggs in April, and the hatch will occur usually in May or early June. In other parts of the United States, where the climate is a little colder, the breeding period will begin in April and will extend through May, and the hatch will take place sometime in late May and into June.

The breeding period for turkeys is easy to determine by the activity of the turkeys themselves. A trip into the woods during the early morning hours will tell you whether or not the breeding period has begun. Normally, the first indication is that the male turkey, commonly referred to as a gobbler, is beginning to gobble on a tree limb during the late winter or early spring. Male turkeys gobble to attract hen turkeys. When the male turkey begins to gobble, he is ready to breed. If he can attract hens to him, he will start breeding. When the breeding period is at its peak, the gobbler will be gobbling and the hens will be calling to the gobbler. This activity begins with the gobbler gobbling on the roost early in the morning before he flies off the roost and having hens respond to his gobble by calling back to him. On many occasions, I have seen a gobbler remain in a tree for two or three hours after daylight gobbling every time he heard a hen cluck, purr, yelp, cackle or cut.

The gobbler, in many instances, will remain in the tree until he sees the hen pass under it. Then he will pitch out of the tree to the hen and will commence the courtship. This courtship usually consists of gobbling to attract more hens, going into a full strut with his feathers fluffed out all over his body, and his head pulled close into his body with his tail feathers in a complete fan. The gobbler will continue to do this until the hen submits to him.

Once the hen has been bred, she will generally leave the gobbler in his strutting area and he will continue to gobble. However, I have observed gobblers following hens through the woods or in open fields. This usually occurs when the gobbler has more than one hen with him and is able to attract a half dozen or more. In many instances, before he has bred the hens, he will follow them around in the woods hoping to get them to submit to him. In every instance I have observed this behavior, the gobbler has remained in a full strut for long periods of time dragging his wings on the ground, doing what is known as drumming, which is a spitting sound and a low hum. This spitting sound is a vocalization made by the turkey, but the humming sound is either a vocalization or is caused from the vibration of his feathers while he is in a full strut. It is not known for sure just how this sound is made. This activity will eventually cause the hens to submit to him.

When a hen is ready to be bred, she will squat on the ground with her breast on the ground and her feet folded up beneath her. At this point, the gobbler will walk up on the hen's back, and will, in most instances, use his beak to grab the skin on the head of the hen and will then breed the hen.

The breeding process may not take more than thirty seconds or a minute. I have seen it last longer than that. But, usually after the turkey gobbler mounts the hen, the breeding process is over very quickly. One time, I observed three gobblers and five hens in a strutting area. Apparently, the boss gobbler was in a full strut walking around the five hens, and periodically one of the hens would squat and the boss gobbler would breed her. Only the dominant gobbler bred the hens while the other two gobblers walking in a full strut observed. In each case, as the gobbler finished breeding a hen, the hen would get up, shake herself off and walk away. None of the hens left the area until the boss gobbler had bred them all. When the last hen was bred, the five hens went off in one direction and the three gobblers left together in the opposite direction.

Within a few days after the hen has mated with the gobbler, she will commence laying her eggs. She will lay one egg per day, every day, until an entire clutch of eggs has been laid. The clutch may consist of eight to fifteen eggs. After the hen completes laying the eggs, she will then begin to set or incubate them for about twenty-eight days, at which time the eggs will begin to hatch. There is something very unique about the way a turkey's nest hatches out. Even though all the eggs were not laid on the same day and there may be a ten to twelve day span between the first egg and the last egg, all eggs hatch within twenty-four hours.

The eggs of the wild turkey are easily recognizable. They are slightly larger than a chicken egg and they are basically white in color with brown spots on them. The spots on the egg are very small, which makes the egg a white and brown speckled color.

Keep in mind that a single breeding of a hen by a mature gobbler is sufficient to fertilize every egg she will lay during the spring season. A single breeding is sufficient for a renesting attempt by a turkey hen in the event it becomes necessary for her to lay a second clutch of eggs. This occurs when the first clutch is destroyed by a predator or by a natural disaster, such as flood or snow. Hens may lay fertile eggs up to four weeks after the first breeding - even though hens may be bred every day during the spring breeding season (Dickson 87).

There is a misconception among some turkey hunters that turkey hens will hatch two different clutches of eggs in the same season. This misconception stems from seeing small poult turkeys late in the summer. What has actually happened is that the turkey hen's first nest was either destroyed by predators or by some natural disaster late in the incubation process and before any of the eggs could hatch. When that happens, the turkey hen will build a new nest and lay a second clutch. The second clutch will normally contain fewer eggs than the first clutch. Of course, after the hen finishes laying, she then has to incubate those eggs for about twenty-eight days until they hatch. When this happens, it is not unusual to see very small poult turkeys from mid-July to mid-August.

Many people who have seen this believe that the turkey hen they see with the small poults in August has already raised a group of poults and has renested. This is not the case. What has happened is what has been described above - either a predator has destroyed her nest, or some natural disaster destroyed her nest and she renested and successfully hatched a clutch of eggs. If there was a large natural disaster in a particular area, you may see many hens with young poults during July and August. So, it is not unusual to see young turkeys of different sizes during the summer months.

After the hen starts to set the eggs, she will no longer have anything to do with the gobbler. Gobblers have nothing to do with nesting or brood rearing. Once the eggs start to hatch, the young turkeys, better known as poults, will come out of the eggs able to stand. They are covered with a yellowish natal down which also has brown markings. Poults are able to walk and to run at the moment of hatching (Dickson 40).

During the first few days of a turkey's life, normally for the first two weeks, the poult is most vulnerable to predation. It is during this time that the poult is most susceptible to disease and most likely to die of natural causes. If, during this time, the poult is exposed to severe cold or large amounts of rainfall, it may die of exposure. It is also during this time that poults roost on the ground under the hen, and are vulnerable to predation by nocturnal predators such as the bobcat, the fox, and the great horned owl. During the daylight hours, poults are vulnerable to predation by bobcats, hawks, owls, domestic dogs and other animals that can catch them because of their inability to escape by flight. The worst possible thing that can happen is for one of those predators to kill the brood hen, for the poults will surely die.

Beginning on about the twelfth to fourteenth day of a poult's life, it can jump or fly a short distance, and will begin to roost on bushes or on low limbs of trees. Predation of the poult begins to lessen at this stage of their lives. At about two weeks of age, the poult has developed sufficient plumage to fly and has no trouble going to roost with adult hens but will rarely roost in the same area where adult gobblers roost. After about three months of life, the poult has taken on the full plumage of an adult, with certain exceptions. For example, the poult gobbler, for the first year of its life, will have three feathers on both sides of his fan which will be shorter than the feathers located in the middle of the gobbler's fan. The fan of a turkey gobbler will contain either seventeen or eighteen feathers, which means that there are six feathers, three on each end, which are shorter than the middle feathers.

From the moment of birth, a poult will begin to fend for itself. In most instances, the poult will remain with the hen for the first year of its life. From the date it hatches, it will look for food on its own. Its primary diet at this early stage of its life is grasshoppers, crickets and other insects. As it develops, the diet of the poult becomes very similar to that of the adult turkey and it will begin eating acorns, seeds, berries, insects of all kinds, grass and leaves, and even small snakes, grubs, lizards and worms. During the fall, a major portion of the juvenile's diet is acorns and other mast crops (pecans, beechnuts, fruits) that have fallen from trees.

An interesting phenomenon occurs among turkey hens between mid-July and late-September to early October. After the turkeys are hatched in May or June, the hen will keep her poults with her throughout the summer months. During this time, hens that have not nested or lost their nest begin to congregate with hens that have successfully hatched a nest, forming a flock. These flocks consist of adult hens, jennies and jakes. These turkeys will normally stay together in this flock throughout the fall and most of the winter until the early spring. Some time in the late fall or early winter, jakes will split off from the flocks and form their own small bands. These bands will normally remain together throughout the mating season, and in many instances, until the next spring when the turkeys are two years and old enough to gobble and breed, at which time the bands will break up.

Flocking provides security in numbers. A turkey has extraordinarily good eyesight and can hear nearly any movement within one hundred yards. Where there are seven to ten hens and six to fifteen poults with them, this large number of turkeys provides a great deal of security for all of the members of the flock. It is likely that one of the turkeys in the flock will spot a predator, or any other form of danger, soon enough to warn the others and permit them to escape. The warning is an alarm putt which will notify the other turkeys in the flock that there is something wrong, causing them to disperse usually by either running or flying short distances away from the danger. In many instances, the entire flock will pitch into nearby trees until the danger has passed.

Once the flock has been scattered by the predator, the turkeys will call to one another and regroup as a flock as soon as the danger has passed. These flocks will remain together until early spring or late winter when usually the jakes will split off from the flock and form small bands of six to ten. Hens will sometimes stay together over into the spring, but in many instances the hens will disperse into small groups.

A unique behavior characteristic that distinguishes the juvenile hens from jake gobblers is the hens will usually breed their first year but the jake gobblers will not have the opportunity. This occurs because the older or mature gobblers will not permit them to do so, or the jakes are unable to gobble to attract hens to them. I have heard jakes gobble as well as mature gobblers, but that is not usually the case. Most jakes are unable to make the gobble of a mature gobbler.

Jakes are also not physically mature enough to fertilize a hen. In addition, the jake turkey has no spurs to fight, is much lighter in weight, has no experience, and is no match for a mature gobbler with spurs. In nearly every incident when a jake gobbler and a tom or mature gobbler fight, a mature tom gobbler will prevail. Although some jakes can gobble as well as a mature gobbler and some jakes will breed hens, this is the exception and not the rule (Dickson 85-86). In addition to all of these factors, the ornaments or waddles on a jake do not have the same appearance as those of a mature gobbler, and this will cause a hen to reject a young turkey.

Some time between twelve and eighteen months of age, the young turkey gobbler will molt, developing a full fan and all the tail feathers will become the same length. During this time, his spurs will continue to grow, and at two years of age, his spurs will usually be about 3/4 inch in length, but will not have a real sharp point. As he continues to age, his spurs will continue to grow in length and will come to a very sharp point and will begin to turn up.

Once a jake reaches nine or ten months, he has at least a ninety percent chance of surviving, if left alone by hunters. Hunters will kill more jake gobblers than all other predators combined. If hunters would discontinue taking jakes, there would be many more gobblers in the woods today and hunters would have a greater chance of taking a mature gobbler in the springtime (Hurst and Godwin).

Juvenile hens do not have the same chance of surviving as jakes because they must lay eggs and sit a nest. The most vulnerable time for the hen is the reproductive period. There have been no scientific studies that confirm that the nesting period creates a greater danger for the juvenile hen; however, a hen of any age sitting a nest is at a greater risk of being caught by a predator than turkeys that are moving around in the woods. This is especially true since most of the predators of a turkey are nocturnal and can slip up on a sitting hen at night and catch her off the nest. It is documented that turkeys cannot see as well at night as they can during the day. It would, therefore, follow that a hen incubating eggs on the ground is extremely vulnerable to predation during the nighttime hours.

Sometimes in the fall, you may observe jakes associating with a flock of mature gobblers, but this is the exception rather than the rule because jakes usually remain in their flocks during the fall. In the spring, when the mature gobbler groups break up, it is very rare to see a jake associating with a mature gobbler, but I have seen it. In those instances, the mature gobbler would always chase the jake off when he approached hens. Usually when jakes approach mature gobblers with hens, they will keep a respectable distance. On one occasion, I observed a tom gobbler strutting and displaying with several hens, and while I was watching the gobbler, seven jakes approached him and began to fight him. At that point, the old tom broke away from the jakes and I watched the jakes in hot pursuit of the old gobbler as they went out of sight. Later that same day, I went to the spot where the jakes had run off the gobbler and the gobbler was once again strutting and displaying for the hens. That is the first and only time I had ever seen jakes gang up on a full grown gobbler and run him off. I guess I was responsible for that happening because I was calling to the turkeys when the jakes appeared. All of the turkeys were coming to my calls and once they met, the incident described above occurred.

I have had people tell me that they have seen a band of jakes gang up on mature gobblers and run him off, but I have never seen that occur before, and I have never seen it happen since then. In any case, I believe it is a very rare circumstance that jakes gang up on mature gobblers, but even when they do, they do not take over that gobbler's harem of hens. The gobbler will return to the hens and he will continue to breed the hens and the jakes will play no part in the breeding process as a result of having run the mature gobbler off.

Normally, when a mature gobbler just runs at a jake or a group of jakes, the jakes will run off and will not stand and fight. Usually this is just a slight charge; the mature gobbler may run eight to ten yards in the direction of a young jake turkey, the young jake will move out of the mature gobbler's way as quickly as he possibly can, and then the pursuit is over. In the case of one mature gobbler attacking another mature gobbler, I have seen these fights go on for some time, but usually the pecking order has been established - that is the boss gobbler has already established himself as the boss and normally just a slight charge even toward another full grown turkey gobbler will result in the boss gobbler running the other gobbler off.

3

SAFELY HUNTING THE TURKEY

Hunting involves the use of guns. The use of guns by its very nature is dangerous to you and people around you. Safety, therefore, is essential to good hunting and good sportsmanship. Hunting accidents come in many forms, ranging from accidentally self-inflicted fatal wounds, accidentally self-inflicted non-fatal wounds, to accidental wounds of hunting companions and strangers. Causes of these injuries vary, therefore every aspect of hunting safety should be carefully considered before a person takes a gun out of his closet or gun case and loads it. When picking up a gun, the first thing the hunter should do is check that gun to see if it is loaded. This is a very simple procedure which takes only a few seconds to complete. It can be done with a single barrel shotgun or rifle simply by unbreaching the gun, or opening the bolt in the case of a rifle, to see if there is a cartridge in the chamber. In the case of a bolt action shotgun or rifle, again it is just a simple matter of opening the bolt, checking the magazine or clip and the chamber to make certain there is no shell or cartridge either in the magazine, clip or chamber. To check a pump shotgun or rifle, it is a simple matter of pushing the pump release button which is installed on every pump gun; pulling the pump back toward the receiver, thereby opening the bolt, which makes it very simple to look inside to determine whether or not there is a shell in the chamber or magazine. In the case of a semi-automatic shotgun or rifle, it is a simple matter of pulling the bolt back to the locked position, and looking to see if there is a shell either in the chamber or magazine. This procedure can be completed in less than ten seconds, and may save your life or the life of another.

When checking the gun to determine whether it is loaded or not, the muzzle of the gun should always be pointed in a safe direction. It should be pointed either straight up or straight down and never pointed straight away from the person. The safety should remain in the safe position while checking to see if the gun is loaded or unloaded. However, there are some guns which require the safety mechanism to be in the "off" position before the bolt will open. Please make sure that your gun is pointed in a safe direction.

If the gun is loaded, make sure that you unload it before you do anything else. When unloading a bolt action, semi-automatic or pump gun, always make certain that you did not accidentally put a shell in the chamber while attempting to unload the gun. After the gun is unloaded, check the safety once again to make sure it is in the safe position, and the trigger cannot be pulled.

Another important step in checking your gun is to always make sure that the barrel is free of obstructions. Remove the barrel and look through it, or insert a ramrod with the bolt open, checking to see that the ramrod comes unobstructed all the way through the barrel to the open bolt. The safest and surest way to make certain there are no obstructions in the barrel is to remove the barrel and look through it. In the case of a bolt-action gun, the bolt can be removed, and you can merely look through the barrel without removing it, to determine whether or not there are any obstructions. Many hunting or firearm accidents have occurred because of an obstruction in a gun barrel, causing the barrel to blow up after the gun had been shot.

Once you have removed the barrel, always make sure it is properly seated in the receiver before you attempt to replace it. Never force the barrel into the receiver. The barrel is built to easily slide into the receiver, and when properly inserted there is no need to force it.

Always make sure that the safety on your gun is operating properly. If it is not, do not use that gun; it can cause death or injury to you or other people. The easiest way to check the safety on your gun is, with the gun unloaded, cock the gun, put the gun on safety, aim the gun at a target and attempt to pull the trigger. Then, take the gun off of safety, operate the bolt, put the gun back on safety, point it at the target again, and attempt to pull the trigger. If you are unable to pull the trigger, your safety is probably functioning properly. If the trigger pulls, then you have a defective safety and that gun should be taken to a gunsmith immediately for repair. If the safety is improperly functioning, remove the bolt from the gun, place the bolt in a safe place, separate from where the gun is stored, and as soon as possible, take the gun for repairs.

Always keep the safety in the safe position until the moment before you shoot. If you do not shoot after taking the safety off, remember to put the safety back in the safe position. If you do shoot, always bolt another round in the chamber and place the gun back on safety. This is done so that you are ready for the second shot, if it is necessary, but the gun is in the safe position before the second shot is taken. Of course, in the case of semi-automatic guns, the gun itself will reload, and you must remember to put the gun back on safety after the shot. Constantly check the safety on your gun to make certain that it remains in the safe position. Sometimes you may accidentally knock the gun off safety without realizing, so it is always necessary to check and recheck the safety.

Always be conscious of where you point the gun. Too many times, I have seen hunters walking through the woods with their gun on their shoulder and the gun pointing directly at a person walking behind them. I have also seen hunters carrying their gun by their side with the gun pointing directly at a person walking in front of them. Always make certain that your gun is either pointing straight up or straight down toward the ground. I recommend that you have a sling installed on your gun and always carry the gun in the slung position. This insures that the barrel of the gun will always be pointed straight up to reduce the risk of an accident.

You should always try to avoid running while carrying a gun. There are just too many things that can go wrong when you are running through the woods with a loaded gun. There are roots and vines that can trip you. There are always slippery places and stump holes that you can fall in while running with the gun, which could lead to a serious or fatal accident.

When crossing fences or foot logs, you should always, without exception, unload your gun. When you come to a fence, slide your gun under the fence on the ground until you can get across the fence. If you are hunting with someone else, always unload your gun; hand your gun to your partner and let him hold your gun while you cross the fence. Then he should hand you your unloaded gun, unload his gun and hand it across the fence to you while he climbs the fence or goes through it. Once you are on the other side of the fence, you can reload your guns and resume your hunting.

When crossing a foot log, it is very easy to lose your balance or slip and fall off. It is also absolutely necessary that you carry your gun with you, therefore, you should unload your gun. In addition, there are other hazards on a foot log such as vines and limbs that may be in your way. Sometimes, the most prudent way to cross a foot log is to sit down and straddle it, and scoot across it. Any time you are going to walk a foot log, you need to find a limb that is long enough to reach the bottom of the stream or water you are crossing and use it as a staff to help you maintain your balance. Always remember, if your gun is unloaded, there is no chance that your gun is going to discharge and kill you if you happen to fall off the log. If the gun is loaded, you place yourself at unnecessary risk.

Always make sure of your target before you shoot. I have heard many horror stories about people who shot at sounds or movement without knowing what was causing the sound or movement. These shots, in many instances, resulted in the injury or death of other hunters. If you are a turkey hunter and you only hunt long beard mature gobblers, you will eliminate this problem because you will know what your target is when you shoot. Turkey hunters must be admonished never to shoot a movement in a bush, because it may be another hunter hiding from a turkey. And never shoot at a turkey sound, because it may be another turkey hunter attempting to call a gobbler to him. Turkey hunting results in injuries every year because people shoot at movements or sounds thinking the movement or sound to be a turkey. Not knowing that it may be a human being, the hunter shoots and injures or kills another hunter. This is probably the most common cause of injuries during turkey season.

Be especially careful to identify your target. Always check the area behind your target to make certain that there is no danger beyond it. A rifle shot or shotgun pellet does not stop when it reaches the target. It continues to travel. It is essential that you make sure there is nothing, or no one, beyond your target that you might injure if you have a missed shot.

Never, and I emphasize never, lean your gun against a tree, a fence, an automobile, a truck, a house or anything else. It is too easy to bump the gun causing it to fall and discharge, or for the gun merely to slide off a fence or tree, hit the ground and discharge killing or injuring someone. If you must put your gun down, lay it down flat so that there is no chance the gun can fall.

Never carry a loaded gun in a vehicle. This includes ATVs and boats. There are just too many things that can go wrong with a loaded gun in a vehicle. Since it is illegal to shoot from a vehicle, there is absolutely no reason to have a gun loaded while in the vehicle. When carrying your gun in a vehicle, make sure the muzzle is always pointed toward the floor board. If the gun is loaded and it does discharge, at least it will discharge into the floor board and not into the passenger compartment.

If you see a friend or a child doing something unsafe with a gun, please bring it to their attention. It is extremely difficult for us to tell people that they are committing unsafe acts. Remind them of safety tips, or bring to their attention things they are doing wrong. It may not only save your life, but their lives as well. So, please do not hesitate to remind friends, and especially children, how to safely handle a gun if you see them doing something unsafe. Most people will appreciate your bringing it to their attention because usually they are unconscious of the unsafe act they are committing and most hunters want to be safe.

Before you leave to go hunting, always notify someone of the location you are going to hunt, and the approximate time you expect to return. If you decide to change your hunting location, always call and notify someone that you have done so. You want to make sure somebody always knows where you are. There can be no more lonesome feeling than being involved in a hunting accident in the woods alone and that there is no one who knows where you are or how to find you.

You should be familiar with the area you are hunting and you should especially know the location of any occupied dwellings or any public roads in the area. You should never shoot your gun in the direction of a house or a public road. Because of the negligence of some hunters, turkey hunting can be a very unsafe sport. While you are turkey hunting, you should always be mindful that there are other hunters in the woods that will shoot any turkey and those hunters create a very serious problem.

Some of the unsafe things you are required to do while turkey hunting include making turkey hen sounds, remaining perfectly still while making those sounds, and concealing yourself (as opposed to hiding); and some turkey hunters will gobble to either get a turkey to gobble on the roost in the morning or to get a gobbler to come to them. It is essential, while turkey hunting, that you make hen sounds to the gobbler if you expect that turkey to come to you; but when making those kinds of sounds, you expose yourself to danger.

You must remain perfectly still while hunting, because a turkey can see any movement you make. The result of remaining still sometimes causes a hunter to shoot at the sound because he is unable to locate the animal making the sound. To enhance your chances of killing a turkey, it is necessary that you conceal yourself, and this is done by using camouflage to blend into your surroundings. Thus, you become much more difficult to locate by other hunters and sometimes this results in hunting accidents.

You should never hide from a wild turkey. If you are hidden from the turkey and in a position where the turkey cannot see you, you are also concealed from other human beings. Hiding from the wild turkey while hunting is one of the greatest causes of hunting accidents. It also means that your own visibility is obstructed and it is difficult for you to see other hunters slipping up on you. Being unable to see other hunters may result in your being unable to notify them of your presence, or resulting in your accidentally shooting a hunter.

Always put your back to a tree that is large enough to completely cover it. You should also select a position where you can see for a long distance to your left, to your right, and in front. This way you can see other hunters slipping up on you or coming through the woods as you are calling. When you have your back to a large tree that completely covers it, a hunter coming up from behind you will not be able to shoot you from behind. This practice has probably kept me from being shot several times. I cannot tell you the number of times that I have seen hunters attempting to slip up on me. This has also helped me harvest turkeys, because I could see them coming in plenty of time to be ready to shoot once they got in range. I could see the turkey at a far enough distance so that when the turkey walked behind a tree or some other obstacle, I was able to get my gun in a position to shoot and be ready when the turkey got there.

As you already know, a turkey has many colors in its plumage and on its head, but the most dominant colors of the wild turkey are the white patch on the top of the turkey's head, the red waddles on the turkey's neck, and the blue color along the side of the turkey's face. For this reason, you should never wear anything in the woods, during turkey season, that has any red, white or blue in it. I am very careful to make certain that any paper towels or other paraphernalia that I carry in the woods are concealed - especially if those items have any red, white or blue on them.

If you are sitting in the woods yelping like a turkey, and you have any item of clothing, or anything on you, that has any red, white or blue in it, you increase your risk of being shot. Another mistake that many turkey hunters make, is to gobble on a gobble box or any other device. In the spring, most hunters are listening for the sound of a turkey gobbler.

If you are walking through the woods gobbling, you are certainly going to attract the attention of other hunters. There are only two reasons why you should ever use the gobble. One reason is to use the gobble as a locator call to make the turkey gobble to you on the roost, or to make him gobble to you after he has flown off the roost; and the second reason is to use the gobble as a method of calling the turkey to you.

Some hunters believe that you can gobble while you are calling, and the turkey you are attempting to call will believe that another gobbler has invaded his territory, and will come to the gobbling sound. There is absolutely no reason for you to ever have to gobble to a turkey early in the morning, since there are many devices on the market now to make a turkey gobble from the roost. There is certainly no reason for you to be gobbling to a turkey to which you are calling. You should be able to call that turkey in by the use of hen sounds, but in the event you are not able to do so, some devices on the market now will help you call him in by using what is referred to as aggravated purrs of turkey gobblers, which mimics the sound of gobblers fighting. It is preferable to use those sounds, rather than a gobble box, not only for calling the turkey, but also for safety reasons.

Using decoys while hunting can be a very unsafe practice, especially if you are using gobbler decoys. While hunting turkeys, you are making turkey sounds with other turkey hunters walking around the woods looking for turkeys. Many times, the other turkey hunters will hear you making turkey sounds and attempt to slip up on you. If, when they slip up on you, they see a gobbler decoy standing close to the spot where they heard the turkey sound, it increases the likelihood that a hunting accident can occur. Using decoys makes it even more important that, when setting up to call to a turkey, you choose a site where you can protect your back and have an unobstructed field of vision to both sides and front. Always sit next to a tree that is large enough to completely cover your back when you are using decoys. After you are set up, be alert so that you can hear and see any hunter slipping up on you. Once you see the other hunter, notify him immediately of your presence.

Finally, to make turkey hunting a safer sport, keep in mind that if you only shoot long bearded gobblers, then you will never run the risk of shooting another human being, and that alone would make turkey hunting a safer sport. You would not be shooting at movement or sounds, because if you are only going to be shooting a long-bearded turkey, you have to see the beard on the turkey before you take the shot. And if all turkey hunters would only shoot long bearded turkeys, it would totally eliminate the possibility of anyone mistaking a human being for a turkey.

Another important thing you must remember is how to transport your turkey out of the woods. Some people have been shot leaving the woods with a dead wild turkey slung over their shoulder. To a hunter at a distance, this appears to be a turkey either flapping his wings or a turkey running through the woods. Other hunters can see the head flopping, they can see the red, white and blue on the head and they can see the wings dangling by the side of the turkey. The turkey is what they are hunting, and many times their attention is focused only on the turkey and they shoot, thinking they are shooting at a live bird. The result is that the turkey hunter gets shot. The safest way to carry your turkey out of the woods is to carry a green or brown garbage bag with you and place the turkey in the bag, sling it over your shoulder, and carry your turkey out.

In some states, hunting accidents during turkey season have reached a point where they are now requiring hunters to wear hunter's orange or a blazed orange color during turkey season. This will probably not reduce the number of accidents and may even increase the number. The major objection to the blazed orange while turkey hunting is that the color is easily confused with the red in the waddles of a wild turkey and may result in people being shot. In addition, all hunters will then be expecting everyone to be wearing the blazed orange, which is not always the case. A person making turkey sounds who was not wearing his blazed orange would increase the chances of a hunting accident. This is simply because every hunter would be expecting every other hunter to be wearing the blazed orange vest, and if a hunter fails to wear this vest, he would be putting himself in great danger.

I feel the adoption of regulations or laws requiring the use of blazed or hunter's orange while turkey hunting are going to have an adverse effect on the sport itself. It is extremely difficult to harvest a wild turkey under the most favorable conditions because of the turkey's visual abilities. There is absolutely no question that the wild turkey can distinguish colors, and if he sees a blazed orange jacket or vest sitting next to a tree in the woods, he is certainly not going to come close enough for you to get a shot. Such a regulation would make it more difficult to harvest a turkey, thereby resulting in the frustration and disgust with the sport because of one's inability to be successful, causing many people who enjoy the turkey woods to abandon the sport.

One of the things that can be done to make turkey hunting a safer sport is to require every person, regardless of his or her age, to complete a hunter education course. In some states, if you were born before a specified year you do not have to take a hunter education course to obtain a hunting license. It is not unreasonable to expect people who are going to be in the woods with loaded guns to take a hunter education course before they enter the woods.

4

ETHICS

If hunters would be more ethical in their approach to hunting the wild turkey, accidents would be nearly eliminated. If hunters would practice the safety tips that have been set out in this book, it might eliminate all hunting accidents. If hunters would make certain of their target and shoot only long bearded, mature gobblers, the hunting accident rate among turkey hunters would be much lower. In addition, states should require everyone applying for a hunting license to pass a test on hunting safety, hunting ethics, and hunting methods of the wildlife the hunter expects to pursue.

The states should also have an administrative procedure available to them so hunting licenses can be revoked for whatever period is necessary when people are negligent in the commission of a hunting accident. Every state should also thoroughly investigate any hunting accident. If alcohol is involved, the person who caused the accident should have his hunting license revoked immediately and for the duration of his lifetime. There should also be the option of referring the case to grand juries for indictments and jail penalties, especially in those cases where alcohol is a factor in the hunting accident.

When we take to the woods to hunt wildlife, we should all set standards of conduct for ourselves and promise to abide by them at all times. We should always respect our natural resources, which includes the wildlife and the environment. We should always conduct ourselves in the woods as ethical hunters, respecting other people and their property, and the wildlife we hunt. If we are going to preserve this sport for future generations, then we must be willing to make a commitment to set an example for other hunters so that everyone not only respects the wildlife and the property of others, but also abides by state laws. We should certainly set an example for young hunters or future generations of hunters who will follow us in the woods. Unfortunately, there are those among us who have no ethics and who will hunt wildlife out of season, who will kill more than the limit set by the states, who will trespass upon the property of others and destroy private property in the process, and who will do such things as headlight deer and other animals without regard for the consequences of their acts. These people are commonly referred to as "slob" hunters, and should be condemned by the entire hunting community.

We should all be willing to report those people who conduct themselves in unethical or illegal ways, and to make certain that those people are put under pressure from other hunters to change their hunting habits. We must remember that the newspapers report hunting violations and convictions. When you read the newspaper, all you will ever see regarding hunting are court decisions involving people who are convicted of killing more than the limit or who have failed to wear proper clothing, such as hunter's orange during deer season and who have been caught headlighting or violating other game laws. It is incumbent upon those of us who consider ourselves ethical hunters to make the general public aware that the people they read about are the exceptions, and that most hunters are ethical, abide by the laws and respect the game they pursue.

There are certain methods of hunting the wild turkey which, although may not be against the law, are considered by most turkey hunters to be unethical and do not constitute what is commonly referred to as "fair chase." Such conduct as "limbing" or shooting the wild turkey off the roost is considered unethical. It must be remembered that a wild turkey during the daylight hours has excellent eyesight. However, just before dark and just after daylight, a turkey's eyesight is poor. Although that turkey may be gobbling on the roost, he cannot see the ground beneath him. When he gobbles, it is very easy to locate his position and if it is just at daylight, it is very easy to slip up under the tree where the turkey is roosting to shoot it. Any hunter who would do this is not worthy of calling himself a turkey hunter, and this certainly could not be considered a "fair chase."

Many turkey hunters consider it unethical to hunt turkeys with high powered rifles such as a 22-250 or 243. The challenge of hunting a turkey is to call him in close enough for you to take him with a shotgun. This gives the turkey an opportunity to locate you and to take advantage of his sense of sight and hearing. To kill the turkey with a rifle at 100 yards or 150 yards does not give the turkey the opportunity to take advantage of his sense of sight and hearing in locating the hunter. In addition, hunting turkeys with a rifle enhances the opportunity for the hunter to shoot the turkey off the roost. The turkey can be located by his gobble, spotted by telescopic sight on the rifle, and shot at 100 or more yards from the roost. This certainly cannot be considered a proper way to hunt the wild turkey. It also must be kept in mind that in many states it is now illegal to hunt turkeys with a rifle. You should check your local state laws and regulations to determine whether or not it is prohibited in your state.

In some states, it is legal to hunt turkeys in the fall with a dog. Hunting the turkey in the fall is extremely difficult, and it takes an excellent hunter to do that. The hunter has to be able to recognize turkey sign, and have the ability to follow that sign to locate a flock of turkeys. Once he locates the flock, he has to break it up, and then call the individuals back, and pick out the turkey he wishes to harvest.

The use of a dog takes most of the work out of hunting the turkey. The dog can scent the turkeys, run into the flock and break it up. In many instances, the dog will cause the turkeys to fly into nearby trees, and the dog will then bark at the turkeys giving the hunter their exact location. He can slip up on the turkeys while they are preoccupied with watching the dog, and shoot one out of the trees. This certainly is unethical and should not be condoned.

Because dogs have the ability to trail turkeys by scent and find turkey nests, they should not even be allowed in the woods in the spring, whether for the purpose of turkey hunting, or any other purpose. When this happens, the dogs will flush the hens from the nest causing the hen to abandon her eggs. In addition, many times the dog will catch turkey hens and kill them and break up turkey nests. This affects your turkey population, therefore dogs in the woods in the springtime should be prohibited by state law.

There are many turkey hunters who consider it macho, or proof of their ability as hunters to kill more than their limit of turkeys. Certainly, those of us who want to see the turkey population flourish would never do such a thing. I once had a hunter brag to me that he had killed a dozen turkeys in a season and that he had killed several long bearded gobblers and several jakes. I pointed out to this hunter that, in Mississippi, when he told me this story, there were only about 400,000 turkeys and 60,000 turkey hunters. If each of those turkey hunters killed ten turkeys during the season he killed the twelve turkeys, there would be 600,000 turkeys killed in that year, thereby wiping out the entire turkey population in Mississippi. If every turkey hunter ignored the limits, the day would come when there would be no turkeys to hunt. Limits are placed on wildlife for the purpose of conserving it for future generations of hunters, and hunters who do not understand that, should be the subject of the scorn of all hunters, and it should not be tolerated within the hunting community.

Some slob hunters pay no attention to the seasons established by the states, and will kill wildlife during the entire year. These people fail to understand that seasons are established for a purpose, and one of those purposes is to limit the number of wild animals that are killed every year. Another purpose is to give the wildlife an opportunity to raise its young during the off season.

It is generally accepted that people who hunt out of season do not take into consideration the sex of the animals they kill. People who kill turkey hens during the spring or summer probably guarantee that fewer poults will be raised. Killing more than the limit of wildlife and hunting out of season are problems that exist throughout the United States. We should make sure that those who commit these acts should be turned in to the local authorities so that they can be observed, caught and punished for their acts.

Some people who call themselves turkey hunters are either too lazy or incapable of learning how to use some of the products to call turkeys in. Those people, therefore, resort to the use of bait for hunting turkeys. In many instances, these hunters will erect a blind or hunt from shooting houses in close proximity to the bait. They have absolutely concealed themselves from the turkey, not giving it the opportunity to take advantage of its sense of sight or hearing, and will shoot the turkey when it comes to eat the bait. This certainly cannot be considered a "fair chase" and has to be considered among one of the most unethical ways of harvesting wild turkeys. There is absolutely no way that baiting could be considered hunting the wild turkey. The best that can be said about baiting is that it gives one the opportunity to kill a turkey, not to hunt a turkey.

There are states where hunting the wild turkey with the rifle or over bait is perfectly legal. I assume that, in those states, they have made a determination that hunting the wild turkey in that way is consistent with their approach to management of the turkey, and I would not be critical where the biology dictates that this method of hunting be permitted. In some states where the use of rifles and bait are permitted, it may be allowed as a method of controlling turkey populations, and be perfectly consistent with sound biological and game management practices, and in that case I certainly have no quarrel with being able to hunt with bait and rifles.

Under those circumstances, I have very little objection to it, although I do consider the use of bait and rifles unethical, simply because the other factors that I mentioned such as the instinct of the animal, the natural defenses, such as its eyesight and hearing, do not come in to play, and the hunter simply shoots the turkey without there being a "fair chase" involved in the hunt.

When I talk about the concept of a "fair chase", I am talking about actually hunting the turkey as opposed to killing the wild turkey. By this, I mean that the animal is given a chance to use its superior physical qualities; such as its superior ability to see and hear and to use its instincts, together with its speed and other attributes - which contribute to its survival - to escape the human being. The human being pits his knowledge of the animal and his ability to think against the animal's natural defenses to harvest that animal in what is considered a "fair chase" approach to hunting.

Conversely, if the animal you are hunting is not given the opportunity to use his superior sight, superior hearing, or whatever other qualities he has, such as his ability to climb trees or his ability to escape by using his superior speed or ability to fly; if the animal is never given the opportunity to utilize those characteristics it has in the chase part of hunting, then there is not a "fair chase" in the harvesting of that animal. For example, if you are sitting in a shooter house concealed from the wild turkey with bait on the ground, and the turkey walks up to eat the bait, and you shoot it, the turkey is never given the opportunity to use its ability to see, its ability to hear, its speed afoot and its speed of flight to escape. The hunter merely sticks the gun out of a window in the shooter house, pulls the trigger, and the turkey is dead. That cannot be considered a "fair chase" within the concept of what we generally refer to as hunting the wild animal.

To the purist, the question of ethics comes into play at this point because it is unethical to kill a wild animal without the "fair chase" concept being a part of the pursuit. In effect, ethical pursuit of a wild animal includes the concept of hunting and included within the definition of hunting is the ethical consideration of whether or not that animal was taken in a "fair chase" pursuit. So you have ethics, hunting and "fair chase" all considered as a part of the same concept, and unless all three are involved in the taking of a wild animal, the hunt is really not a hunt; it is merely a kill and there is a distinct difference for the purists who call themselves hunters.

Many hunters now are hunting all species of game with a bow because they believe that is the purest form of hunting and always involves the "fair chase" concept. They consider bow hunting to be the most ethical method of hunting wildlife. It is easy to wound a wild turkey with a bow and arrow. Before you undertake to hunt the wild turkey with a bow and arrow, you should become extremely proficient with the bow, and have the confidence that you can make a clean kill. Otherwise, leave your bow and arrow at home.

Probably the most serious threat to hunting today, is the "slob" hunter who disregards property rights. These slobs will go on private land, shoot the wildlife on that land, in many instances destroying private property such as fences and gates, and sometimes even resort to shooting domestic livestock. Such conduct on the part of hunters has caused many property owners to no longer grant permission to hunt their property.

In addition, many private property owners pressure state legislators to increase restrictions on hunters. I personally know of instances where private land owners have granted others permission to hunt, and the people who were granted the permission to hunt would actually bring their friends. Of course, this resulted in the land owner revoking permission for all to hunt, and then refusing to grant others the permission to hunt on his property simply out of fear that the same thing would happen again. It is essential that, if the sport of hunting is going to continue to exist, hunters must respect private property and remain off that property unless they have the express permission of the owner.

It is also unethical for a hunter to take a shot that he knows will not result in a clean kill of the animal. Too many times, hunters will take fifty and seventy-five yard shots at a gobbler with a shotgun. I personally do not know of a single instance where anyone has ever killed a turkey at seventy-five yards with a shotgun. However, I know of many instances where turkeys have been shot and wounded at long distances and then got away. Many of those animals will not survive the wounds.

It is essential that you pattern your shotgun and know which shell loads it shoots the best, or which size shot it shoots the best; and never try to extend the range of your gun. Always shoot within a distance where you know you can make a clean kill. If you think you may not be able to kill the turkey that you are going to shoot at, let that animal walk away. You can hunt him another day. If you shoot that gobbler at a distance where you know you are probably not going to kill him, you have taken away from yourself another day of hunting that turkey. Always remember that the wild turkey has many predators, among them are fox, domestic dogs, coyotes, bobcats and you. A wounded turkey has very little chance of escaping his predators.

Each of us, as individuals, has the right to establish for ourselves our own standard of ethical conduct as hunters. I would merely suggest to you that you set a high standard for yourself, thereby setting an example for others. If you do that, you will become a better hunter and you will have the respect of your fellow hunters. Your conduct may be the example that turns a "slob" hunter into an ethical hunter.

There is a minimum ethical standard that hunters can follow in the woods. The concept of the "fair chase" should be uppermost in every hunter's mind. Exactly what does a "fair chase" mean when hunting the wild turkey? What it means to most turkey hunters is that they would never kill a turkey that they had not called up to them. The art of using a turkey call to reverse nature and make a turkey gobbler come to you is one that gives every hunter who has accomplished that a great deal of pride.

I have been asked many times whether I thought ambushing turkeys was consistent with the concept of "fair chase." There are instances when I consider ambushing to be ethical, and there are instances when I consider ambushing to be unethical. To ambush a turkey, in many instances, requires the hunter to be an extraordinarily good woodsman and turkey hunter. In some instances, you actually outsmart the turkey and are able to move into a position on the turkey without being seen.

Your chances of ethically ambushing a turkey are nearly zero, simply because once the turkey is on the ground and gobbling, you have to be able to anticipate exactly where that turkey is headed, and exactly which path that turkey is going to take. Then you have to be able to move into a position ahead of that turkey and wait for him to come to you. I would estimate that 99.9% of the time, even if you are right about where the turkey is going, you will be wrong about how the turkey is going to get there. Your best chance to kill a turkey is to call that turkey to you and get him within gun range. I certainly think that ambushing a turkey off the roost, or ambushing a turkey over bait is unethical, and do not consider people who do that to be turkey hunters. Those people are turkey killers.

The longest shot that I believe a person should take on a turkey is forty yards and even that is a long shot. The best shot and the surest shot is between twenty and thirty yards. In almost every instance of a shot that close, you will harvest your turkey.

You should always take a head shot because the head is a vital spot and is the easiest place to get penetration of your shot. Never take a body shot. Even if you do penetrate the feathers, it is highly unlikely you will penetrate the breast to reach a vital organ.

If you are going to be an ethical hunter, then you must know the gun you are shooting. You must have shot that gun enough to know its exact limits. I would not recommend hunting the wild turkey with anything less than a 12 gauge shotgun shooting a three inch magnum shell. I further recommend that you use the size shot that best patterns in your gun and usually that will be either 6's, 5's or 4's.

For instance, if you are shooting a three inch magnum twelve gauge shotgun using Winchester copper coated three inch magnum shotgun shells with maximum powder drams and two ounces of shot, the #4 shot will have approximately 270 pellets; the #5 shot will have approximately 340 pellets; and the #6 shot will have approximately 450 pellets. It stands to reason that because you have 450 pellets in a shotgun shell shooting #6 shot, as opposed to 270 pellets in a shotgun shell shooting #4 shot, you are going to hit the target with more pellets using #6 shot than you are using #4 shot. However, that may not be the determining factor in what shot you use since the #4 shot will get greater penetration at a greater distance than the #6 shot. If you are putting between 30 and 40 pellets in a turkey head target at forty yards using #4 shot and you are putting 45 #6 shot in the turkey head at the same distance, you may want to use #4's simply because you are going to get greater penetration with the #4's at the longer distance. This is a choice you must make after you pattern your gun.

To determine which shot your gun patterns the best, you should buy a box of 6's, a box of 5's and a box of 4's, and you should shoot each of those shells with a full choke, a modified choke or an extra full choke at various distances. You should pattern your gun at a distance of forty yards. To do that, you should shoot each of the chokes to determine which choke and which shot would give you the best pattern at that distance. The probabilities are, that the extra full choke is going to give you the best pattern at forty yards, but there are instances with some guns where other chokes pattern better at forty yards. Whichever shell and choke patterns work best for you at forty yards is the one you should use.

When attempting to pattern your gun, use a commercial target that has actual, life-size turkey heads. This will help you determine exactly how many shots you can expect to hit the turkey in the head, and the distance you should shoot; but more importantly, it will help you determine the distance beyond which you should not shoot. I will emphatically and unequivocally say that I do not believe any one should ever hunt the wild turkey using #7 1/2 or #8 shot. These types of shot are too small to be effective.

Another subject debated among turkey hunters is whether or not it is ever ethical to hunt turkey hens. There are some who argue that taking hens is necessary in areas where there is overpopulation. This argument concludes that if a certain number of hen turkeys are not taken, there is a chance for overpopulation of turkeys, thereby increasing the chances of disease. This is a perfectly valid argument, recognized by many biologists as being a sound method of controlling turkey populations, and reducing the chances of disease. On the other hand, there are those who believe that hens should never be killed. Their argument is that turkeys are very susceptible to weather conditions and natural disasters such as floods and heavy rains or storms. Therefore, to insure that there will always be sufficient turkeys, hens should never be taken.

As has already been mentioned, turkey populations fluctuate a great deal from year to year. This is due to many factors, but mostly due to predation, disease and weather conditions after reproduction. Because of these factors, taking of hens should be closely monitored on an annual basis to make certain that turkey populations remain stable or continue to increase. During those periods when turkey populations are down, the taking of hens should be absolutely prohibited so that the population can recover.

The suggestion has been made that in those states where hens are permitted to be hunted, the estimated number of hens that would be killed should be trapped and relocated or restocked in areas where turkey populations are low. This procedure would accelerate the return of turkeys in areas where populations have been slow to recover.

Hens could be relocated to those states with presently low turkey populations, and where turkey hunting permits are granted, even to residents, by lottery. Turkey hents from states where hunting them is legal could be used to restock those states with low populations and it would hasten or accelerate the day when all the turkey hunters in all states would be issued permits and could enjoy this sport. It would seem this would solve the problem.

If turkey populations are controlled by trapping and restocking, then you reduce the possibility of disease among the turkey flock. In addition, you make a contribution to other areas where turkey populations are low. Cooperative efforts between states in financing trapping and restocking of turkeys would make it financially feasible to accomplish this goal, and suit the purposes or meet the needs of each state. A state with an overpopulation would benefit from trapping and moving the turkeys, and the state with the low population could soon have a turkey season open for all hunters.

There is currently a debate within the turkey hunting community concerning the ethics of using decoys. The "purists" believe that the use of decoys is an unethical method. It is their argument that once the turkey spots the decoy, his attention is diverted from the caller to the decoy. When the turkey's attention is directed solely at the decoy, his sense of hearing and sight are no longer as keen to danger as they would have been if the decoy were not present. Use of the decoy certainly gives the hunter an advantage he would not otherwise have, and probably results in the taking of more turkeys than without the use of decoys.

Those who advocate the use of decoys argue that it permits the hunter to get the turkey in close enough to make a clean shot in every instance. If the decoy is placed well within gun range and the turkey comes in to the decoy, it is certainly going to reduce the possibility that the turkey will be wounded. It gets back to the argument of whether or not the use of decoys constitutes a "fair chase" hunt of the wild turkey. There is certainly room for disagreement about this, and every individual must make up his or her own mind about whether or not the use of decoys is an ethical method of hunting the wild turkey.

Nearly all turkey hunters I know would agree that using decoys while bow hunting is consistent with the "fair chase" and is an ethical way in which to hunt the wild turkey. It is difficult to take a wild turkey with a bow and arrow, since the hunter must bring his bow to a full draw after the turkey gets in range. I do not know a single hunter who is capable of bringing a bow to full draw with a turkey standing within twenty yards without the aid of blinds and decoys. I would estimate that one hundred times out of a hundred, a turkey will spot a hunter attempting to draw a bow at that range. The result is that a bow hunter would never get a shot at a wild turkey. Even with the use of decoys and blinds while bow hunting, it is still extremely difficult to get in a position to take a wild turkey with a bow and arrow. The turkey is just too keen, and his sense of sight and hearing too good for hunters to be able to consistently take them with a bow and arrow.

I know of instances where decoys have cost hunters a shot at a wild turkey. In one particular instance, a decoy was being used and there was a wind blowing. When the turkey spotted the decoy and started to it, the wind caused the decoy to spin around on its stake. When that happened, the gobbler knew that no turkey hen could make such a move; it was immediately alerted that there was "something rotten in Denmark" and left in a full run. In that particular instance, the decoy actually saved the life of a wild turkey. Had the hunter not been using the decoy, the turkey would have probably come into range of a shot. If a turkey is responding to a caller, and the hunter remains still - and is undetected by the gobbler - in most instances, once the turkey gets in sight of the hunter, he will usually come on in, close enough for the shot with or without the aid of the decoy.

Another instance where the use of decoys prevented the killing of a turkey occurred when I was calling turkeys for two hunters in Kansas. On this particular morning, I was unable to get a turkey to gobble at daylight, but I had seen a gobbler in the area where I had taken the hunters. I decided we would set up and "dry call" (calling without knowing if there is a turkey in the area in hopes that you will get a turkey to respond.) The hunters were sitting to my right, facing different directions, and I had the video camera. The hunters were both sitting on either side of the same tree. We put one jake decoy and two hen decoys approximately twenty yards in front of us. The two hen decoys were placed about a foot apart, and the jake decoy was placed behind the two hen decoys about ten yards to make it appear that the jake decoy was following the hen decoy.

After calling for about twenty-five minutes, I turned, looked to my left, and saw a big gobbler coming in. This turkey had not made a single sound, but was coming to my calling. I was between the two hunters and the turkey. Since I was attempting to video this hunt, I did not have a gun. With the turkey coming in to my left, and the hunters sitting to my right, I was directly between the gobbler and the hunters - which prevented the hunters from getting a shot. When the gobbler got in range, he stopped and looked at the decoys. Once he spotted the decoys, he would not come any closer. I decided to do a soft purr and some very soft yelps in the hopes that one of the hunters could get a shot. The very moment I completed the soft yelping, the gobbler gobbled at the decoys. This is the first time this gobbler had made a sound, and in my opinion, the only reason this turkey gobbled at this point was to get a response from the decoys. If we had not been using decoys, this gobbler would have continued to come on in looking for the hens he had been hearing.

When this turkey gobbled and the decoys did not respond or react to the gobble, the turkey turned and left without a shot being fired. As the gobbler was leaving, I heard him cluck two or three times, saw him strut and then walk away.

There is absolutely no doubt in my mind, that the use of decoys prevented the gobbler from coming in and giving one of the hunters a shot. This gobbler was looking for the hens he had been hearing. Once he saw the decoys and they did not respond to the gobble, he knew something was wrong and he left. As a result of my experience using decoys, I have now decided that I will no longer use them unless I am hunting with a bow, but I will continue to use them when I am attempting to video a hunt.

There is much evidence that clearly shows decoys can be an effective way of taking wild turkeys. I have seen videos, and I have actually videotaped turkeys coming in to decoys, and I know that there are times when hens and gobblers alike will attack decoys. I think the most effective way to use a decoy is to place two hen decoys in close proximity of one another and a jake decoy about ten to fifteen yards behind them to make it appear that the jake decoy is following the two hen decoys. When the adult gobbler comes in and sees this, he will invariably challenge the jake decoy.

I have seen it happen time after time and I know that the adult gobblers, instead of going to the hens, will walk over to the jake and start to strut around it. A friend of mine, Thomas Neuberger, showed me this trick, and it was certainly helpful when I was videotaping turkey hunts. It is also very helpful to hunters who are attempting to kill wild turkeys and at the same time have that hunt videotaped. Sometimes, when you are videotaping a turkey, you will have three or four people on the same hunt. You will have a guide or someone to call the turkey, the videographer and the hunter, and in some cases two hunters, and with that many people it is virtually impossible to call the turkey up and kill him without being spotted. The decoy is certainly helpful under those circumstances.

The decoy does divert the turkey's attention away from the place where the calling is coming from, making it easier for the hunter to get in a position to shoot. This is a debate that will continue among turkey hunters. Each turkey hunter should make his own decision about whether he considers the use of decoys an ethical way or tactic for hunting the wild turkey. If you, as an individual, are satisfied in your own mind that there is nothing unethical about using decoys, then use them. If, on the other hand, you have strong feelings about the ethics of it, and believe it is unethical, then you should not use decoys to hunt the wild turkey.

The states, in adopting statutes and regulations concerning the harvest of the wild turkey, have an obligation to impose minimum standards on the entire hunting population. It is up to individuals to establish their own standards that do not violate state laws or regulations. Many states presently require, or have implemented, a tagging system for taking turkeys. It is my view that every state should have a tagging system. Once a hunter has used his tags, he is no longer eligible to hunt, and to be caught in the woods with a gun without your tags is a violation of the law. It is a well known fact that in the northeast and northwest, severe winters will cause increased mortality in turkey populations. In the southeast, springtime flooding causes increased mortality. If the northeast and northwest experience a severe winter, bag limits should be reduced and seasons should be shortened. If the southeast has springtime flooding, the bag limits should be reduced in that area, as well as shortening the seasons. These measures should be taken to assure that hunting does not contribute to an overkill of turkeys and they have a chance to replenish.

5

TURKEY HUNTING EQUIPMENT

To be a successful turkey hunter, it is almost necessary that you have certain hunting equipment. Probably the most expensive item is the shotgun. There are many excellent shotguns on the market, and some shotguns are even designed specifically for turkey hunting. These special purpose guns are usually short barrel guns with extra full chokes and completely camouflaged. There are also special turkey guns that come in gauges ten and twelve and are designed to take three inch or three and one-half inch magnum shotgun shells. Many guns available to turkey hunters are not special purpose guns and will also do the job. You should shoot the gun with which you are most comfortable and in which you have the most confidence.

A growing number of people enjoy hunting the wild turkey with black powder and bow and arrows. Many bows on the market are well suited for turkey hunting, and many varieties of black powder shotguns will take the wild turkey at thirty or thirty-five yards with no problem. In addition, you should practice with the bow and arrow and with the black powder gun by shooting turkey targets.

The second most important thing you will need to hunt the wild turkey is effective camouflage. Head-to-toe camouflage -- from boots, pants, shirts and T-shirts, to face mask, gloves and hats -- should be worn while turkey hunting. This camouflage will be your best friend for concealment. If you use an effective camouflage, you can avoid the need for hiding in thickets or bushes. You can merely sit against a big tree and blend in, regardless of the type of tree you choose to sit by.

To demonstrate the effectiveness of camouflage, I would like give you two examples that helped me to harvest gobblers. On one occasion, I was hunting wild turkeys in west Texas, in a wide open oak flat on the edge of a small creek that runs into the Rio Grande River. I managed to call up a turkey gobbler and several hens. Once the hens were within about forty-five yards of me, they would come no closer and the gobbler would not leave the hens to come to my calling.

This left me no alternative except to attempt to get closer to the turkey on my own. So, I rolled over on my stomach, cradled my gun in my arms and began to low crawl toward the turkeys yelping and clucking as I crawled along the ground. I was fully camouflaged from head-to-toe. I managed to crawl within about twenty yards of this entire flock of turkeys without being detected.

Once I was within shooting distance of the gobbler, I was able to slide upon my knees, get my gun to my shoulder and kill one of the biggest Rio Grande turkeys I have ever seen. There is absolutely no doubt in my mind that, had I not been camouflaged, I would not have been able to accomplish this. I was in the open. The turkeys could see me with no problem, but the camouflage was so effective that none of the turkeys ever became suspicious of my presence, which allowed me to get in position to make a kill on this gobbler.

Author with camouflage shotgun designed for turkey hunting and fully dressed in camouflage clothing.

When I did this, I was hunting on a 50,000 acre private ranch where I knew this tactic would be safe. If you hunt public land, I do not recommend that you try this, because it can result in a serious hunting accident.

On another occasion, I spotted a turkey in the middle of a ten acre field. After calling to that turkey for about an hour, I was unable to get him to leave the hens that were with him, and I was unable to call the hens to me. The only chance I had to take this turkey was to get to him across the open field. I got down on my hands and knees with my gun in my right hand and started to crawl out into the field. I never took my eyes off the turkeys the entire time I was crawling, and every time the turkeys would look up I would stop and yelp to them. I managed to get within about two hundred yards of the turkeys and figured that was as close as I could get without scaring them. I then managed to sit down in a ball so that I would appear to the turkeys to be a stump in the middle of the field.

I then called to the turkeys using soft clucks, to purrs, to excited cutting. There were two hens, a full grown gobbler and a jake in the field. I eventually got the attention of the jake and within a few seconds he was standing within six feet from me looking directly at me. When he did not spot another turkey, he turned and walked right by my side and left the field. When the hens looked up and saw the jake in the area from which I was calling, they then started toward me.

After the hens started toward me, the gobbler followed. Once I got the hens started in my direction, I continued to call to them using soft yelps and clucks to keep their interest. The turkeys came right to me, never realizing what I was. The only thing that I can figure is that the camouflage fooled the turkeys, giving me an opportunity to take this gobbler.

I am absolutely convinced that the camouflage you use in turkey hunting is just as important as your ability to call or your ability to shoot. On this particular hunt, I was hunting on my own land so I knew this tactic was one I could use without any danger to myself.

In selecting the apparel that you are going to wear, it is important that you have an effective camo. You must also be able to break up the contour or silhouette of the human body. I use a hat with a wide brim that will turn down in front of my face to help break up the silhouette of my head, as opposed to a baseball cap which does not. In addition, it is a solid cap and mosquitoes have a difficult time biting through the cloth.

The three places on your body that you want to keep mosquitoes away from are your ears, the back of your legs and your ankles.

If you are hunting with a mesh baseball cap or one that is adjustable with an open back, mosquitoes will not only bite through the mesh, they will also get in between your hat and your head from the open rear side of the cap, causing you to have to move around to swat them. If you are moving to fight mosquitoes while turkey hunting, you are wasting your time in the turkey woods.

The next item you need is a good face mask, preferably one that does not fit your skin tightly, but is loose around you. This way, the mosquitoes cannot bite through the face mask and will only fly around it. They may light on it, but because it is not touching you, the mosquitoes cannot bite through it. The face mask should also fit you fairly tightly around the eyes, so that when you move your head, it does not obstruct your vision.

I use a face mask with an elastic band inside that is connected right to the eye holes. When this elastic band is put around your head, the eye holes remain in place, regardless of the movement you might make while looking for a turkey or for other hunters slipping up on you. The face mask also has an elastic band around the bottom to prevent mosquitoes from flying under it and getting inside.

I prefer to hunt with a mask without a nose hole cut in it because a nose hole will sometimes fray and the threads will tickle your nose or mosquitoes will fly in. I prefer to sew up the nose hole in any face mask I use. If you wear glasses, however, it is almost necessary that your face mask have a nose hole to prevent fogging them up. That is the reason most face masks have nose holes in them.

I also prefer a face mask without a mouth hole in it. This keeps you from breathing in mosquitoes when you inhale air to blow your diaphragm. One disadvantage is that you have to reach under the face mask to change the call you are using. When changing calls, you should always look all around you to make certain that there is no turkey in the area.

I have been in the process of changing calls, only to look up and see a gobbler standing there watching me. I can assure you that once a turkey gobbler sees you move, he is not going to stick around to see why you moved or what you are. He is going to be in the next county before you can get your gun to your shoulder.

I try to always pick very loose fitting undershirts and outershirts. I always try to wear long sleeve undershirts and I never go in the woods without a long sleeve outershirt. Two long sleeve shirts make it virtually impossible for a mosquito to bite through your clothing, especially if the clothing is very loose and does not make contact with your body. Loose fitting clothing also allows you to stay fairly cool while hunting on warm days and it does not restrict movements.

Effective camouflage is essential. The long sleeve T-shirts under my outershirt and the outer shirt are the same camouflage. I prefer a T-shirt with a pocket and an outershirt with two pockets. I always carry my emergency paper in the pocket of my T-shirt, and I carry other items such as my glasses, extra turkey calls or whatever I need in the two pockets in my outershirt.

Over those shirts, I always wear a turkey hunting vest with four pockets inside for my flashlight and miscellaneous items such as insect repellent. The vest also has several pockets on the outside designed to carry most equipment you will need. I carry my face mask until I am ready to use it, and my gloves. I also carry turkey calls in a specially designed pocket for turkey calls. It also has a pocket with elastic in it for carrying shotgun shells. The pockets are also large enough to carry a locator call, such as a hawk call, crow call or owl hooter. The vest also has a specially designed pocket to carry a striker if you use a friction call that requires one. It also comes equipped with a game bag which is ideal for carrying my Niff-T-Seat.

While calling to a turkey, I always wear a pair of thin gloves with high wrist cuffs on them. I never wear mesh gloves turkey hunting. These very thin gloves permit you to feel well enough to pick up diaphragm calls without removing your glove and changing mouth calls while calling. In addition, these gloves permit you to feel the safety on your gun, and do not put you in any danger of accidentally squeezing the trigger after you have taken the safety off. It is essential that you have a very good pair of camouflage gloves when turkey hunting. When a turkey comes into sight, the only thing that you should ever move on your body is your hands to get your gun in a position to shoot. If your hands are well camouflaged, you can get away with a great deal more movement than if they are not.

You'll always want to wear the thinnest gloves possible. Since you never want to jerk the trigger on a shotgun when shooting, the thinner the gloves, the easier it is to tell the amount of tension you are putting on the trigger as you squeeze it. The gloves that I wear while turkey hunting are the only piece of apparel that I want to fit tightly. I want to be able to feel everything that I touch, including the tape on the diaphragm call, and sometimes even how the call is made so that I can tell which side of the call goes up or down in my mouth without having to look at it. On all the calls I use, the tab on the frame in the back of the call is always on the bottom of the call. With the sensitivity provided by thin gloves, I can actually feel the tab on the call and can always tell what side I should put in my mouth facing down.

Since my gloves are going to be the tightest fitting and thinnest clothing that I will be wearing, I always spray my gloves with insect repellent before I leave my truck and start walking to the place where I intend to listen for a gobbler. I like the long wrist cuffs on my gloves because those cuffs will fit under the sleeve of my shirt and prevent mosquitoes from biting me around my wrist.

In choosing pants, I try to have the pants legs a little bit longer than I would normally wear because when I sit down I do not want them to ride up over the top of my boots. I want my pants to fit loosely for the same reasons I want my other clothes to fit me loosely. I always like my pants to have as many pockets, and as deep, as possible. Your pants and all the clothing you wear while turkey hunting should be as soft as possible so that you can walk through the woods without making much noise.

One of the places you will always be attacked by mosquitoes is the back side of your leg behind your thighs. This is where it hurts the most for a mosquito to bite you. I always spray the back of my legs with insect repellent as an added precaution. It is virtually impossible for a human being not to react to a mosquito that bites him on the back side of his leg. One of the things you do not want to do while turkey hunting is to be calling to a boss gobbler, and all of the sudden have to scratch a place where a mosquito bit you two or three days ago.

I do not know of a human being alive that can withstand an attack of mosquitoes on his ankles under any circumstances. I can withstand a great deal of pain while hunting, but it is impossible for me to restrain myself from scratching or killing mosquitoes biting me on my ankles, even if the largest wild turkey gobbler in the world is coming in to me.

To keep mosquitos from biting my ankles, I always wear green socks that reach up to just below my knees. Long socks cover my lower legs if my pants are too short, and ride up above the top of my boots. In addition, it gives me an additional layer of clothing under my pants, from the top of my boots to the top of my calves, where mosquitoes would have to bite through two layers of clothes.

I never hunt in regular shoes or 3/4 boots or shoes. I always hunt in high top boots for several reasons. The first, and most important reason, is that I am protected to some extent from snake bite at least to the height of the boots. Secondly, I can wade in water, probably six to eight inches deep, without the water getting over the top of my boots.

Finally, high top boots always protect your ankles from mosquito bites. Plus, in the southeastern part of the United States in the spring, ticks and redbugs are beginning to crawl, and high top boots will give you some protection from them.

I personally do not like boots that have cleats or lugs on the bottom. I find that they contribute nothing to your traction once they are filled with mud. The mud that accumulates on the bottom of a pair of boots adds weight to the boot, and if you have to walk long distances, as you do many times, it just contributes to tiring you out.

I do not recommend boots that have hooks instead of eyes for lacing up. You would be constantly snagging those hooks on briars and vines and bending them, causing your shoe laces to become loose and untied. Not only is it uncomfortable to walk through the woods with loose or untied shoestrings, it is dangerous. I do not know a single hunter who has not at sometime in his experience stepped on his own shoelace and tripped.

In addition to the equipment you need in preparation for turkey hunting, you need other equipment to move into the woods to get in a position. The first, and most important thing is a flashlight that is compact and lightweight, so that it is not a burden to carry. It should be fairly bright to enable you to see for a reasonable distance.

If you are going to properly hunt the wild turkey in the spring, you must go into the woods before daylight and be in the position where you intend to listen for a turkey gobbler before the sun comes up. To reach the place before daylight, it is absolutely essential that you have a flashlight. I do not know of a single hunter who can find his way through the woods to any specific point on a cloudy or overcast morning with no light.

You should always make sure that it has a good bulb, lights and batteries, so that you do not get in the woods and find yourself with a bad flashlight. When walking to the point that you want to listen to your gobbler, you should use the light as little as possible, but you should also try to walk as quietly as you can to the point where you intend to listen for the turkey. Once you reach that point, turn the flashlight off and put it away. You never know whether a turkey may be roosting within ten or fifteen yards or a hundred or two hundred yards of you.

Once you have reached the point where you intend to listen for a turkey to gobble on the roost, you need to stand there perfectly still and quiet until it starts to get daylight. I use two tests to determine when I should first try to get a turkey to gobble. Number one is when I hear the first birds start to chirp. If other birds are waking up, then turkeys are waking up, too. Sometimes you can get a turkey to gobble very early if you hear other birds making sounds in the woods and start using your locator calls. If you do not hear any other sounds in the woods, then the moment that I can see the hands on my watch, I know that it is light enough for turkeys to be awake and making sounds on the roost.

Once it gets light enough for you to attempt to get a turkey to gobble, you should get prepared to make the sounds to locate a turkey gobbler. There are four basic "locator" calls available on the market today that you should always have. The first, and most frequently used, is an owl call. If you cannot make the sound of an owl with your natural voice with enough volume to carry for a long distance, then you should absolutely have an owl call.

If a turkey gobbles when you owl to him, get prepared for the hunt. If the turkey does not gobble when you owl to him, then it is a good idea to try a crow call. Again, if you cannot make the sound of a crow with your natural voice, purchase a good call.

After you have owled two or three times and nothing responds, then you should try a crow call and do three or four repetitions. If that fails, then you should try the hawk call. Personally, I very rarely ever get to that stage. Either I have had a turkey gobble, or there is already enough daylight that I am going to start calling to a turkey with a diaphragm or friction call. But, in any event, sometimes a turkey will respond to the squeal of a red-tailed hawk.

As a last resort, and I mean absolutely as a last resort, you can use the gobble box. Using the gobble box is extremely dangerous. As an alternative, you may want to try using whatever calls you have with you. One of the most effective calls is a very low and very soft tree call. The tree call can be done on almost any friction call and on most diaphragm calls. I have never had a turkey respond to a tree call that I did not eventually kill. If a turkey does not respond to a tree call, then the final locating call that you would want to use is the fly down cackle. This particular call can be done best with a diaphragm, although I have heard many people use a friction call to get an excellent fly down cackle.

To review this, you are now at the point where you want to try to locate a gobbler. You have made it into the woods, where you fully expect to listen for a turkey gobbler. Now you need to make the turkey gobble so that you can get set up on him. You need an owl call, a crow call, hawk call, and have at your disposal a gobble box or some other gobble device to try to shock a turkey to gobble.

If all of those fail, then you want to go to the call that you use best, that will not only make a very soft tree call of a turkey hen, but that can be done with a diaphragm call or a friction call. If the tree call does not get a response, then the next locator call that you want to make is the fly down cackle of a turkey hen. That, in my opinion, can best be done on a diaphragm call. If, for some reason, you cannot use a diaphragm call, and many people with denture plates

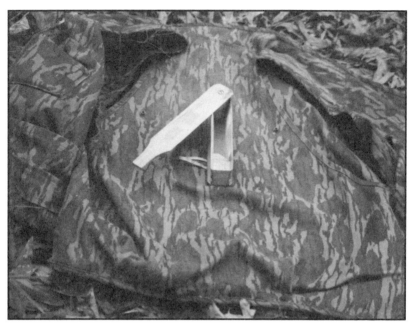

A gobble box. This box will also make hen sounds, but when vigorously shaken, will make the sound of a turkey gobbler.

cannot, then you need to learn to do the fly down cackle on a tube call or a friction call.

If you have heard a turkey gobble, get ready for the most exciting and important element of turkey hunting -- getting the turkey you heard gobble to come to you. To do that, you need to have a turkey call that you are proficient at using. Probably the most common type of call used today is the diaphragm call. These calls come in many different varieties, with many different cuts in the latex or rubber that is used to build the calls. The calls come in many different sizes and kinds of tape on them. You should choose one that fits most comfortably in your mouth, and one that you can use to make the kind of sounds necessary. Diaphragm calls come with as few as one reed -- that is, with one stretch of rubber or latex across them -- up to as many as four reeds. I do not

An assortment of diaphragm calls. These calls come in single frame or stack frame. They also have different tensions of stretch on the latex rubber and the latex rubber may have a variety of nicks or cuts in it to give a variety of different sounds.

know of any manufacturer who makes a five reed diaphragm call, but there are some manufacturers of turkey calls who make stacked frame calls. You need to experiment with all of these calls to determine which one best fits your mouth, and which one makes the sound that you like the best for calling. To use these calls, it is necessary for you to put them in your mouth, place them against the roof of your mouth and blow air across them until you can produce the sound of the wild turkey.

The next type of call that is used -- and are not classified as friction calls -- is known as the tube call. This is a derivative of the old snuff can calls. These calls have a piece of latex stretched across one-half of a tube and a solid other

A snuff can. Made by cutting the bottom out of the can to get the sound chamber, and by cutting one-half of the top of the lid out. The latex rubber is then stretched across the top of the can, and the lid with the cut-out side placed down over the latex rubber.

half. A turkey sound is made by placing the call against your mouth, getting it moist, and blowing puffs of air across the latex or rubber, producing the sound of a turkey hen. The other most commonly used non-friction, non-diaphragm call is the wing bone of a turkey hen. This call is made by taking the wing bone, extracting the marrow from that wing bone, then scraping the wing bone down to where it is fairly thin. Place one end of the wing bone in your mouth between your lips and suck on it to make the sound of a turkey hen. It has been said that the turkey hen wing bone is the only one that can be used to call a wild turkey gobbler. Personally, I believe this is a myth, and that the hollowed out wing bone

The wing bone of a turkey. Hollow out the wing bone of a turkey, and then by sucking on the wing bone you can make the sound of a turkey hen.

of any turkey will do, whether it is a domestic or wild turkey.

The last category of turkey calls available on the market today are what are known as "friction" calls. These include one-sided box calls, which only make the sound of a turkey hen, or two-sided box calls, which will make the sound of a turkey hen on either side, or when vigorously shaken, will make a gobbling sound. Other friction calls include: slate calls, which require the use of a striker rubbed across the slate to make the sound of a hen; glass calls, which are sanded to become coarse, and use a striker to make the sound of a hen.

Many different kinds of push button calls are available. Some make the sound of only one hen, while others will

Homemade slate friction calls with homemade wood strikers.

make the sound of two hens. These calls can also be used to make contented purrs of hens feeding, or aggravated purrs of gobblers fighting. Push button calls require relatively little or no skill to use. All that is necessary is the ability to push a peg, which will produce a sound similar to that of a hen. Push button calls are simple to use, and, in many instances, require the use of only one hand, and do produce results for many turkey hunters.

You need to experiment with all of these calls to determine which of them best suits your needs and produces for you the sounds, you believe, will make you a successful turkey hunter. By far the most versatile call that you can use is a diaphragm. Not only can you make every call that a turkey hen makes, you can make those calls with your hands free. Except for the gobble, there is no turkey sound that cannot be made on a diaphragm. It is easy to do the yelp,

A one-sided box call. This box call will not allow you to gobble and it will only make the sound of a hen turkey.

cluck, tree call, kee-kee, kee-kee run, purr, cackle, cut or cutting, putt, and lost call on the diaphragm call. There are very few people who can totally master the diaphragm, and those who cannot must rely on friction calls and tube calls as well as the diaphragm calls.

Those who have mastered the diaphragm perfectly do all of the calls mentioned above, and therefore can call most any turkey by using the diaphragm alone. Some who have totally mastered the use of the diaphragm use no other calls. However, they will use other calls, such as the box call, to locate turkeys. The box call will give you much more volume than you can get out of a diaphragm, and it is an extremely valuable tool in locating turkeys. Once the turkey is located by doing a gobble or a yelp on a box call, most hunters who have mastered the diaphragm will use it

Commercially produced glass call with plexiglass striker. This call makes an excellent cluck, purr and yelp.

as their primary method. It is much easier to make a mistake using a friction call than it is using the diaphragm. For that reason, those hunters who have mastered the use of the diaphragm rely heavily on it.

You will find that there are times when a turkey will only respond to certain kinds of calls. That is, you can be using a four reed diaphragm and a turkey will not respond at all, and you can replace that call with a three reed diaphragm and the turkey will respond every time you call. If you go back to using the four reed, the turkey will stop gobbling. The same is true with respect to friction calls and tube calls. There are times when turkeys will not respond to any diaphragm, but will respond to every call you make on a box call. You need to keep this in mind before deciding to depend solely upon one of these calls to the exclusion of all

Homemade slate call with homemade corn cob striker. This call is used mostly to make a turkey yelping sound.

others. It is a good idea to have an assortment of calls with you while hunting the wild turkey, just in case the turkey is not responding to your favorite call.

While using the diaphragm, all of the calls mentioned above can be made with a minimum of movement and with your hands free to get your gun in position to shoot. Even after you have your gun in position to shoot, with both hands on the gun and the safety off, you can do very soft purring and clucking to coax the turkey into range. If there is any way possible for you to learn to use the diaphragm call, you should do so.

Another piece of equipment every turkey hunter needs is something to sit on once they have picked a place to set up on a wild turkey. Some hunters use cushions and others use nothing, but those who use nothing usually end up being

Commercially produced trough call with plexiglass striker.

very uncomfortable. If you pick a spot and sit down using nothing, you may sit on roots, acorns, pine cones or anything else that may be under you, which will make it impossible for you to remain comfortable while calling. Some turkey hunters use cushions to prevent them from sitting directly on the ground and getting wet or sitting on some object that may be or become uncomfortable to them.

I use a seat known as the Niff-T-Seat which is ideal because it keeps you off the ground, and there is never the possibility that water or moisture will soak through your cushion. Just like everything else in turkey hunting, each individual has to make his own decision about what type of seat to use. Every turkey hunter knows that after a rain, if you do not have some sort of cushion or seat, it can become extremely miserable sitting on the wet ground for two or three hours attempting to call a turkey in to you.

Nearly every turkey hunter, and when I say nearly I mean 99 out of every 100 turkey hunters I know, uses something to sit on while hunting. I will not go in the woods without my Niff-T-Seat. It is the driest, most comfortable and most effective seat I have ever used.

The seat is lightweight, very portable and easy to assemble. In addition, you can rock up on your knees off the seat and get circulation back in your legs and butt and then just sit back on the seat. Without the pedestal, the seat permits you to swivel so that you can see turkeys coming up on your blind spots. If you use the seat with the pedestal, it gives you even greater flexibility to swivel and stand up without being concerned about the seat falling over. This seat has helped me on many occasions to remain in one spot with the minimum amount of movement and to eventually harvest a turkey.

6

SCOUTING AND PREPARATION FOR THE HUNT

As I have pointed out earlier, turkey hunting is an individual sport -- not a team sport. When scouting for the wild turkey, you should try to do as much of your scouting as possible alone. In this way, you do not have two or three people moving through the woods harassing the wildlife and scaring the turkeys. You can also scout in your own way and at your own speed.

When you find turkey signs or spot turkeys, they will be your turkeys, and you can hunt them. Everyone has his own method of scouting for turkeys and you should develop your own method by scouting alone whenever possible. The more experience you gain as a turkey hunter, the more you will understand the need for doing all of your scouting alone, and for turkey hunting alone. It is not being selfish. It is merely the best method of hunting the wild turkey, since the fewer people there are in the woods, the greater your chance of success.

The first and most important thing when preparing to hunt the wild turkey is to know the area. Any little change in a terrain feature, or any man-made obstacle, can create problems. I am going to list several things that you need to

This is a picture of some excellent turkey hunting woods which show very good turkey habitat and is an area where I have called up many turkeys.

familiarize yourself with, before you hunt. Every piece of property has unique features that can either help or hurt you in hunting the turkey. For example, you need to know where every fence is located, because a fence can sometimes be an obstacle to a turkey.

I have hunted turkeys where there are fences around the perimeters of the area, and then cross-fences across the area. If you are not aware of the location of these fences and you set up at a distance where you cannot see them, then you may call a turkey to that fence and sometimes you will be unable to make him cross it. Always attempt to be on the same side of the fence as the turkey.

I will give you four examples of what can happen when a turkey reaches a fence. I have seen turkeys come to a fence, and it did not make any difference whether it was an old or new fence, whether it was grown up or in good repair, nor does it make any difference whether the fence is barbed or hog wire. I have seen them gobble and strut and walk up and down the fence on the opposite side of where I was calling them, for a distance of a hundred yards or so. In the case of a barbed wire fence, it would have been a simple matter for the turkey to walk under the fence and come on to me. But once the turkey reached the fence, it would not cross it. After it got to that fence, the turkey acted like he wanted the hen to be the one to cross it. He displayed and gobbled and remained there, so I was unable to kill that turkey.

On one occasion, I was calling a gobbler and he was coming to me, and I was on the opposite side of a fence. When the turkey got to the fence, it did not pose an obstacle to him at all. Instead of flying over the fence or jumping over it, the turkey merely squatted, and crawled under it. So, sometimes they will go under a fence, and sometimes they will not. It depends on the mood the turkey is in on the particular day. A good general rule is to always be on the same side of the fence as the turkey.

One morning while turkey hunting in Texas, I had not heard a turkey gobble, so I set up to do some dry calling, not knowing if there were any turkeys in the area. I could see a cross fence not far from me. In a few minutes, three turkeys started gobbling to me.

Later, I saw three turkeys, on the opposite side of the fence, and they were all coming to me gobbling. I could see the turkeys coming for a long distance, and I watched them as they made their way to the fence. They reached the fence at a point almost directly in front of me. About a hundred yards to my left, I could see an old road that ran through this area and a closed gate. The fence was a mesh, or hog wire fence, with three strands of barbed wire at the top. When the turkeys reached it, they spent about fifteen or twenty minutes walking up and down, gobbling and strutting and would not cross it. After about fifteen or twenty minutes of this, the turkeys started walking straight down the fence row until they reached the old road. When the turkeys reached the gate, they jumped on the gate, and then jumped off to my side of the fence. Then they came back up the fence and right straight to me.

On other occasions, fences have not been an obstacle because some turkeys do not hesitate to fly over a fence. It has been my experience that once a turkey hangs up on a fence, you can forget trying to call him across it. Under those circumstances, you must change positions. You must quit calling to the turkey, try to leave the position that you are in, circle around, cross the fence away from the turkey and start calling to him again.

Water is another very important factor in turkey hunting. You must know where every stream, creek, river, lake, slough, bayou, or pond is on the area. You need to be on the same side of the water that the turkey is on because most of the time a turkey will not fly across water. One day I was hunting turkeys in an area where I had seen an awful lot of turkey sign. The spot I picked to set up was a big tree right next to a slough that was about fifty yards wide. I picked the slough because I did not think the turkeys would come from behind me. I thought the turkeys were going to come to me from the front.

I had been calling there for about forty-five minutes when I heard a turkey clucking behind me on the other side of this slough. There was no way for me to get around to see or kill the turkey and I did not know whether this was a hen or a gobbler.

I did not believe that I could make the turkey fly the slough so I just quit calling for about twenty minutes hoping the turkey would leave before it spotted me. I was afraid that it would alert other turkeys in the area of my presence. Since I did not believe I could make the turkey fly the slough, I did not want to take the chance that it would put other turkeys on the alert.

After about twenty minutes, I did a series of yelps, and just as I finished the yelps, the turkey landed about two feet from me. I turned to look and he saw me. His feet had hardly touched the ground and he was gone. When that turkey hit the ground, his wings almost touched me, and it scared me so bad that I literally shook for about five minutes. The turkey was there just long enough for me to see that I had screwed up a hunt on a long beard!

On another occasion, I only had about two hours to hunt. I heard a distant turkey gobble. I knew that I did not have time to get down through the woods to him, so I decided to set up on him and start calling.

The turkey was gobbling from his roost in a beaver pond that was about a half-mile long. The turkey sailed down off the roost on the opposite side of the beaver pond from me, but he was answering me every breath. I could barely hear him gobble on the ground, but he kept getting closer and closer to me coming up the opposite side of the beaver pond. Eventually, I could see him coming and he was in a full strut most of the time.

Soon, he was directly across the pond from me, but too far to shoot. I would call to him and he would walk right up to the edge of the water, turn around and walk back. He would do that every time I called to him. Eventually, the turkey turned and started back down the beaver pond the exact way that he had come. I could barely hear him gobbling when he reached the end of the beaver pond.

I kept calling and calling to the turkey. Eventually, I could hear him coming up the woods on my side of the pond. This turkey had come to me on the opposite side of the beaver pond -- did not fly the water to me -- turned and walked all the way to the end of that pond, walked around the end of it, and was now coming to me up my side of the pond. He was taking his own sweet time about getting to me, and as my two hour time for hunting that morning ended, I could still hear the turkey gobbling and coming on to me but at a very slow pace. Since I did not know how much longer it was going to take to get this turkey in close enough to kill, I decided to leave the turkey gobbling and come back the next morning to see if I could position myself better.

One of the hardest things I have ever done in my life was to get up and walk away from that turkey, but not being on the same side of the water cost me that gobbler. The next morning when I went to that spot, there was no sound of a gobbler.

On another occasion, I was sitting on the edge of a large pond and calling. I had been calling for about forty-five minutes and had not heard a gobble, then the thunder of a gobble came roaring through the swamp. Of course, I was facing away from the pond because I had not expected a turkey to gobble on the opposite side of the pond. I changed my position and was able to get situated so that I could see across the pond. I felt certain I could make this turkey fly across the pond.

The more I called, the more the turkey gobbled and he was just as ''hot'' as he could be. On several occasions, he would interrupt my yelp with a thunderous gobble and sometimes double and triple gobble. As I gazed across the pond, I saw him coming in all of his splendor - his head solid white on the top, his waddles fiery red and his feathers puffed out like a big balloon. He came walking right up to the edge of the water, and I think he even stuck his toe in the water, but he would come no further. He stood in one spot, strutted, drummed and spit; and responded to every

A logging road through some excellent turkey hunting woods, and a road I have used many times to look for turkey sign.

yelp and every call that I made to him, but he would not fly over the water.

After about thirty minutes of this, one of the most disgusting and disappointing things that could possibly happen to a turkey hunter, happened to me. As I looked across and watched the gobbler, I saw a real turkey hen come walking up to the spot where the gobbler was standing. Needless to say, my chances of killing this turkey had just ended, because as the old saying goes, "a bird in the hand is worth two in the bush" and in this case a hen at hand was worth two hens on the other side of the slough. I was helpless. I had to sit there and watch this hen "take" my gobbler and disappear down through the river swamp.

Turkeys flying off the roost into an open field or pasture.

The following was told to me by a good friend of mine, Tommy Bourne. In 1987, Tommy won the Mississippi State Championship Turkey Calling Contest, and also won the Mississippi State Owl Hooting Contest, and is the only person to have ever accomplished that. In addition to being a great turkey caller, he is one of the best complete turkey hunters I know. Tommy related to me a story that is an example of how you can make a turkey gobbler fly water to you, and it also verifies that if you are in a place that a turkey wants to be, you can call him to you.

As Tommy tells the story, he was hunting with an older gentleman who could not climb the hills and negotiate the hollows of Jeff Davis County, Mississippi. On this particular morning, they had heard several turkeys gobble, but because of the older gentleman's inability to negotiate the terrain,

A turkey roosting site. This is a large gumpond where turkeys regularly roost and where I go often to owl to turkeys in the spring.

they could not get to the bird. They decided to set up on the edge of a big corn field that had a creek on one side.

After he had been there for a while, periodically dry calling, all of a sudden he heard a turkey gobble, but unfortunately the turkey was on the other side of the creek from Tommy. The old man Tommy was hunting with assured him that there was no way he could make the turkey fly the creek.

The turkey continued to get closer and closer as Tommy called to him. The more Tommy called, the more the turkey gobbled. So Tommy decided the only way he was going to make the turkey fly the creek was to quit calling, and that is what he did. Shortly after Tommy quit calling, he looked up and saw the turkey coming to him. The turkey finally got within gun range and Tommy was going to let his partner kill the turkey.

Unfortunately, when his partner shot, he missed the turkey and it escaped. This story indicates that sometimes it is better not to call to a turkey. As long as Tommy called to the turkey, the turkey gobbled but would not fly the creek. Once Tommy stopped calling, the turkey flew the creek and came right on in to him. You can call turkeys across water if you are set up in a place where a turkey wants to be.

In addition to the features already discussed, you need to know where every hill, valley, depression, logging road, main road, pasture, cutover, pipeline, power line and other topographical features of the area you are hunting are located. Many times turkeys will fly down to power lines or pipelines or out in the middle of big fields or cutovers. If you know where those places are, and how to get to them, you definitely have an advantage.

You should know where old logging roads or woods roads are because many times a turkey will travel these roads. Go to these spots, sit down and start to call. On more than one occasion, I have had a gobbler walk right up to me on an old woods or logging road. Turkeys will use power lines, pipe lines, fields and pastures to strut. When a turkey is strutting, he wants all the hens in his territory to see him strut and be attracted to him by his display. It is much easier for a turkey hen to see a gobbler strutting in an open area such as a pipeline, power line or pasture than it is for a hen to see a gobbler strutting in the woods.

It is not just important to know where these areas are, it is also very important to know how you can get to all of these areas, and the quickest way to get to them. Many times you will have to get there before daylight in pitch dark, and if you do not know the woods you are not going to be able to find your way.

Gobbler track found in the mud located in a logging road in some excellent turkey woods.

Many times I have found myself turned around in the woods before daylight and have had to stop and wait until daylight so I could figure out where I was. When that happens to you, you have lost the most important time to turkey hunt -- the moment right at daylight when the turkey might gobble on the roost. If you know your woods well enough, that should never happen to you.

While scouting for wild turkeys, one of the most important things to look for is a roosting site. Roosting sites are extremely difficult to find if you are not in the woods at daylight or at dusk. In the springtime, at daylight and just at dark, you can hear turkeys on the roost. At daylight, you can hear the gobbler gobbling on the roost, and you can hear turkey hens calling to him. Just at dark,

Scouting And Preparation For The Hunt

you can hear the flapping of the wings as they fly up to roost, and many times the gobbler will gobble. Finding these places before the season opens is a big advantage.

When turkeys roost over water, their droppings fall in the water making it more difficult to find them. When turkeys roost over land, their droppings fall on the ground and a nocturnal predator can more easily find the roost. The predator can then climb the tree and catch the turkey while it is on the roost.

Generally speaking, turkeys prefer to roost over water and they prefer roosting over ponds which have standing timber in them such as gumponds, cypress ponds and beaver ponds. They will roost around the edges of lakes and on the banks of creeks. The reason turkeys prefer roosting over water is that it protects them from nocturnal predators that are able to climb.

In areas where there is not an abundance of water, turkeys prefer to roost in or around elevated sites such as hills and mountains. When the weather is still and dry, they will roost higher in trees on the tops of hills or mountains. When the weather is windy, rainy or cold, generally speaking, turkeys will roost down on the sides of hills and on the lower limbs of those trees. They seem to know instinctively what the weather conditions are going to be and choose their roosting sites accordingly.

I have seen them return to the same roosting place day after day and fly up to roost. I have also watched them fly up to roost, and in many instances, watched them fly to the same tree. Depending on what the weather conditions are, I have watched them hop from limb to limb before deciding on a particular limb until they have found a place where they feel safe and comfortable.

When scouting the area you are going to hunt, it is extremely important that you find roosting areas and know the terrain of those areas where the turkeys are flying down off the roost early in the morning. If there is no water over which turkeys can roost, you can find roosting sites by looking for large amounts of turkey droppings on the ground under trees. These roosting sites will usually be found up on tops or on sides of hills. Turkeys rarely roost in bottoms, but they will do that from time to time.

I have often heard experienced hunters say that you should always study a topo map of the area you are going to hunt. Learn the elevations and the depressions and every land feature outlined in the map. It certainly does not hurt to get a topo map of the area you are going to hunt, however, there is absolutely no substitute for walking over the area before the season.

Look for turkey signs and know where you are going, and how you are going to get there. Topo maps will not show you how deep a creek is, or whether that creek is on the rise or where the foot logs that you may have to use to get across that creek are located. The only way that you are going to find the foot logs or the shallow places in the creek that you can wade, is to go to that creek and find out where you can cross it.

Topo maps are not going to show you feeding areas for turkeys or roosting sites where turkeys might be. They are not going to show you turkey sign like scratching, feathers, and droppings. You need to get in the woods and find out where the turkeys are ranging and what they are doing. Find roosting areas where they are coming down when they come off the roost. All of this information will help you determine where you are going to have to be in the morning when the sun comes up.

Once you familiarize yourself with the terrain, then it is time to do some serious scouting. It does not make any difference what time you are in the woods, you will always want to be looking for turkey sign. Turkeys will be in one area one day and in another area the next.

Scouting And Preparation For The Hunt

Gobbler tracks found in the mud in the turkey woods.

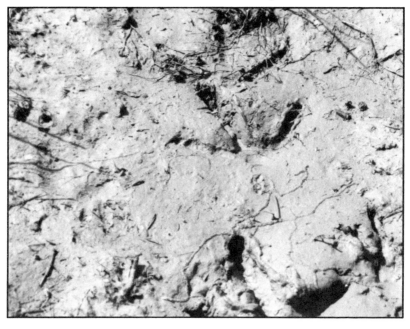

102 *Turkey Tracks*

However, if you consistently find turkey sign in one area, that means they are pretty well staying close, and that is an area you may want to hunt in the spring. When you are deer or squirrel hunting, you always want to have your eye out for turkey sign. Of course, you want to look specifically for gobbler sign, but if you find hen sign or just turkey sign in general, you can bet the gobblers are not far away.

As a general rule, you will find more turkey sign in the fall and winter while the turkeys are in flocks than you will during the spring and summer, when the turkeys have dispersed into smaller flocks. When turkeys are traveling in groups, usually anywhere from twenty to seventy-five in a flock, it is much easier to find sign such as scratching, droppings, feathers, dusting sites and tracks. If you do not see the sign, it does not mean that turkeys are not there.

Tracks are probably the easiest sign to find. Turkeys will walk on roads, and it does not make any difference to them if they are walking in mud. Wherever they have to go, they will not let a little mud stop them. They like to dust in sandy areas, and it is always a good idea to check out these areas.

While walking on old roads, always go to every mud puddle and check it out. There is a big difference between a gobbler and a hen track, and once you have seen both of them, you will never have any trouble recognizing and distinguishing the tracks. Gobbler tracks are always much larger than hen tracks. Even a jake track is longer than a hen track, so you will not have any trouble distinguishing the two tracks.

In addition to looking for turkey tracks, you always want to look for turkey feathers. Turkey feathers are easy to distinguish from any other bird in the woods -- especially the feathers around the tail of the gobbler. They are iridescent, and as the sun hits them from different angles, they show different colors like green and blue. It is just unbelievable how beautiful those feathers are when you hold them up. Wing feathers are long, brownish in color, and will have little white streaks across them.

If you find a wing feather in the spring, and it looks like somebody cut the end off it, there is no question that it is a gobbler feather. Gobblers will wear those feathers down by strutting and dragging them on the ground and you can tell from a wing feather if a gobbler has been strutting.

Another sign of a turkey gobbler or hen is droppings. Gobbler droppings will usually be shaped like a question mark or a walking cane; the hen dropping will usually be sort of a blob with a little white color on top of it or mixed in it. So any time you are walking around in the woods, you want to look for turkey droppings, because you can establish whether a gobbler or hen has been there.

One morning I was calling to a gobbler and had him coming in to me. I was watching him, but he was not close enough for me to shoot him. I actually saw him defecate. Once the gobbler left, and I had given up on hunting him, I went over and examined his droppings. It was, just as plain as day, a walking cane shaped dropping.

A dusting area is a great place to find turkey sign and they are fairly easy to find. The best place to look for a dusting site is in loose ground, primarily in sandy areas where turkeys can scratch out bowls in the sand, get in them and kind of roll around and flop their feathers around. They do this to groom their feathers and rid themselves of insects, and they do it all year round. There are always going to be a lot of turkey tracks, so you can tell whether or not gobblers or hens were there. You will usually also find feathers because when they are flopping around and picking on themselves, they pull feathers out.

Scratching, done by turkeys is fairly easy to detect, and it is always something you should be looking for. I have heard people say that turkeys leave certain marks in the

A hen track found in a sandy area near a turkey dusting site.

woods when they are scratching, but it has been my experience that turkey scratches will not always look the same every time.

Sometimes turkeys will go through the woods scratching. Their scratching looks like one foot reached out and pulled the leaves back in one direction and then the other foot reached out and pulled the leaves back at a slightly different angle forming a perfect "V" in the leaves. The point of that "V" is the direction the turkey was heading. I have seen areas just torn completely up, and I knew turkeys were responsible because I could find their tracks and droppings in the areas they scratched.

Another scratching sign that turkeys leave looks like a little circle. There will be an absolutely clean space about six inches in diameter or maybe a little bigger than that, where a turkey scratched out a complete almost perfect

Scouting And Preparation For The Hunt

A dusting site of a turkey.

circle on the ground. On other occasions, you will come up on scratchings and you will not be able to tell whether they are from turkeys or not. Usually, if you have a large area of disturbed leaves, turkeys are responsible. After you have watched turkeys scratch and go to examine the area, you will be able recognize turkey scratching any time you see them in the woods.

If you are ever in the woods and you happen to spot turkeys before they spot you, just sit down and be real still, and watch them. When the turkeys leave and get out of sight, get up and examine the area where the turkeys went through and see what kind of sign they left. You will be better able to tell what kind of sign they are leaving when you spot it again in the woods, and you will know for sure if the sign was left by turkeys.

A dusting site where turkey feathers have been shed.

In the spring, you will want to look for strutting areas. This is nothing more than the place a gobbler travels to just about every day where he struts and drags his wings around. Turkeys like to strut in places where they can be seen from a long distance by hens. They will pick open woods, and a lot of times, they will pick pipe lines, power lines, open fields and pastures, so that hens can see them for a long way. You should always examine these places for areas where turkeys are strutting.

When a turkey struts, he always drags his wings on both sides of him, so you should look for the tracks and on both sides of the tracks, look for drag marks on the ground where the turkey has been dragging his wings. If you find a strutting area, then you are going to want to try to hunt it sometimes. A lot of times in the morning, you will hear a

A gobbler dusting site. Gobbler tracks leading away from the dusting site tell me this is where a gobbler dusted.

turkey gobble in the tree and you will start calling, but you'll hear him fly out of that tree, hit the ground and start gobbling going straight away from you. When that happens, in many instances that turkey is headed to his strutting area for one or several reasons.

Strutting areas are sort of like dusting areas. You are always going to find gobbler and hen tracks, and probably turkey feathers, in a strutting area because that is where turkeys do a lot of breeding. The way a turkey gobbler breeds a hen is to crawl up on her back. It is sort of a violent process when that gobbler starts to get up on that hen's back. When he starts to mount her, he will scratch and peck at her. I have even see the gobbler slip off the hen's back.

A gobbler dropping. You can see that this dropping is in the shape of a question mark or a walking cane, and this is generally what turkey gobblers drop and how turkey gobbler droppings appear.

When the breeding process is over, the hen will always get up and shake off. I have watched turkeys breed many times and I have never seen a hen get up and just walk off. She will always get up and shake her body real good. Many times, feathers will fall off of her from where the gobbler has scratched all over her back.

The strutting area is also where the gobbler goes to call the hens to him, and sometimes he will stay there all morning long. It is not unusual for him to leave the strutting area in the middle of the day and come back late in the afternoon. So, you want to know where these strutting areas are, if you can possibly find them.

Hen droppings found in a chufa patch.

As I have already mentioned, you always want to look for turkey sign all year long -- whether you are deer hunting or squirrel hunting or rabbit hunting. Whatever you are doing in the woods whether it is gathering fire wood or anything else, you always want to be looking for turkey sign. It is just something you do when you are in the woods.

About a month before turkey season opens, you really want to get serious about scouting. You need to start getting up before daylight as often as you can, and going in the woods, walking around and looking for turkeys flying off the roost, and listening for turkeys gobbling from the roost. You want to get in the woods before daylight and go to the spots where you think there may be turkeys, so that when the season gets started, you will be used to walking in those woods in the dark. You will know what obstacles

A dead turkey hen found by the author while preseason scouting. This was a very small or young hen. I could tell by the size of the breast bone that it was a small turkey.

will be in front of you - if there are any tree limbs in your way or whether there is any water or whatever you may have to cross, so you can be prepared for it.

You will also want to do some late afternoon scouting. That means you need to be in the woods by 3:30 or 4:00 PM, an hour or two hours before dark, looking for turkey sign all the time, and walking through the woods without disturbing anything and without scaring any wild animals. Get to some place where you think turkeys might be flying up to roost, just before dark. Sit down, be real still, and sometimes turkeys will come walking right by you and fly up to roost, that will give you an idea where turkeys are roosting. It is always best that you see gobblers flying up to roost because then you know they are in the area.

Scouting And Preparation For The Hunt

The tail feather of a turkey gobbler found by the author while scouting.

If you see hens fly up to roost, that is just about as good because usually gobblers are going to find the hens in breeding season. Many times gobblers like to roost very close to hens so that when they wake up in the morning and start gobbling on a tree limb, the old hen will fly down and she will come walking right under the tree where the gobbler is roosting and he can just pitch right on down to her.

In addition to that, even if you do not see a turkey, sometimes when a gobbler flies up to the roost he will gobble on the limb. Sometimes he will sit on the limb, just before dark, and gobble several times. I have heard them gobble fifty or seventy-five times on the roost in late afternoon after they have gone up. I think they do that so they can let other gobblers know that they are the cock of

Breast feather found by the author while scouting.

the walk in that particular area that they claim that as their roost. They also gobble on the roost to get a hen to answer to them so that they will know hens are in the area. The next morning when he gobbles he knows hens are close and he will have no trouble getting with a hen.

If you want to kill a turkey gobbler on opening morning, it's a good idea to leave all your calls at home when you are in the woods scouting. If you are like me and you have turkey calls with you and you hear a gobbler gobble, you are going to want to talk to that turkey. That is not a good idea in pre-season because he will get used to your calling. He might even come in on you and spot you, then your chances of killing that turkey on opening morning are not very good. If you just like to look at turkeys, and it is not a big deal whether you kill one, then take the calls with you and call

Scouting And Preparation For The Hunt

Wing feather found by the author while scouting.

him up and look at him. However, if you play with them like that before the season starts, it is going to decrease your chance of killing a turkey during the season.

In the preseason scouting, you want to be very careful not to scare the turkeys every time you go to the woods. If you are constantly scaring these turkeys, or you are in the woods all the time, it is going to make it that much more difficult for you to harvest a turkey during the season. One thing you certainly do not ever want to do is scare a turkey off the roost, either in the morning when you get in the woods, or in the late afternoon in the preseason. If he is scared off the roost too many times, and sometimes it does not take more than one time, that turkey will leave the area. Then all of the work that you have done is for naught, and you are not going to kill that turkey when the season opens.

If you are in the woods in late afternoon, and the turkey flies up to roost close to you and you can see him sitting on the limb, you should wait until it gets dark before you leave the area. If you get up and leave at a time when the turkey can see you, he is going to fly off that roost and you just messed up a good turkey hunting spot.

In preseason scouting, as I have already said, leave your calls at home. There are only a couple of calls that you can take with you and they are your locator calls. I would not carry a gobble box with me to locate a turkey in the preseason, but I would carry an owl hooter or a crow call or a red-tail hawk call with me to see if I could locate a turkey in the morning.

You get in there at daylight, and right after that first bird makes a sound if you start blowing that owl hooter or that crow call and that turkey gobbles, you know about where he is, then you do not have anything else to do. You might want to go back in that area one or two more times before the season starts and owl to him again to make sure he is still in there. Leave that turkey alone until after turkey season starts. After you find a turkey and he has gobbled for you a couple of mornings on the roost, then you need to be looking in another spot for a second turkey.

7

HUNTING THE WILD TURKEY

So far in this book we have been through many topics. We have covered a little bit of the life cycle of the wild turkey starting when a turkey begins to breed to when the poults are hatched out; what the hens do and what the gobblers do during the breeding season and during the time that the hens are setting the nest; how the hens raise poults; how important the hen is to the poults; and what will happen to a turkey nest in the spring . Then we took you through the life cycle of a poult, when it started growing its feathers, when it stopped roosting on the ground and started roosting in trees, when it grew its adult feathers, and about what time of its life it was able to fly up in a tree to roost.

We have talked about how many eggs a hen will lay and what the predators of a wild turkey are, so you know a little bit about the wild turkey and what makes it such a wary bird. When everything in the woods is after him, raccoons and opossums and crows and skunks and coyotes and owls and hawks and fox and domestic dogs and bobcats, snakes - how practically everything in the woods will attack and kill the wild turkey from the time it is a little poult until the time it gets to be a grown bird. So all of these predators have made the turkey one of the keenest animals in the woods and one of the most difficult to hunt.

In addition to that, we talked about the importance of safety and why you should follow safety rules while turkey hunting. Everybody knows that turkey hunting is one of the most dangerous hunting sports in the United States, and it is important for all of us to be safe and remember these safety rules. Nothing can ruin a hunt faster than to have an accident happen. I have actually known situations where people give up hunting altogether after being involved in a hunting accident. We do not want that to happen to anybody, so please read and reread the chapter on safety. If you apply these safety rules to your everyday conduct in the woods, you will be a better hunter for it, and you will enjoy hunting. Best of all, you will never have to regret having shot somebody or shot yourself or hopefully, you will not ever have to worry about being shot. So, always remember the safety rules.

We also talked a little bit about how important hunting ethics are. The impact hunting has on the general public, and why we should establish standards for ourself and stick by those standards. We should not kill more than the limits and insure that when we go in the woods to hunt any animal, but especially the wild turkey, we engage in practices that could be classified as a "fair chase". As I pointed out in that chapter, you should always abide by the laws of the state where you are hunting, but you should always set a higher standard for yourself than the minimum required by the state. If you do that, you are going to give hunting a good name, and you are going to be respected by your peers. You will set an example for others to follow. I encourage everybody to develop these standards and do not forsake them under any circumstances.

I also talked about understanding the terrain where you are going to be hunting, familiarizing yourself with all of the obstacles you are going to confront and all the things that you might be able to use to your advantage. How to use water and how to use roads, fences, cutovers, pipelines and

Paul Rishel with 21 lb. Eastern turkey which had a 9 inch beard, taken in Pennsylvania. Paul is one of my very good friends and one of the best turkey hunters with whom I have ever been in the woods. His philosophy is "If I don't call it, I don't kill it."

power lines and more to your advantage in hunting the wild turkey, and why it is important that you know where these terrain features are and how to get to them. Then I talked a little about how to scout for a wild turkey; when to scout, and what to look for when you are scouting. I told you how to locate a turkey in the first two or three weeks before the season opens, and what you should do after you locate a turkey.

All of the things I have told you up to this point in this book are going to make you a better and more successful turkey hunter. Plus you will enjoy turkey hunting much more because this advice is going to increase your chances of killing turkeys every spring. But whether or not you kill a turkey is going to depend to a great extent on your own skill and ability as a hunter.

Only experience can teach you some of the things that I have told you so far. You are going to have to apply all of this material yourself, by going in the woods and actually putting it into practice when turkey season opens. If it is your first year to turkey hunt, the probabilities are you are not going to kill a turkey because you lack the experience necessary to get on him and call him up. I have known people who have hunted turkeys three or four years and some as many as five years before they ever killed a turkey gobbler. That's because if there has ever been a hunting sport where you can make a mistake, it is in turkey hunting. It is very easy to do, very simple to do and it takes one mistake for your hunt to be over for the day.

Only experience in hunting the turkey will make you conscious of your mistakes and make you correct them. You need to get in the woods, learn about the wild turkey, practice your turkey calling, learn how to be a good woodsman, how to sit up on a turkey and you will be a successful turkey hunter. You will have to get some experience to become an expert turkey hunter.

In this chapter, I am going to try to teach you how to hunt the wild turkey. I am going to tell you things you need to do when hunting the wild turkey, and I am going to try to tell you some stories about experiences I have had in hunting the wild turkey. I will relate some mistakes I have made. I do not believe there is a mistake that you can make that I have not already made. So if you listen to what I have to say in this chapter, you should not make the same mistakes I did. Your chances of killing a turkey are going to be greatly improved if you will just put into practice the things I tell you to do in this chapter.

There are some things you need to know about the way turkeys behave in the early part of the turkey season; how they behave in the middle part of the season; and how turkeys behave at the end of the season. At the beginning of turkey season, the turkey hens have not yet started to nest and are being bred on a daily basis by the turkey gobblers. As a result, turkey gobblers do a lot of gobbling early in the morning. The purpose of this gobbling is to attract hens to them. Once the turkeys have attracted a number of hens to them, they will usually stop gobbling and start breeding the turkey hens. Usually they will not gobble again until they have bred all of these hens.

In many instances, in the early part of the season, since the hens are not laying and have not gone to the nest, the hens will stay with the gobbler all day long, or the gobbler will follow the hens around all day long. Consequently, after that turkey gobbled early in the morning for the first thirty-five or forty minutes or maybe the first hour of the morning, and he has attracted several hens to him, he may not gobble any more that day because the hens will be with him all day long, or until he has bred all of them. He may gobble when he flies up to roost in the evening.

In the early part of the turkey season, from opening day to the first few days of the turkey season, it is very important for you to be in the woods before daylight to listen for a turkey to gobble on the roost, so that you can call that turkey to you before he calls hens to him. Once a turkey gets hens gathered up with him early in the morning, it is one of the most difficult things in the world to call that gobbler away from them. As a matter of fact, it is next to impossible and the probabilities are that you are not going to call a turkey to you if he has hens with him. He is probably not going to gobble much after he gets two or three or four or five hens with him.

That means you have to be in the woods early in the morning, and you have to call that turkey straight off the roost to you before he has a chance to call hens to him. As a matter of fact, about the only way you are going to kill a gobbler after he is "henned up" is to call the hens to you; and to do that you have to know how to call a turkey hen. If you can get the hens to come to you, then usually the gobbler will follow the hens right up to you, and you can take the gobbler.

Hens start laying eggs in about the middle part of the turkey season (of course this varies in different parts of the country). Early in the morning the turkey will gobble on the roost and call hens to him. He will continue to breed hens during this time. During the day, after the turkeys have bred and the hens have had a chance to feed a little, the turkey hens will leave the gobbler and go to the nesting site where they lay their eggs. They will spend several hours, or at least a good portion of the middle of the day, on the nest laying eggs. Sometimes a turkey hen will fly off the roost and go straight to her nest. She will lay an egg, and then she will leave her nest, go back in to the woods to feed and get with a gobbler.

Usually the gobbler gobbles in the morning and the hens answer him while they are in the tree. They will fly down and yelp to him, and after the gobbler hits the ground gobbling, the hens will come to him. The hens will stay with him for a little while, and then they will move off and go to

A flock of turkeys feeding in an open field.

the nest. When this happens the gobbler is usually left alone and he will continue to gobble to attract more hens.

During the middle part of the season, a gobbler is more likely to gobble up in the morning and you will have a better chance to hear a turkey gobble if you call to him later in the morning. During this time, you should be in the woods early in the morning and you should stay in the woods to see if you can hear a turkey gobble later on in the day.

The third period of time that I mentioned is when hens are setting the nest. In some parts of the country, that will take place while the turkey season is still going on. After spending some time with the gobbler in the morning, the hens will leave himr and go to the nest. Unless the hens are laying eggs, they spend most of the time away from the nest (Dickson 51). They feed away from the nest, they roost just as they usually roost -- not around the nest. As a hen lays more and more eggs, she spends more and more time closer to the nest. That means they spend more and more time away from the gobbler.

Once a hen lays her last egg, she will immediately start to incubate them, and in most instances a hen will never leave the nest. She will stay on the nest night and day for the entire period, with the exception of a short time during each day, when she may leave for an hour or maybe two to go get some water. She will usually feed and defecate when she is away from the nest so that she does not soil it.

During the time they are away from the nest, they are not interested in gobblers and they do not respond to gobblers. Once the hen starts incubating her eggs, the breeding season is over for her, and her primary interest is in the hatching of the eggs. As more and more hens start incubating the eggs, the gobbler spends more time alone looking for hens. During this time, the gobbler has a tendency to gobble a little more, and he will answer your calls all day.

From the day she lays her first egg, the hen will return to her nest every day until she starts incubating her eggs. Every day she goes to that nest, she spends a little bit longer on it and of course that is more and more time she spends away from the gobbler (Dickson 52). Right around this time, in the spring, all the hens start laying. Some hens lay earlier than others, some later than others.

Sometimes during this time, while some hens are laying eggs, some are setting the eggs. Many of the hens will be laying or setting, and while they are doing that they are away from the gobbler. This means there are fewer and fewer hens to entertain the gobbler, which means that the gobbler has to look harder for hens. The way the gobbler finds hens is to gobble to them, and get them to come to him. But once the hen goes to the nest to lay eggs or to incubate the eggs, she is not going to respond to the gobbler.

This is when it is easier for you to call up a turkey, or at least it is easier for you to make that gobbler gobble back to your calling. When hens are setting the nest, they are extremely difficult for the gobbler to find because they are in thick areas hidden from predators and from the gobbler. They do not yelp to the gobbler while they are on the nest. They sit there perfectly quiet so they do not attract predators, therefore, the gobblers have an extremely difficult time finding hens at this time. During this time, gobblers will gobble all day long in an effort to find turkey hens.

It would seem that, as the season goes on and the hens start laying or incubating eggs, it would be easier to call a turkey to you. In some instances, that is true. But, by the time the hens start incubating the eggs, many of the turkey gobblers that you hear gobbling have been "educated" and are very reluctant to come to the calling of a hen.

Many of these gobblers have been called in to hunters and they have been scared by the hunter. From that point on, those gobblers will either go to a strutting area and call the hens to them, or they will stop gobbling altogether. Usually the turkey will go to a strutting area and will call hens in to him. He will not go to a hen after he has been scared by a hunter, or after he has been shot at and either wounded or missed. For these reasons, it is just as difficult to hunt a turkey in the late part of the season as it is to hunt a turkey in the early part of the season.

There are times that a turkey gobbles on the roost and no hens come to him, and he will fly off the roost and hit the ground gobbling. He will continue to gobble then until he attracts hens to him. This is the gobbler that you can call to you. Usually when a turkey gobbler hits the ground gobbling and no hens come to him, he will then go in search of hens. If he hears a hen yelping and she will not come to him, you can reverse nature and make the gobbler come to the hen.

As you can see from the "get go", you have an insurmountable task ahead of you to call a turkey in to shooting range. As we have already mentioned, there are all kind of terrain features and other factors that you must take into account when setting up on a turkey. After you get set up on the turkey and start calling to him when he is gobbling in the tree, all of these factors come in to play. Such things as hens going to him before he flies out of the tree, and him pitching off to them.

Even after he pitches off the limb and no hens have come to him, when you start calling to him and he starts gobbling back to you, he may attract hens to him before he is able to get to you. I have called turkeys, had them coming right to me, and looked out in the woods to see a hen within twenty-five or thirty yards of me going right straight to the gobbler I am calling.

Once hens get to a gobbler or get between you and a gobbler, then the probabilities are that you are not going to call that gobbler up to you. If you see hens headed in the direction of a turkey gobbler and then that turkey quits gobbling, you can rest assured that those hens went to that turkey and you might as well wait and hope that he will get through with those hens in a hurry and come over to you. But, you never know what he is going to do, because sometimes even after he gets through breeding the hens, he might leave with them and follow them around all day long strutting and displaying himself for those hens. If he does that, he is never going to come in to you.

When you get up in the morning to go hunt the wild turkey, you need to get up in plenty of time to make sure you have all of your equipment together, and to make sure that you get all the necessary things done at home that you need to get done. Turkey season is hard on a turkey hunter because he has to get up very early every morning to be in the woods before daylight. From time to time, it happens to every single turkey hunter, he will oversleep some mornings. When that happens, he is in a big hurry to get in the woods before the sun comes up or as soon after the sun comes up as possible. Invariably when that happens to a hunter, he will run off and forget his turkey calls or he will forget his face mask or his shotgun shells or some other very important piece of equipment.

You need to get up in plenty of time to get all your diaphragm calls out, and make sure that the reeds are not stuck together. Put them in your mouth, get them wet, and run a series of yelps or two on each one of them to make sure they are making the right sound. If you are using friction calls such as a box call or a glass or slate call, you need to get them chalked and sanded before you leave home, so that you do not have to do that in the dark in the woods. You need to also make sure you have plenty of emergency paper with you when you head out to the woods to turkey hunt, especially if you have slept late and you have not had time to take care of all your business at home before you leave to go to the woods. Nothing is more uncomfortable than to be in the woods and have to go to the bathroom and be out of emergency paper.

On opening day, and on every day you are going to hunt the wild turkey, you want to decide the day before where you want to go the next morning. You need to sort out all the places that you have seen turkeys, and run through your mind where you want to be the next morning. You need to set your clock to get you up so that you can get to that spot about fifteen or twenty or thirty minutes before daylight. You do not want to get there an hour before daylight because that is just too long to stand around and wait. You want to get there at least fifteen minutes before any daylight, but thirty minutes is better.

When you are walking through the woods and it is dark, you want to walk as quietly as you can, and you want to take your time getting in. You do not want to make a lot of noise, and you do not want to get tangled up in bushes and step on big sticks. That is the reason you need a good lightweight flashlight to help you find your way to where you want to go. It is always a good idea to park your vehicle as far away from the spot you are going to hunt as possible. I would never drive my truck any closer than a half-mile to three-quarters of a mile from where I am going to hunt. If you can park further away than that, then you should do so.

Before you leave your vehicle, check to make sure you have all your equipment, and that your gun is loaded (and safety on.) You want to do everything at the vehicle that you can possibly do, such as making sure your gun is already loaded before you leave your vehicle, getting the head net on, getting out the calls that you are going to use, getting out insect repellent if you think you are going to need it, and anything else that you can do to avoid doing much after you start to hunt. Once you have all your gear ready and everything is the way you want it, then you start walking at an easy pace to the place where you are going to listen for a turkey to gobble. You want to walk at a careful pace so you do not make a lot of noise. You do not want to scare turkeys off the roost when you are walking in.

When you get there you want to stand there as quietly as you can, you do not want to move around very much. A lot of times in areas where you are going to be turkey hunting, there will be deer in the area. You do not want to spook deer and get them running through the woods snorting, knocking down trees, running through water and that sort of thing. But, in the event you do spook a deer, you want to be there in plenty of time so that the woods have time to settle down again after the deer has made all the commotion running away from you.

Once you get to where you are going, then you stand there and you listen. Do not do a lot of moving around. Keep your ears wide open. Of course, you are not going to be able to see anything because it is going to be dark. The minute you get to the spot you know you want to be, and

Young buck deer crossing the field where turkeys are feeding.

you know you are there, turn that light off, put it in your pocket and leave it there. You should already know that there is a turkey somewhere in this area, because in your preseason scouting you should have already been to this spot early in the morning and heard a turkey gobble there. So you know a turkey is somewhere in this general area, or at least one has been roosting there before the season opened. Then you just stand there and wait for it to get daylight.

A lot of times I sit and listen for the first birds to start chirping. When I start hearing these birds wake up in the morning and start to move around, I wait until I see the first bird fly off the roost. If you stand there and wait until you see the first bird fly, (not a turkey), usually the chirping of these other birds will wake up a wild turkey, and he will be sitting on a limb wide awake. The minute that I can see the hands on my watch, I know its light enough for me to start owling or using whatever type locator call I am going to use to try to get the turkey to gobble.

When you get to the spot and it starts to get daylight, if there are real owls already owling, there is no need for you to do anything. You just stand there and listen and hope the real owls will get the turkeys to gobble. If an owl just hoots once or twice, and that is not enough for you, then you get out your owl hooter, or you can use your natural voice to owl two or three times to see if you can get the turkey to respond to you.

If a turkey does not respond to the hoot of an owl, I will sometimes use a crow call to try to get a response. There will be some mornings when you go in the woods and there is a turkey gobbler within two or three hundred yards of you or even closer, and he just will not respond to either the owl hoot or the crow call. Some people like to use other calls, such as the coyote call or the red tailed hawk call, but I stick mainly to the owl hooter and to the crow call to get them to respond to me.

In fact, if I have tried the owl hooter and the crow call and I have not had a turkey gobble back to me, I will get my diaphragms out, and the first call I am going to make is a very soft tree call, just about three or four real soft yelps or clucks, and then just stand there and wait a few minutes. If you can get a turkey to respond to that tree call, then you have that turkey's attention and there is a good probability that turkey is going to come on to you.

So, that tree call is very important. It is the first thing you want to do in the morning after you have used your other locator calls. I want a turkey to respond to that tree call, because like I say, once he starts responding to the tree call, that turkey is focused on you. Then all you have to do is set up on him and do the right things from then on, and you are going to probably kill that turkey. But, getting a turkey to respond to a tree call is hard to do and I have not had many turkeys do it. I have had some do it. It is a very effective and good call because you are the first thing on that turkey's mind early in the morning if he answers your tree call.

In the event that turkey does not answer the tree call, then try the next call that a hen is usually going to make. She might yelp or purr on a limb before she flies down, so you might run a couple of short series of yelps and purrs to try to get a turkey to respond to you. But the call that is going to work for you, if any call is going to work for you, is a fly down cackle. When the hen flies out the tree early in the morning, many times she will do a fly down cackle all the way from the limb to the ground. When she hits the ground, she will usually start walking and she will do a series of yelps behind that fly down cackle.

After you have done those tree calls, yelps and purrs and nothing happens, wait a few minutes, then do a fly down cackle and do it just long enough for that hen to sail off that limb and hit the ground out there. Usually, from the time a turkey leaves the limb until it hits the ground is from one to three seconds, so the fly down cackle should be very short. She will start walking the minute she hits the ground. Sometimes they will stop and fluff off a little bit, but usually they will walk four or five steps and then stop and fluff off. Whenever she walks those four or five steps she might do five or six yelps right behind that cackle and that is what you want to do. If there is a turkey in the area, he should respond to the cackle.

When turkeys, both hens and gobblers, fly off the roost, they do it in two ways and you should be familiar with both. The turkey will sometimes spread its wings and sail off the limb to the ground. When a turkey does this it will not flap its wings and will make no wing noise when it flies down. When a turkey sails off the limb without flapping its wings, it may or may not do a fly down cackle. When the turkey sails off the limb, you will not hear the turkey fly down unless it does a fly down cackle. Most of the time when the turkey leaves the roost it will flap its wings and fly to the ground. When a turkey flaps its wings, if you are close enough to it, you will hear him. The sound a turkey makes when it flaps its wings is a sound you will not mistake. You can imitate this sound by slapping your leg or you can use your hat to slap your leg.

There is a product on the market called a "fly down flapper" which, if properly used, makes a sound identical to that made by a turkey when it flies off the roost. If you can make the sound of a turkey flapping its wings at the same time you do the fly down cackle, many times a gobbler will resound to it. Sometimes a combination of these two sounds will cause a gobbler to fly right to you from the roost.

I am going to assume two things here, and try to talk you through what to do under both circumstances. Early in the morning, when you get in the woods, you are trying to locate a gobbler. I am going to assume first, that after you have done your owl hoot or one of the other locator calls, the turkey responded to you. He either responded to you when you did your owl hoot, or he responded to you when you did your crow call, or he responded to you when you did your tree call or he responded to you when you did your fly down cackle. I am going to go through what you need to do from that point forward.

After a complete discussion on what you should do if you get a response from a turkey using a locator, I am going to come back and discuss with you what you should do after you have gone through all of your locator calls and have had no turkey gobbler respond to you. It is a very disgusting feeling to get up before daylight, go to a place where you know there should be a turkey, and to go through your locator calls and have no response. It is a big let down not to have a turkey gobble to you first thing in the morning, but it does not mean the hunt is over. There is still a possibility of killing a turkey if you go about it properly from that point forward. At this point, many factors come into play including all that I have talked about concerning knowledge of the area you are hunting and how to really hunt the wild turkey.

8

TURKEY RESPONDS ON THE ROOST

When you use your owl hooter or your natural voice to owl hoot, and a turkey responds by gobbling on a limb, then there are things you have to do right away that cannot wait. Immediately start moving toward that turkey, depending on how far away he is. Let's say that turkey gobbles at you and you estimate he is around two or three hundred yards away, and you want to set up on that turkey and call him into you. At that point, you must move closer to that turkey.

If the turkey responds to you when you owl hoot, there is usually a little darkness left, it is not quite daylight yet or it is right on the verge of daylight. You are in a position where you can move fairly close to that turkey without being seen or heard by the turkey. When you start to move toward the turkey, you need to be very careful and you need to move as quickly as you can, and as quietly as you can to a spot hopefully within about a hundred yards of the turkey. You do not want to get any closer to the turkey than a hundred yards in most circumstances. If you get any closer than that, the turkey is going to hear you. He is sitting up in a tree where he has a good vantage point for seeing everything around him and he might see you. If he either sees you, or hears you walking through the woods, then that decreases the chances of calling that turkey to you. Some hunters would say you want to get seventy-five or fifty yards from that turkey, but that is living dangerously, and it is not advisable to try to get too close.

Now, when I say you have to move to that turkey in a hurry, I do not mean you go running through the woods to the turkey. You want to move quickly, but as quietly as you can --which means that you do not want to step on any big sticks or rustle dry leaves.

Once you get fairly close to that turkey, let's say a hundred yards from him, you should start looking for a place to set up so that you can start calling to him. Do not start calling to that turkey until you get set up or that turkey might fly out of the tree and land right out in front of you, before you are ready. Find a big tree that you can sit down next to, hopefully one that will completely cover your back. Or, sit down next to the largest tree you can find. You should try to sit down in a place where you have a good field of vision to both sides and in front of you.

When you find a tree that you want to sit against, it is a good idea to clean things out from around it. Get the leaves and sticks out of the way, so that whenever you have to make any movement you are not going to make a lot of noise. You want to be sitting up against a big tree with your back against it so that the tree helps camouflage you.

Remember, whenever you sit down next to that tree, you want to get as comfortable as you can because you may be there for several hours calling to that one turkey. Do not make any calls to that turkey until you are sitting down and you have your face mask and gloves on, your gun is in the right position and your turkey calls out and ready to use. You want all of that ready before you ever start calling to that turkey.

If you start calling to the turkey before you are ready, and he comes sailing out of that tree and lands out there

Thomas Newberger with Rio Grande gobbler taken in West Texas. Thomas Newberger is an excellent turkey hunter and a professional turkey hunting guide.

Turkey Responds On The Roost

about fifteen yards from you, you are in deep trouble. You are not ready and you are not going to kill that turkey because when you try to get your gun on him, he is going to spot you and he is going to be gone. Before you ever call to the turkey, make certain that you have everything exactly the way you want it, and only then are you ready to start calling.

I actually had that happen to me more than one time, but one day in particular, I was hunting a turkey and I walked up to this spot at the edge of this big gumpond and owled. The turkey gobbled right back to me the very first time I hit that owl hooter. He was about a hundred and fifty yards from me, roosting out in the middle of a big gumpond. I could not get any closer to that turkey. All that was left for me to do was to sit down right where I was standing. At that point, I was standing right on the edge of the gumpond itself. I backed off about thirty-five or forty yards and found a big tree to sit next to. I was facing the way the turkey was gobbling. I did not say a word to that turkey until I was completely ready, i.e. finding a place to sit, getting my face mask on, my gloves on, and my calls arranged exactly the way I wanted them. I started calling to him and every single time I called to that turkey, he answered me. The beautiful part about that was, I knew the turkey was in a tree because I knew he was out over a gumpond.

The first call I made to that turkey when I sat down was a tree call. When I did that, the turkey gobbled back at me as hard as he could gobble. I knew that if nothing else happened, if no other hens started calling to that turkey, he belonged to me. He was focused on me, he was interested in me and he was going to come to me when he flew out of that tree. So after I made that tree call and that turkey responded, I sat there for about five minutes before I did anything else. After about five minutes, I did a fly down cackle to tell that turkey I was out of the tree and on the ground, and I was ready for him to come to me. As soon as I finished the cackle portion, I did a little short series of yelps right behind it so that the turkey would know I was on the ground and I was walking around. I did not get that call completely finished before the turkey answered me, and there was no question in my mind that, even if some other hen started calling to that turkey, he was definitely interested in me and he was probably going to come to me. All I had to do was wait for it to get light enough for that turkey to see the ground and I felt fairly certain that turkey was going to sail out of that tree and land right out in front of me.

The turkey continued to gobble and as soon as he would finish his gobble, I would light into him with some calls, so that if any other hen made any sounds out there in that gumpond or anywhere around there, I would be the first hen that turkey heard and I would be the one he would respond to. I did not want that turkey to be diverted away from me by some other hen, so I did not wait for him to gobble two or three times before I called back to him. The minute he gobbled I called to him. It might be soft yelps, it might be some purring, but as soon as that turkey gobbled, I called right back to him because I did not want any other hens to interfere with what me and that turkey had going on. From where I was sitting, I knew about where the turkey was in a tree, but I could not see him. There were too many trees between him and me, but I kept my eyes straight in the direction where that turkey was gobbling.

At ten minutes after six that morning, I looked out through that gumpond and I saw that turkey come sailing off the limb and down through those trees, zig-zagging around missing limbs, never flapping his wings but in a glide coming straight to me. The turkey hit the ground on the edge of the pond about twenty-five yards from me, threw his head straight up and started walking around looking for the hen that had been calling to him. The turkey was standing in the wide open, and there was nothing I could do but sit there perfectly still and wait for the turkey to walk behind a tree so that I could get my gun up to my shoulder. There was one tree between us big enough to conceal me from him when he walked behind it. As soon as he walked behind it, I put my gun on my shoulder. When the turkey stepped out from behind the tree, I was able to end that hunt. On that particular morning, it did not get daylight until about six o'clock and that is about the time I owl hooted to him the first time. By 6:15 I was on my way back to the house with a fine twenty pound turkey gobbler that had a ten and one-half inch beard.

If you can get the turkey responding to you with a tree call, then you are in a position to have that turkey's undivided attention. Once you get it, you do not want to lose it. As long as he is in the tree and he is gobbling to you, answer him every time he gobbles so that you can keep his interest. You do not want some other hen to take him away from you.

Once the turkey sails out of that tree or pitches down out of that tree and hits the ground, if he has not sailed down directly to you, then you are going to have to start doing some different things. Your strategy to get that turkey to come on in may change two or three different times before you finally get him to come in, but you need to develop a strategy for that turkey. You can always tell when a turkey has flown out of a tree by the way the turkey sounds when he is on the ground. Many times, when you are within a hundred yards of a turkey and you have not spotted him in the tree, if you listen very closely you can hear him when he flies down. If you keep your eye on the tree, you can see the turkey and hear him flap his wings when he flies out of the tree. I have seen turkeys, though, that whenever they pitched out of the tree, they would not make a sound; all they would do is spread their wings, jump off a limb and just pitch straight out of the tree right down to the ground. In that case, when you do not hear the wing flaps, you have to

Author set up to video turkey hunt.

listen for the turkey to gobble when he hits the ground. If I know that a turkey has left the tree, then I am going to start calling to that turkey immediately.

The first time that turkey gobbles and I know he is on the ground, I want to keep him interested in me. I am going to call to him the very first time he gobbles. I want to be the first thing that makes him gobble after he is on the ground. I have heard the old timers say that once a turkey flies out of the tree, all you need to do is cluck to him a couple of times and if he gobbles to you, then you just put your call down and shut up because that turkey is going to come right on to you. He may not come straight to you, but some time during the day, that turkey is going to come to where he heard that first hen. I have heard that said by the old timers time and time again, but that is not the way that I personally hunt the wild turkey.

The first thing you should do is make up your mind that when the turkey hits the ground and he gobbles to you, you are going to be in for a long wait. You need to get yourself psychologically prepared that the turkey is not going to come straight on in to you. But you also need to be prepared and to be ready to get your gun up because sometimes the turkey will come on a dead run to you. He will be standing there looking at you, and you will not be ready. Your expectation must be that he is going to come right on in to you and you have to be prepared for that; but in addition, you have to be ready to have the patience to wait that turkey out. Sometimes it will take two or three or four hours before that turkey will finally decide to come on in to you.

When a turkey flies down out of a tree, if he is within a hundred yards of you and he continues to gobble to you, it is my opinion that you should never move on that turkey. You should hold your ground and not make any effort to get closer to the turkey. At a hundred yards, a turkey can see you bat your eye, and if you get up from the position you are in and you start moving around on that turkey, 99 times out of a 100 and probably a 100 times out of a 100, that turkey will spot you and your turkey hunt will be over for that particular gobbler.

Once a turkey is on the ground, then you need to find out what you have to do to keep that turkey interested in you. You have to start calling to that turkey by doing some soft yelps. You can do some soft purrs or you can do some cutting or lost hen calls or whatever you think you need to try to keep him interested. I personally let the turkey determine how I am going to call to him. I always mix up my calls, but after I have determined which call he responds to best, I use it the most. Sometimes, it is even necessary to quit calling a turkey altogether.

One of the ways to tell when a turkey has a lot of interest in you is if that turkey walks on your calling. That means that before you finish your yelps, the turkey is gobbling. If he is interrupting your calling, then he is definitely interested in what you are doing. Make absolutely no mistake about it, just because that turkey is answering you every time you call to him, and he is double and triple gobbling to you, that does not mean that you are going to finally end up getting that turkey. I have seen it happen too many times with a hot gobbler (one that is gobbling every breath and double and triple gobbling) where he has been able to call hens to him before he gets to me.

Once he gets the hens in with him, then it is extremely difficult to make that gobbler come on in to you, or to make him leave the hens. While you are calling to that gobbler and you hear other real hens yelping, not other human beings, or if you see real hens go to the turkey that you are talking to, then you need to change your strategy. You are probably not going to call the gobbler away from the hens, but you can call the hens and make the hens come to you. If you can do that, the gobbler will probably follow the hens right to you.

I have been caught in that situation many times and I have had the good fortune to be able to observe hens with gobblers. That is, I could see the gobbler and I could see the hens that had gone to the gobbler, and I could watch what was going on.

When that happens to me, the first thing I do is start experimenting with the hens, making calls directly to them trying to get their interest. I want to see every hen's head come up or at least two or three of their heads come up when I make that call. Then I want to be able to watch the hens to see if they are responding and if they are moving in my direction.

One time I was hunting a turkey in Texas, and he was "henned up." I could not do anything with the gobbler because he was with the hens. I started to kee-kee to the hens, and that got their interest. I just kept kee-keeing and soft yelping to them, and the hens came right on to me and brought the gobbler in with them. I had to do some other things in that situation that I have already mentioned in this book, but the kee-kee, in that particular instance, got the turkey hens interested in me.

On another occasion, the gobbler had five hens with him. Everywhere the hens would go, that gobbler would follow. Since there was absolutely nothing I could do with the gobbler himself, I started calling to the hens trying to find out what they were interested in, and to get them interested in me. After trying several different calls, such as the kee-kee, the lost hen call, a string of yelps, some purring, on a variety of different calls, I was unable to get the interest of the hens. I started doing some real quick cutting, but not a long series of cutting. It was three or four notes of just real fast cutting. The first time I did it, every one of those hens threw up their head and looked straight in the direction I was calling. The hens began to feed in my direction. I continued to do this little quick cutting to them periodically, and eventually the hens came right on in to me. The gobbler stayed in a full strut the entire time, followed the hens right up to me, and I was able to kill that turkey. So you have to experiment with different kinds of calls and things that you can do to get the hens interested in you.

Once the gobbler has hens with him and you can call those hens, in nearly every instance, the gobbler will follow them right up to you. Sometimes it will be kee-keeing that will get their interest, sometimes it will be cutting, sometimes you may have to do some soft purring and clucking to them, and other times you may have to do some aggressive calling and some yelping, but you need to find out what the hens are responding to and then get them to come on in to you.

If you can actually hear the sound that the hen turkeys are making, it is always a good idea to mimic that sound exactly the way the wild hens are doing it. That is not only a good idea for the purpose of calling the hens, it is also a good idea to use that very sound when hunting other gobblers. The gobblers in the area you are hunting are responding to the sounds the hens in the area are making and if you can make the identical sound, then your chances of taking a gobbler dramatically increase.

Human beings have established a vocabulary for turkeys, and within that vocabulary are a given number of calls that human beings refer to as purring, clucking, yelping, kee-keeing, cackling, the tree call, the lost call, the assembly call, gobbling, the kee-kee run, putting and cutting. However, there are sounds that turkey hens make in different areas of the country that do not fall within the vocabulary assigned to turkey sounds by human beings. When you hear these different sounds, you need to be able to immediately adjust to them and start using them to call turkeys in the area where you are hunting.

I have heard turkey hens make sounds that no self-respecting human being would make on a turkey call. I have heard turkey hens make sounds that sounded so awful that I would be embarrassed to make those sounds on my turkey calls in front of other human beings who hunt turkeys. These sounds that are made by the actual wild hens are the sounds you need to use to hunt the wild turkey. You need to be constantly listening for whatever different sounds you can hear from wild hen turkeys and not pay quite so much attention to what human beings say you should be doing in terms of the sounds you make calling a wild turkey.

When no hens go to the turkey who has flown out of the tree and he is interested in you, you want to make absolutely certain that you set where there are no barriers between you and the turkey, no creeks, lakes, streams, fences, thickets or anything else between you and the turkey that would prevent him from coming on in to you. Then you must find out what that turkey is interested in, what he was responding to when you called to him. You should mix up your calls a little bit, but always go to the call or calls that he responds to and keep him interested. If no other hens come to him and there is nothing to obstruct him from coming in to you, then you will probably end up killing that turkey. All you can do is hope that there is not a coyote or bobcat that comes to his gobbling, (or comes to your calling) or that no deer walks by or anything else happens that could spook the turkey. Everything has to be nearly perfect, because there are just too many things that can happen.

I am going to go back and talk about when the turkey gobbled to you while you were using your locator calls. If you were using a crow call, a tree call, or a fly down cackle as a locator call, then you have to do some things different, in my opinion, than you would do if you were using an owl hooter. Usually, when you get a turkey to respond to you using an owl hooter, it is still kind of dark. You can move on a turkey a little easier, get a little closer to him, set up on him and get ready to call. If you are using some other kind of locator call, like a crow call, or you have done a tree call or a fly down cackle and that is when the turkey responds, then you usually have daylight to contend with, and you have to be very careful when you are moving on a turkey. By the time you do these other locator calls, it is light enough that the turkey can see you moving through the woods, and he can hear you. Always remember, if you can see a turkey, that turkey can see you. If you can hear a turkey, that turkey can hear you. Of course, he can hear you whether it is light or not, but once it becomes daylight and his vision is no longer obscured or obstructed by the darkness, he can see for a long way and you are going to have to be very careful when moving in on that turkey. You will have to use your own judgment about how close you want to get to him.

I do not recommend that you try to get within a hundred yards or closer than that to a turkey after it gets daylight, but you definitely want to be closer than two hundred yards. That depends on where you are hunting and how high the turkey is roosting in the tree, and whether or not you think he might see you moving to him. It is better to call a turkey at three hundred yards away and have a chance of calling him in without scaring him, than it is to try to get two hundred and fifty yards from a turkey and have him see you coming through the woods. If he sees you, it will scare him off the roost. Once you scare the turkey, he is going to fly off and you are not going to be able to do anything with him. So, it is always better to call a turkey a long way, than it is to try to get too close to him and scare him out of the tree.

In my opinion, you should not try to get as close to a turkey after daylight as you would try to get just before daylight. If the turkey has gobbled to you after good daylight, then I would not try to get as close to that turkey as if he had gobbled to me just before daylight or right at daylight. You need to take that into account when you set up on a turkey. You want to be as close to the turkey as you can get, because the closer you are to the turkey then the less likely it is that his gobbling is going to get hens to come to him, before he comes on in to you.

Getting close to a turkey is important. But, it is just as important not to scare the turkey out of the tree before you ever get a chance to call to him. When you get set up on a turkey after daylight and he has responded to your locator call -- whether it is a tree call, fly down cackle or crow call -- you are going to do the same things you would do if you had located him with an owl hooter just before daylight. The only difference is, you are not going to be as close.

Probably the most difficult decision you are going to have to make if that turkey does not come right on in to you is whether or not you should move on that turkey. A lot of turkey hunters will not move at all, because they believe once that turkey is gobbling to them, he is going to come on in at some point during that day. That is not always true and it does not always happen that way. At some point it may become necessary for you to move on that turkey. The most difficult part of making that decision is that you have a turkey out there, and you cannot see him. You have not heard or seen any hens go to him. The turkey just shuts up and will not say another word. The turkey will not respond to anything you do, and he, just all at once, quits gobbling.

There can be many things that cause a turkey to do that. Among them, is that hens may have come to him from a direction that you could not see, and now he is very contented to have hens with him. He is no longer interested in what you are doing.

The second thing that could have happened is that something could have spooked the turkey. He could have been gobbling to you or coming to you and he could have walked up on a bobcat or a coyote, or a domestic dog could have spooked him. An owl or hawk could have swooped down on him, or a deer could have snorted him or run by him and you never knew it or saw it, and that could have spooked the turkey.

Anything could have spooked that turkey and caused him to shut up. So you are in a situation where you have been calling to the turkey and he has answered you and double and triple gobbled. Then he just shut up and did not say a word or do anything. You called to him for a while longer and that turkey would not respond to you in any way. You have to make a decision about what you are going to do. Is the turkey still out there with hens? Has the turkey been spooked by something? Is the turkey coming on to you, just taking his time and not saying anything? This is the dilemma you are in, and a lot of times the decision you make can determine whether or not you are going to be able to kill that turkey.

I have been in that exact situation on many occasions. On more than one occasion after I have sat there and decided it is time for me to move, I start getting up or moving my feet, all of a sudden I hear the most awful sound you have ever heard. It sounds like a helicopter taking off.

You look to see your gobbler is flying out through the trees. At that point, you want to kick yourself in the posterior because you know if you had waited another five or ten minutes, that turkey would have come right on in to you and you would have been able to take him. I do not care who you are or how long you have turkey hunted, that is going to happen to you if you go in the turkey woods on a regular basis.

If you decide to move, the worst mistake that you can make is to think that you are going to be able to ease through the woods and slip up on that turkey in the last place you heard him gobble. I know of many turkey hunters that have tried this, but I do not know any turkey hunter who can consistently slip up on a wild turkey in the woods. I do know of situations where people have slipped up on the edge of fields, pastures or pipelines, and have been able to kill turkeys by doing that. But, to slip up on a wild turkey in the woods is virtually impossible. If you think you can do it, then you know something about slipping up on turkey gobblers that I do not know.

When moving on a turkey, you may want to check the area around you to make sure there are no turkeys standing within killing distance, or standing out there looking at you when you start to move. You need to check the woods carefully. I mean look all around, look at every bush, look at every tree; closely examine anything out there that might appear to be a turkey. If it appears to be a turkey, it probably is a turkey. I have seen them stand in one spot and look for five minutes or longer, and never move anything. They will just stand and look. Sometimes it will appear to be a stump or something out there, and then all of the sudden when you start to get up, that stump you were looking at takes off and flies. After you have checked everything and made sure there is no turkey out there, then you can get up and gather all your paraphernalia.

One tactic you can use to get closer to a turkey is to move about a hundred and fifty or two hundred yards away from the turkey and yelp to him or make some call that might get some response out of him, and hope that he will answer. The purpose of moving away from the turkey is to make him think that the hen he was once interested in is leaving the territory. If he is interested, he is going to have to respond to you and get you to stay, so that he can get with you at his leisure. If he gobbles to you under those circumstances, then try to move back up where you had originally set up and start calling to him again. The turkey will think you are coming back to him, that you are moving in his direction, and he may come on in to you then. It has been my experience that it is bad turkey hunting practice to move straight in the direction of where you last heard the turkey. Many times the turkey is still there and has hens with him and you might end up scaring him. If moving away does not work, circle to the left or right around the turkey, and try to get close to him. You should move to a different position within a hundred and fifty or two hundred yards from where you last heard the turkey gobble. At that point, you should sit down and call to him again, so he will think it is a new turkey or the old turkey has moved and is trying to locate him. Sometimes that will make him gobble and you can renew the chase at that point.

Sometimes you will know the turkey is not interested in you because you will hear him gobble when he hits the ground. He may gobble to you five or six times while he is on the ground, then all of a sudden, when he gobbles to you the next time, he sounds like he is a little bit further away. You keep calling to him and he gobbles to you and next time he sounds even further away. You know that the turkey is moving away from you, but you want to make certain that the turkey is not just walking up and down in the strutting area -- that is he is just not moving away from you for the moment. You can do that by continuing to call the turkey.

Troy and Belinda Ruiz with Rio Grande turkeys taken while hunting in Oklahoma.

Then if he starts getting closer to you again and he stops, and then all of a sudden he starts getting further away from you, you can almost bet that turkey is either hung up on something or he is in a strutting area. When I say hung up I mean there is a fence between you and him, or there is some kind of water between you and him, or there is some obstruction like a depression in the ground or just some kind of terrain obstruction that turkey has found, and he just does not intend to come any further.

But if he is in a strutting area, he is not hung up, he is merely trying to call hens to him. When he was answering you, getting further away from you and then closer to you, then going away from you again and coming back to you, he was telling you he is in a strutting area and he is probably not going to come to where you are. He wants you to come on in to him. Sometimes you can sit in one spot and call to the same turkey for three or four hours and he will gobble to you every time you call, but in one gobble it sounds like he is getting closer to you, and the next time he gobbles it sounds like he is getting further away from you. You can carry on with a turkey like that for most of the morning and the probability of you calling that turkey out of that strutting area is not good.

You are going to have to devise a plan to get him to leave that strutting area. Normally, that cannot be done no matter what you try, but a couple of tactics will work some times. One is to change your position. That is, you circle away from that turkey at a distance far enough away so he cannot see you or hear you walking through the woods. Then you try to get yourself positioned within a hundred and fifty or two hundred yards of that turkey from a different position, and call to him. Sometimes he will leave that strutting area and come on to you.

The other thing to do is to use a series of different kinds of calls that make different sounds. For instance, you can use a single reed call that makes a pure sound of a young hen, all the way up to a four reed diaphragm call that makes a sound of an old raspy hen. Sometimes a turkey will only respond to a different call, such as a box call or glass call or diaphragm, and will not respond to any other call. What you want to do is go through a series of calls to make that turkey think there is more than one hen calling to him from your position.

Another way to do that is to get your diaphragm call in your mouth, get one of your friction calls in your hand, (and it does not make any difference whether it is a push button call or whether it is a glass call, slate call or a box call), put one in your mouth that you can blow with your hands free, and then get the other call that you are going to have to use your hands to operate, and start calling on that diaphragm and then come in with your friction call. Start calling with two calls at the same time. Many times you will fool a turkey into believing that you are more than one hen. He will come over to you because he knows that he is not going to separate the hens. What is happening here is that you are making the sound of two hens, and the gobbler knows unless both hens come to him, neither will come. If he cannot get the two hens to come to him, then he will go to them. You are also playing with his competitive nature. He is more likely to be concerned that with all of the calling going on some other gobbler might slip in and get with those hens. The turkey gobbler knows that and many times he will come on in to more than one hen calling to him.

Doing that very thing on one occasion, I actually called a gobbler away from hens. I could see the gobbler in the tree from the position I was in, and I could see under the tree he was in. I got very close to that turkey that morning, of course, I did not have any choice on that particular morning because when I owled to the turkey, the turkey gobbled right on top of me. I just had to find a place to sit down in a hurry, and when I did I was able to get situated without the turkey seeing or hearing me. I looked up in the tree and not far from me, there was the turkey sitting on a limb. Well, I could see down through the woods and I could see the turkey sitting on the limb. The turkey would turn around on the limb and he would strut on the limb and he would gobble on the limb; but that turkey did not intend to fly off that limb until he could see hens under the tree he was roosting in. Of course, I did not want to call to the turkey a whole lot because I knew if I could see the turkey, the turkey could see me. I did not want to do a whole lot of calling because I did not want him looking in my direction trying to find a turkey hen that was not there. After he had gobbled several times that morning, he was still sitting in the tree in a full strut moving up and down the limb he was sitting on. Eventually, a single hen walked right under the tree where the turkey was sitting. Needless to say, the turkey never flapped his wings, he just jumped out of the tree, spread his wings and pitched down to the hen.

I knew at that moment I had to either try to call that gobbler away from the hen, or I had to try to call the hen to me. I tried everything I knew to call the hen, but the hen was having nothing to do with me and was not paying me any attention. Then I had to resort to trying to call the gobbler to me. The only thing that I knew to do was to try to make that turkey think that there were two hens where I was, and only one hen where he was. Hopefully, I could get him to leave that one hen and come to the two hens. In any case, I got my Double Trouble Glass call, a friction call that makes an excellent cluck and a purr, and a diaphragm call. I started working them simultaneously. I would always start with one and then come in with the other. I would never end with both of them at the same time. I would keep calling with the diaphragm after I finished calling with the friction call, or I would continue calling with the friction call after I finished with the diaphragm. I was able to get the gobbler's interest and actually called that gobbler away from that hen. He came right on in to me and I was able to

Author headed into the woods with video equipment.

take that turkey. I guess two hens in the bush can be better than one in hand.

If you ever decide you are going to move on a turkey and you want to move in the direction that you last heard the turkey, then you should circle around to your left or right so that the turkey cannot see you. You should always keep a careful eye out for the turkey because you may be moving in the direction he went or you might be moving in the opposite direction from which he went. Every now and then you want to call to the turkey and see if you can get him interested again.

From time to time, you might want to stop in a spot, sit down, and just spend about forty-five minutes or an hour calling to see if you can call that turkey in, or if you can get some response out of him. If you do not get any response from that turkey and you have hunted him most of the day, then you want to try another tactic that might work for you. In the afternoon about 2:00 or 3:00PM, go back, close to the area where you heard the turkey gobble early that morning, and set up right there and start calling to the turkey. Many times, a turkey will roost in the same tree day after day. That is not always the case because many times turkeys change their roosting spot, but if you do get back to the area where you heard him gobble early that morning, and wait for him that afternoon, if he decides to come back to the area where he was roosting the night before, you can be there waiting for him and call him to you.

Hunting gobblers in the afternoon or evening just before they fly up to roost is similar to hunting a gobbler in the morning just as he is flying off the roost. In both instances, the gobbler is looking for hens. In the afternoon or evening, before he flies up to roost, a gobbler is in search of hens so that he can roost close to them. In some instances, he will even breed the hens before he flies up to roost. In many instances, a gobbler will roost around or close to hens so that when he flies down the following morning, hens will be close to him. The reason a gobbler will gobble when he flies up to roost in the evening is to get roosting hens to respond to his gobble so that he knows they are close to him.

Of course, if it is illegal to hunt in the afternoon in the state where you are hunting, then this is not a tactic that is available to you. You need to check your state laws to determine whether or not it is legal or illegal to hunt turkeys in the afternoon. If it is illegal to hunt turkeys in the state where you live in the afternoon, then you can go in the woods in the afternoon and "roost" a turkey. What that means is, you can go in the woods, sit down, call to them if you want to, or not call to them, but you can listen for turkeys and you can hear the turkeys when they fly up to roost. Most of the time, you can hear a gobbler when he flies up to roost because he will gobble after he gets on the limb. If you can hear that, or you are in the woods when that happens, you can go back in those woods the next morning and get as close to that turkey as you can before daylight, and then you are in a position to call the turkey up to you.

As you go to the turkey the next morning, you might want to come in on that turkey from a different direction and see if you can get him to come to you, calling to him from a different spot. If you are calling to a turkey and that turkey is gobbling to you as you are calling to him, but you can hear him getting further and further away from you as he answers your calls, then he gets on out of hearing or he just quits gobbling to you and you know the turkey is walking away from you, then it is fairly safe for you to get up and move on that turkey.

Many times, you want to move very quickly on a turkey to make up some distance, but you want to be very careful not to scare him. If you decide to adopt this tactic to hunt the turkey, and when the turkey gobbles to you it sounds like he is coming back to you, then you want to sit down, and get ready because that turkey will probably come on in.

Sometimes this is a tactic that will work on a turkey who is leaving. The turkey believes that the hen is coming to him, and he then gets interested in the hen and will sometimes come back. Sometimes he will not, but that is a chance you will have to take. If he is going away from you, you have nothing to lose by trying some other tactic to make the turkey change his mind and come on in to you.

There could be several reasons for a turkey to leave you like that. That turkey could have called hens in to him, and the hens are leaving him, so he decided to follow the hens away from you. Another reason could be he may have a strutting area some distance away from where he is roosting, and may be headed there. If he is headed to a strutting area, you are probably not going to call that turkey back. Another reason a turkey will leave you is if he has heard other hens call him in the direction he is headed.

If the turkey is going away from you gobbling, there are two things of which you can be certain. First, he is not with other hens, simply because turkeys do not gobble a lot when they get with hens. Instead, they begin to strut and drum and spit to impress the hens, so that the hens will squat for them and they can breed them. They will gobble when they are with hens, but they do not do a lot of gobbling and some turkeys will not gobble at all, once they get with hens.

The second thing of which you can be certain is that this turkey has not been spooked. If he was spooked, he would have run or flown and he would certainly not be gobbling. The turkey is still looking for hens, or he is headed to hens that he can hear in a different direction, or he is headed to a strutting area. At this point, you just have to make a decision on whether or not you want to move on the turkey. It is my view that you have absolutely nothing to lose because the turkey is headed away from you anyhow, and you are going to need to get closer to the turkey but you do not want to scare him.

Another tactic to use on a turkey like that is to take a friend with you. One of you can walk down within a hundred yards of the turkey, but not call to the turkey, and the other one stay a couple hundred yards away from the turkey and do all the calling. This gives the hunter closest to the turkey the opportunity to get a shot. He might get close enough to the hunter who is not calling for him to get a shot, but never get close enough to the hunter who is calling.

Another tactic that you may want to use if you bring a friend with you to hunt the turkey is, if the turkey flew down away from you on the first morning you hunted him, then you may want to get your friend to set up on the turkey in the direction that he flew down, hoping he might fly down to the friend or that he might fly down to you. You can split up, but if you do, you want to make certain that you get far

Verona Inabinette (left) and Liz Barthel (right) with Rio Grande gobblers taken in the eastern part of the Texas Panhandle. Verona is probably one of the best lady turkey hunters in the United States today, and is an excellent videographer. She has called up and videoed turkey kills while also guiding the hunt.

enough away from one another that there is no danger of one of you shooting the other.

Another tactic you can use hunting with a buddy is sitting fifteen or twenty yards apart so each of you can see the other while calling to the turkey at the same time to make that turkey believe two hens are calling from the same location. Many times, that will be enough to make the turkey come on in. If you are going to use this tactic, remember that one of you should be calling when the other is not calling. Then the one who did not call should call while the other does not call. There are times when both of you should be yelping together. That is, one of you will

Turkey Responds On The Roost

start a series of yelps and right after the first one starts, the second one joins in, but never quit yelping at the same time. One of you should continue yelping a couple of notes after the other one stops. As I have already mentioned, I do not like the idea of two people ganging up on one turkey, and I believe you should hunt alone. But there are times when hunting with a friend can be productive. It is also my view that experienced hunters should share their experience with inexperienced hunters, and should always be willing to teach others how to turkey hunt.

9

ROOSTED TURKEY THAT WILL NOT GOBBLE

What happens when you get to the spot where you have heard a turkey gobble before and you go through the whole process of hooting to him, crow calling or tree calling or using the fly down cackle or even yelps, and that turkey does not answer you? You have heard a turkey gobble in this area and you feel fairly certain he is there, especially if you roosted him the evening before, but the next morning nothing you do causes that turkey to gobble on the roost. Then what are you going to do?

Now, we may have two different sets of circumstances. One is you heard the turkey gobble on the roost the afternoon before, so you know the turkey is in there, but he just will not gobble to you in the morning when you start doing your locator calls. Or, you heard turkeys gobble in this particular area when you did your preseason scouting. But when you went in the morning, there was not a sound uttered by a turkey anywhere after doing your locator calls. Now you have to make a decision about what you are going to do and how you are going to hunt.

In the first instance, the choice is not very difficult. What you want to do is get as close to where you were the evening before when you heard the turkey gobble, sit down right somewhere close and start calling to that turkey. You know that turkey flew up the afternoon before and he did not see you, and he gobbled after he flew up to roost. You know that the turkey is not going to see or hear you in that spot.

If he did not see or hear you the previous afternoon, he probably will not again when you go back to that spot the next morning before daylight. You already know about where the turkey is roosted, so you should try to get as close as you can get without letting the turkey know you are there. You want to start with the tree call, and if he does not respond, you want to go to the fly down cackle and see what you can get that turkey to do. If a turkey fails to respond to that, then you just need to wait him out, give him forty-five minutes or an hour or even longer than that if you can, and periodically call to the turkey and hope he will answer you.

Weather conditions can contribute to a turkey getting closed mouth in the morning. It might have rained during the night, or there could be slow drizzle or a light or heavy fog could be hanging in the woods that morning that was not there on the afternoon before. In many instances, drastic changes in the temperature overnight, a storm coming through, heavy fog or any kind of fog that would prevent that turkey from seeing the ground until later on in the day, might cause that turkey to sit on a limb and not gobble early in the morning.

When a heavy fog obscures the turkey's view of the ground, that turkey will sit in the tree until the fog bakes off and he can see that it is safe to fly down. On those mornings, I have also noticed it is hard to get a turkey to gobble. If it is foggy, and you know that a turkey was gobbling on the roost the evening before somewhere close to the spot where you are calling, then just wait for that fog to bake off. As soon as that fog gets to where that turkey can see, start calling to him. It is very probable that he is going to crank up and gobble to you, and hopefully he will fly down right to you and you can get him.

I suggest you not do a lot of calling during the fog because that turkey knows hens are not going to fly down until that fog bakes off. He is not going to respond to a hen that is on the ground on a foggy morning. There is no way he can see that hen through the fog so he is not going to take a chance.

Likewise, if there had been a sudden temperature drop overnight, and that turkey has been cold all night long, he is going to sit in that tree until the sun comes out and warms him up a little bit before he pitches out. The same applies if a rain has come through on the night before and he is sitting up there soaking wet. He will sit in that tree until he can dry out and then he will fly down to the ground.

It is my opinion that the fog will bother a turkey a lot more than cold weather or rain. If it is cold weather but it is clear, and he can see the ground, he might fly right on out of the tree. Or if the rain has already passed through and that turkey up there can see everything, he might pitch out of the tree first thing in the morning. But on a foggy morning, it has been my experience they sit in the trees until late in the morning before they fly down. Sometimes a change in the temperature, a storm passing through, or bad weather passing through the night before will keep them in the tree a little longer, but that does not affect the turkey as badly as the fog does.

After you have called to this turkey for an hour or so, the turkey has not gobbled and you have not heard the turkey fly down, you need to consider your alternatives. There are only two: 1) you stay put and continue to call. If this is your choice, mix up your calls by trying different sounds in a turkey vocabulary and also try several different diaphragm and friction calls. 2) you need to consider changing your location on this turkey or looking for another turkey. Usually after this length of time, the turkey has pitched down and has moved off without responding to your calling, but if it is still foggy, he may still be in the tree and you may want to remain in the area and see if you can get him to eventually respond to you. These kinds of situations will test your patience.

10

THE MORNING YOU DO NOT HEAR A TURKEY GOBBLE

Let's assume it gets daylight around 6:00 a.m. You have been in the woods since about 5:30 waiting to hear a turkey gobble. You find a place to sit, and you sit there for an hour and a half and it is getting to be 7:30 or 7:45 in the morning, and you still have not heard or seen a turkey. By now you have to get up and go find one.

Now you want to know what to do, where to go looking for a turkey, and what to do to find him. You know you are not going to be able to slip up on him so you have to locate that turkey somehow and hear him before you get too close to him. You have to have some idea about where to look. You cannot just go rambling through the woods looking for a turkey, because if you do that the probabilities are you are going to scare the turkey, and then you are really going to be in bad shape. To scare a turkey off can ruin a turkey hunter's day.

You have to have a plan, and your plan has to make some kind of sense. It has to be based on some kind of reason and some knowledge of the turkey. This is why you need to do your scouting in the preseason and you need to know as much as possible about the terrain you are hunting. If you have done that, you know where turkeys are feeding.

The first thing you want to do is to head toward those areas. You can find feeding areas in your preseason scouting by looking for scratching and other turkey sign. Turkeys scratch up the leaves looking for acorns and grubs and other insects, so you know when they have been in that area and found food because there are a lot of turkey signs. Eventually, they are going to go back to that area to do some more feeding. You want to head in the direction of those areas, and about a hundred and fifty or two hundred yards before you get to those spots, you want to do some calling. You want to do some clucking and yelping and maybe some cutting to try and get a turkey to respond to you. Hopefully he is in that area somewhere feeding.

When you move from one spot to another, you never want to walk more than fifty or a hundred yards before you stop and listen. Sometimes by doing that you can hear a hen clucking, or purring, yelping or scratching in the woods. That hen may be yelping to a gobbler, or she may be responding to other turkeys, or she could even see a gobbler. She may even be with a gobbler. You want to listen for all kinds of turkey sounds as you move to pre-scouted feeding areas.

Once you hear a turkey yelping, you want to find a place to sit down and give a series of yelps or do something to try and make that gobbler respond to you, if in fact, the hen you have heard is calling to a gobbler. If that gobbler responds you have to be ready to set down because he is ready to come on in at this time of day. The minute you hear him gobble you need to get set, get everything together and start calling to that turkey.

If you do not find a turkey in these feeding areas, what is left for you to do? Well, I have already told you that you need to know where every pipeline, every field, every open spot in the woods, every power line, and every pasture is

Flock of turkey hens feeding in an open field.

located in the woods because that is the next place you want to start to look. These are areas where turkey gobblers like to go and strut. Many times, they will go straight to those areas and never say a word on their way to them. Consequently, you will not know that the turkeys are there.

As you approach these open fields, pastures, pipelines or power lines, you want to do it very slowly and very quietly or the turkeys will spot you and leave. Once you get within hearing distance of these areas or in sight of them, you want to start calling a little bit to see if you can get a turkey to respond. If you cannot get a turkey to respond, that does not mean that they are not there.

When I get within sight of open areas, I like to glass them before I get too close. I normally carry a set of small binoculars with me. I recommend anything from a 7 x 25 to a 10 x 25 that are very small and lightweight -- something that you can easily carry in your hunting vest. With binoculars, many times you will be able to see turkeys that you just were unable to see with the unaided eye. You do not have to get too close to the field to get a good look at what might be on it.

In addition to that, if there are turkeys on the field you will be able to determine whether they are hens or gobblers. The binoculars will assist you in determining which turkeys are gobblers, and where you need to concentrate your efforts.

When I say that you need to slip up on these open areas, I mean exactly that; if it requires that you get down on your stomach and crawl or get down on your hands and knees and crawl, that is what you need to do. But in most instances, you can ease up to the edge of the field with some underbrush or trees between you, or within thirty-five or forty yards of the edge of the field and look it over. But never go walking out on a field even after you have looked it over. I have done that many times, and as I have stepped out on the edge of the field and looked at an area I was unable to see from the woods, there stands a big turkey looking at me.

You never want to just go walking out on the edge of a field. It is always a good idea to get as close to the edge of the field as you can, look it over carefully, sit down there and call for a little while. If you see nothing on the field and if nothing responds or comes to you, you should crawl out to the edge of the woods looking both ways to see if there is anything in the field.

If, when you crawl to the edge of the field, you cannot see it all, then drop down on your stomach and slide out until you can see the entire field. If you see turkeys in the field, then you need to slide back into the woods, ease around as close to those turkeys as you can get, and find a good place to sit down and start calling to them. If there are no turkeys in the field, then you need to start looking somewhere else for you a turkey.

When you approach one of these fields, power lines, pipe lines or open places in the woods and use binoculars to spot a turkey strutting around in one of these open areas, make sure you do not scare that turkey. Any time you start moving toward a field with a turkey in it, and you can see it, you have to always remember that turkey's eyesight is much keener than yours -- if you can see him he can see you. It does not make any difference if you are in the woods. That turkey can see you moving in those woods and you are going to scare him if you are not careful.

The safest thing you can do at this point is get down on your hands and knees, or get down on your stomach and cradle that gun in your arms. Then you start crawling or low crawling on your belly up close enough to the edge of that field, so that you can get a shot at that turkey. It is not likely you are going to call that turkey out of the field into the woods where you are. You are going to have to get up on the edge of that field, so that when you call him up to the edge of the wood line, you can get a shot at him then.

A turkey gobbler strutting in the open field is the most difficult turkey in the world to call. He is harder to call out of that field than a gobbler with hens is to call away from hens. That gobbler is in the field because he knows that every hen walking up through those woods and on the edge of those woods can see him strutting out there. He knows they are supposed to come to him when they see him out there displaying and trying to seduce them. He is not going to leave that field except under extraordinary circumstances, so you can forget calling him in to the woods to you.

Also, that turkey is in the middle of a field or open area so he can escape from any predator that comes close to him or starts out in that field. Predators can hear him gobbling as well as the hens, so he is endangering himself by gobbling. In open areas and open fields, a turkey can see predators before a predator can get close enough to catch him. For these two reasons, it is virtually impossible to call a turkey out of an open field, especially if he has established that as his strutting area and has been calling hens to him in that field every day.

One day, I was hunting a turkey in a pipeline. I was about 75 yards off the edge of that pipeline and that turkey was using the pipeline as a strutting area. I called to the turkey and he turkey would puff up, strut and drum, and he would just come walking in a fast walk right over to the edge of that pipeline. When he got there, he would strut up and down that tree line but he would not come any closer. He would not leave that pipeline because he knew that a real hen in those woods would see him and she should come on out there where he could see her.

I did kill that turkey, but it was amazing the way it happened. Every time I called to that turkey, he would go into a full strut and start drumming. Well, the only way I was able to get that turkey was for me to call to him and when he would go into a strut and turn his tail toward me with his fan fanned, then I would move on him. As long as he was in a strut facing me or with his side to me, I remained absolutely still, but every time he turned his back to me and had his fan fanned out, I moved on him just as fast as I could. I kept my eyes on him all the time.

When he had his back to me with this fan fanned, I would call to him just as hard as I could call and try to keep him in a strut with his tail toward me. I was finally able to slip up close enough to that turkey so that when he come out of strut and stood there with his head sticking up like a periscope, I was finally able to kill him. It took some patience and sometimes I was in some tough positions, but I just waited the turkey out.

When you see a turkey gobbler standing in the middle of a field, you are probably not going to be able to call him out of that field. If he has hens with him, it is much more difficult to call him out of the field. The only thing that you can do at that point is to start calling to the hens, try to get

Chris Long with a fine turkey gobbler taken in the State of Virginia in an area that Chris refers to as "the toilet bowl."

the hens to move in your direction, and hope that gobbler will follow.

Start doing some soft purring and clucking to those hens. Do that a little while to see if the hens start paying you any attention or responding to the calling in any way.

If they do not, then try to kee-kee to the hens. I know that the kee-kee is a fall call and it is done by young turkeys, but every now and then you will hear turkeys in the spring kee-keeing, and the maternal instinct of a hen is to respond to the kee-kee of a young turkey. It has worked for me and it may work for you. So you start kee-keeing to those hens and see if you can get any of them to start paying any attention. You do not just kee-kee, you do the kee-kee run which means that you kee-kee and then you have a series of clucks or a series of yelps behind that kee-kee. If the turkey hens do not respond to that, then I would start cutting to the hens to see if I could get them to listen to me and start moving in my direction. If they did not, I would try some other calls and I would come back to the purring and clucking. I would just keep trying something until the hens to come to me.

If you cannot get the hens to come to you, then the only alternative available is to wait for the hens to feed off the field or the pipeline and hope the gobbler does not follow them off. At this point, you can go one on one with the gobbler. I can assure you that 95% of the time, when the hens feed off that pipeline or field or whatever the open area is, that gobbler is going to follow them off. Your only chance to get that gobbler on that day is for you to try to circle around in front of the turkeys and ambush that gobbler when he comes walking by. That means that you have to know where the turkeys are going and you have to know how they are going to get there.

I have already indicated that you may know where he is going, and you may think you know how he is going to get there, but you are probably going to be wrong. Or you may think you know where he is going and how he is going to get there, and he may fool you and go somewhere else. In nearly every instance, you are going to be wrong either about where he is going or how he is going to get there.

I find it is a big waste of time to try to ambush a turkey that way. The chances of such an ambush working are very slim, although sometimes you can get around in front of turkeys that are moving away from you and call the gobblers into you. Make sure you allow yourself plenty of room so that you do not walk up on the turkeys and scare them.

Let us say that you have been in the woods since about 5:30 in the morning, and you stood around waiting for it to get to be daylight and no turkey gobbled to you. You called to him for a little while and you got no response. Then you went to these feeding areas we are talking about, and you did not find any turkeys, so you decide to go to the open fields or pastures or pipelines. When you arrived there, you did not see or hear any turkeys. Now what are you going to do?

You have already walked five or six miles that morning, you are tired and it is getting on up in the day and is beginning to get warm, so what are you going to do now to find a turkey? At this point in time, there are only two choices left for you. One of those is to call it off, go to the house, and get a nap and get ready to come back that afternoon. Or, if you are a real turkey hunter, you are not ready to give up and you are going to still look for you a turkey.

When you have not seen a turkey and you have to go looking for him, you have to be very careful. You need to find an old logging road or a place where you can walk very quietly up on top of a ridge, somewhere where you can hear a long way. You have to start walking and calling. What I mean by that is, you never walk and call at the same time. Once you get on the old roads or up on top of a ridge somewhere, start easing along that road for 25 or 50 yards or sometimes maybe 100 yards, stop and stand there for about five minutes and listen. If you do not hear anything, then get out your turkey call and yelp a little, or run a couple of calls of different kinds to see if you can get a turkey to gobble. A good loud box call is perfect when this tactic is used to locate turkeys.

Sometimes, this is a very productive method of locating and killing the turkey, especially later in the season because the hens, in many cases, have left the gobbler and have gone to the nest to lay. A lot of times they will hang around those nests for a fairly long time, depending on how many eggs they have laid. During this time, the old gobbler is lonesome. There are no hens in the woods and they are not responding to him. You can walk through the woods, do a little yelping, walk a little further, stop and yelp a little bit and listen carefully and many times you can get a turkey to respond to you. When that happens, it's usually pretty serious business because you are up in the day, and you know that turkey is talking to you, and by this time the hens have gone to their nests. You are one on one with that gobbler, and chances are, you are going to get to talk to him and he is going to talk to you, without any interference from any hens.

At this point, you want to get set up on this turkey just like you would have set up on him had he gobbled out of a tree early in the morning while he was still on the roost. Since I have already been through all of that, you know how to set up on him. You know how to be in a position where you can see well. You want to get in a position facing the turkey and you want to call him straight on in to you. When you get situated, your calls are in a position where you can change them if you need to, your gun is just where you want it and you are comfortable, you need to start trying to find out what that turkey is interested in, and what is going to make that turkey come in to you.

Now, a lot of turkey hunters will start talking to that turkey, and when he gobbles, they will call back to him. That is a good practice sometimes because you can get a turkey really turned on and gobbling to you every breath. There are some turkeys that will not gobble quite that often and you have to decide what you are going to do. You have to keep trying to figure out where that turkey is, and the only way you are going to know for certain is to get him to gobble to you so you can pinpoint his location.

If he is not gobbling to you, then you have to pay attention to what is going on in the woods around you. You have to constantly keep your eyes on the woods and you have to watch for that turkey slipping in on you from every angle. When that happens, you have to be ready to deal with that turkey. You sit there and hope that the turkey is going to walk by you, or walk off to your side either your left or right, and hopefully, if you are right-handed, he will walk to your left. This will make it easier to get your gun on him. If he walks to your right, then the probabilities are that you are going to have to shoot that turkey off your left shoulder, so you need to be prepared to get that gun around, get it up on your left shoulder, and be ready to shoot. But if a turkey does what most turkeys will do, and you set up on him so he is right straight out in front of you the last time you heard him gobble, he is going to come in to you from that direction.

It has been my experience that, when I am calling to a turkey like that, I want to try a variety of different calls, and sometimes I even want to change calls when I am calling to that turkey. However, there are circumstances when a turkey will not answer but one call and you better stick with that call. A lot of times it will be simple clucking, and that turkey will gobble every time you cluck to him. If that is not what is turning that turkey on, you have to do a string of yelps to see if that is going to make the turkey respond. If that is not what is making him respond, then you want to do some cutting to him.

I am giving you these suggestions in the order that I would try them. If he is not responding to the cutting, you might want to try some cackling to that turkey. Even late in the afternoon or up in the day, cackling is a good call to use for a turkey because it sometimes will heat a turkey up and make him start doing some serious gobbling which can make him start coming on in to you.

Once you find out what that turkey is responding to, that is the call you want to use the most. It may not be the exclusive call you want to use and you may want to use a variety of different calls, but you always want to go back to the particular call that turkey is responding to and see if you can keep him fired up.

If you are calling to a turkey gobbler and that turkey has been gobbling to you, and all at once the turkey stops gobbling, it does not always mean the turkey has lost interest in you. It is not a good sign, but it is not necessarily a bad sign. If this happens to you, and you cannot get the turkey to respond to anything you do, then you might want to try to change the calls you are using. You might want to go from a diaphragm call to a box call or some other friction call such as a slate or glass call. If he does not respond to any of that, then you may want to go to different kinds of diaphragm calls with different types of cuts in them with more reeds, such as from a two reed to a three reed, or from a three reed to a four reed call with a different type of stretch to it. You want to try a number of different things when the turkey quits gobbling to you. I have even heard people owl to a turkey or blow a crow call to get a turkey turned back on, but I personally would prefer to use some turkey calling device.

Although I do not like to do it, I have resorted to using a gobble box to get a turkey to respond to determine his exact location and whether or not he was still interested in me. But the most important thing you want to do at this point is to keep your eyes open. You never want to take your eyes off the woods because that turkey may be coming on in to you. You may be sitting there looking in the wrong direction and that turkey will walk right up on you from one side, or come walking up on you from the front. There you are looking off to the right and when you turn your head around, there stands that turkey. I have had it happen to me many times.

On one occasion, I was hunting a turkey which was gobbling to me every breath, right after I started calling to him. Then all of a sudden, that turkey shut up and did not say anything for fifteen or twenty minutes or maybe longer than that. I kept trying to get that turkey to start gobbling again. On that particular day, I remember it very well, I was using a Black Diamond call and that turkey was responding to it very well, but he just shut up and did not say another word. I did everything I knew to crank that turkey back up.

Well as things would have it, after I could not get him to gobble to me for about twenty minutes, I started getting a little nervous and thought maybe I had lost the bird and he had gone on somewhere else. I decided then, I should change calls and give him a different sound, and maybe I could get him fired up like that.

I reached under my face mask and I took my Black Diamond out. When I had my Black Diamond in my hand, I looked down to where I had my turkey calls laid out. I always lay a piece of camouflage cloth on the ground next to me and lay my calls out in a line on it so I do not have to fumble around with them. I can look and I see right where they are, and I can pick one up and put it in my mouth.

On this particular occasion, I laid my Black Diamond down, and reached to get my Exciter call. Of course, I was watching what I was doing. I had the call in my left hand, and with my right hand I pulled up my face mask, stuck the call in my mouth, removed my left hand from under my mask, pulled my mask back down, and looked out in front of me. About twenty yards from me stood one of the biggest turkey gobblers I have ever seen. I do not know how long he had been standing there or how he even got there, but there he stood watching me change calls. Needless to say, that turkey had seen me put the call in my mouth and when I turned my head to look up, there he stood looking me straight in the eye. It goes without saying that the party was over. The turkey left and my hunt had ended. If I had only waited another minute or two before changing calls, I would have been able to kill that turkey. But that is the way it happens when you turkey hunt.

Another thing that I should have done before I started to change calls is examined the woods around me carefully. I should have looked at every tree and at every bush. I should not have reached up to take that Black Diamond call out of my mouth without having first surveyed those woods thoroughly to make sure there was no movement out there and no turkey anywhere in my vicinity. I did not do it because it had been so long since the turkey had answered me, I figured I needed to change calls right then. I took my eyes off what I was doing and it cost me a fine turkey gobbler. The same thing can happen to you if you are not careful.

After you have changed calls, and you cannot get that turkey to respond to anything you are doing on a new call, then it is probably a good idea, at that point, to go back to the call that you started out with and the turkey responded to in the first place.

Another good tactic when the turkey has not answered back for a long time is for you to wait that turkey out. If you decide to wait the turkey out, then you should stop calling to the turkey altogether. On many occasions, when you stop calling, he will then gobble to try to determine where you are. As long as you are calling to the turkey, he knows exactly where you are. If you quit calling to the turkey, then he loses track of you and he will then start gobbling so that he can locate you. There is absolutely no need for the turkey to continue to gobble to you if you are going to call to him without him gobbling back because you are telling him exactly where you are without him doing anything.

On many occasions when I have been hunting a turkey that had been gobbling to me, and that turkey quit gobbling. I would quit calling, and after about twenty or thirty minutes or sometimes longer than that, the turkey would all of a sudden gobble just to attempt to locate my exact position. Sometimes, it can be a very good tactic to just stop calling to a turkey when he stops gobbling to you. This will sometimes make the turkey gobble to you so that he can find you. You just have to sit there and refrain from calling until the turkey finally gobbles. When that happens, the turkey is looking for you. You need to answer him so that

Author with Rio Grande gobbler taken near Reydon, Oklahoma.

he will know exactly where you are, and will come on in to you.

What you are doing is making that gobbler get reassurance from you that you are still there and you still want him to come on in to you. I have done that a lot of times, and on several different occasions while I was sitting there waiting for a turkey to gobble, I have looked down through the woods and have seen him coming. I never said another word, and that turkey came right on in to me, because he knew exactly where I was and he was just making up his mind whether or not he was going to come.

You can use a similar tactic on a running turkey, one that will move away from you as you move closer to him. Tommy Bourne told me the following story about how he was able to kill a running turkey. Tommy would call to the turkey and the turkey would get further and further away from him. In effect, what Tommy was doing was following the turkey through the woods. Tommy would call, but when the turkey gobbled, Tommy could tell the turkey was moving away from him, so Tommy would try to close the distance on the turkey. The further Tommy went, the further away the gobbler would get. After chasing this turkey for over a mile, Tommy decided to give up on the turkey and started to look for another turkey to hunt.

Tommy walked away from the turkey for a distance of about one hundred and fifty yards. He stopped and yelped, and the turkey gobbled. Tommy decided to set up on the turkey right there because he could tell the turkey was getting closer to him. Tommy called to the turkey three or four more times, and within about five minutes, the turkey walked right up in Tommy's face. In Tommy's words, "I guess he just decided the 'ole girl wasn't going to follow him no more. She was going to find her somebody else and I don't guess he could handle that."

Apparently, when the hen started leaving this gobbler, he decided to come back and find her. This tactic can be used on a turkey in a strutting area, and it can also be used on a turkey that is hung up. If a turkey gobbler believes he is losing a hen, it will sometimes force him to try to find her. I have used this very tactic to kill turkey gobblers on many occasions.

There will be times when you are hunting that you will have the turkey so hot and so fired up that while you are yelping to him, he will interrupt your calling. Right in the middle of your yelp, that turkey will gobble and interrupt what you are trying to say to him on your yelper. When a turkey does that, he is fired up, and a lot of times that turkey will double and triple gobble to you. When I get a turkey double and triple gobbling to me on a regular basis, I will do my best to start calling to him before he finishes gobbling. I have done this in the past, and as soon as I would finish calling to the turkey, he would turn right around and double or triple gobble behind the gobble he was making when I interrupted him. If you can get this to happen to you when you are calling to a turkey, you better get ready because in most instances where a turkey is this hot, he is going to come right on in to you. I have had turkeys do this and come running right straight toward me at full speed.

It is extremely difficult to interrupt the gobble of a wild turkey because the gobble is so short. It can be done but the only way that you can do it is to have your call ready and the very second you hear any sound come from that turkey you have to start your call.

I have told you about some of the tactics and methods I use in hunting the wild turkey. But the thing that I need to emphasize to you, and the thing that you need to fully understand, is that there is no magic bullet when it comes to turkey hunting. There is no one call that can be said absolutely, emphatically, unequivocally, and without any question, is a mating call. The exact sound that a turkey hen makes during the mating season that is a mating call, has never been positively identified by anybody, any place, any time. There is absolutely nothing magic you can do to call a turkey in to you.

The great majority of the times that you go turkey hunting, even when you have a turkey gobbler gobbling and coming to you, you are not going to kill that turkey. That turkey is going to hang up on some terrain feature, or will get with hens, or the turkey will spot you before you have an opportunity to get a shot off. If none of the above happens, you will mess up a call and alert the turkey that you are not a real hen, and he just will not come any closer to you. The point is that the great majority of the time that you go turkey hunting, even when you have turkey gobblers coming to you, you are going to fail to kill a turkey. You might as well reconcile yourself to the fact that no matter how good you are in the woods, or how good you can blow a turkey call, about ninety to ninety-five percent of the time that you go turkey hunting, you are going to come home empty handed. As frustrating as this might be, it makes the successful hunts that much sweeter.

When you become proficient as a woodsman and a turkey caller, and you finally harvest a wild turkey, all of the sacrifice and effort that you have put in to this sport finally becomes worthwhile. There are such things as perfect turkey hunts. Those occur when you walk in the woods, and the turkey gobbles on the roost to you. You then get set down, start calling to that turkey, and he pitches out of the tree and hits the ground gobbling. You then start calling to that turkey and he gobbles to you every time you call. Finally, he comes right on in to you for the kill.

The most beautiful turkey hunts I have ever been on lasted two or three hours. The turkey flies down out of the tree, and then he gobbles to me, and me and him talk to one another for two or three hours before he finally eases his way on in to me. In those situations, you can see that turkey coming a long way. He is out there strutting and drumming and he is walking around looking for you. Your heart starts

Paul Rishel with turkey he successfully hunted in the State of New York.

to beat faster and you know you cannot make any mistakes. You are tired, your legs have gone to sleep and you have no feeling in them, and your butt is sore and numb from sitting on that seat. But there is that turkey, and you cannot get up, and you cannot move, and eventually you bring him on in to you, doing all the right things, and you harvest that turkey. There is nothing more exhilarating, nothing more exciting and nothing more fulfilling in the hunting world than to have that kind of turkey hunt on a cool spring morning!

There is absolutely no call on the market today that you can use to call a turkey in to you every time you use it. There is absolutely no particular call such as a purr, yelp, cackle, a lost hen call, a kee-kee, or any other call, that is going to work for you every time you go in to the woods, so do not expect it to happen that way. There has never been a diaphragm, friction, tube call, or any other kind of call invented that is going to work for you even twenty-five percent of the time, nor is there anything you can say to the wild turkey that is going to work for you even twenty-five percent of the time, so do not expect it to.

What I am saying to you is that it does not make any difference what kind of call you use, or what kind of sound you can make on that call, it is my opinion that you are not going to kill a turkey even one out of every four times that you go in the woods, so do not be disappointed if you do not. I do not know any turkey hunter who can truthfully say that he kills a turkey gobbler or even calls up a turkey gobbler one out of every four times he goes turkey hunting. As a matter of fact, if you kill turkeys or even call up a turkey one out of every ten times you go in the woods turkey hunting, you are a very fortunate turkey hunter.

There are a lot of great turkey callers across the United States who do not compete in turkey calling contests. I have personally been in the woods with many people who are not only good at calling to the wild turkey, but are very good turkey hunters and there is a difference. You can be an excellent turkey caller; that is, you can use all of the calls on the market and you can make all of the right sounds, but when it comes to hunting the wild turkey, there is a special talent needed for that act in and of itself.

The most complete turkey hunter is that person who knows all that he can possibly know about the wild turkey; who is a great woodsman and knows his way around the woods; and a person who has mastered the use of a turkey call, whether it be a diaphragm, friction or tube call. To be a successful turkey hunter, you need to know not only how to call the wild turkey, you need to know how to hunt him. You cannot know how to hunt the wild turkey unless you know an awful lot about him. You have to know about the hen and the gobblers, and frankly it is my view, that the more you know about a hen turkey the better off you are going to be. If you know more about hens than you do gobblers, you are in much better position to hunt a gobbler turkey.

The only way you can become a proficient turkey hunter is to practice with these calls. You need to find someone who knows how to make different kinds of turkey sounds and get him to teach you exactly how to make the sounds you need to make, or you can buy an instructional tape that can assist you in learning to make the kinds of sounds you need to make on a turkey call. But the only way you are going to be able to become a total turkey hunter is to get in the woods and learn something about the turkey. Know what to look for, how to hunt the turkey, and what you have to do to hunt the turkey.

Every single turkey hunt that you go on is going to be totally different. There will be some days when you will see several turkeys and you will call several turkeys in to you. Some of them will be hens, some will be jakes, some will be full grown gobblers. Then there will be other days that you will not see or hear a single turkey. There will be days when you will see turkeys but nothing will cause those turkeys to come to you. The only way that you can possibly understand what I am attempting to explain to you now is for you to become a turkey hunter and go in to the woods to hunt the wild turkey. There is not a single turkey hunter reading these words at this moment who does not fully understand exactly what I am saying.

I have hunted many species of animals in my lifetime, from hunting the elk with a bow and arrow, to hunting mule deer, whitetail deer, and on one occasion, at forty yards had the opportunity to stare down a giant bull moose; but there is not a single experience I have ever had hunting any species of animal that even comes close to the thrill and excitement of hunting the American wild turkey in the springtime.

I can say with absolute certainty that I would consider my existence on this earth to be incomplete if I had never experienced that thrill.

It is not like deer hunting where you go set up in a deer stand by a mast bearing tree, or in an area where there is a lot of acorns, and you sit there and wait for the deer to come to feed. A lot of times, when you are deer hunting in an area, you see the same deer every day. You can go to where a deer has been feeding and you will see the same does, yearling deer, and fawns. You will see the same spike bucks and three points and four points coming to that feeding area every single day that you go there. Then, occasionally you will see the buck that you are hunting come up there, and you will get to harvest that buck. Turkey hunting is not like that.

Every single day you go in the woods, it is going to be different. You are hunting an animal in the wild turkey that is far more suspicious and far more cautious of every single thing that he observes or hears as he goes through his daily routine. So you are going to run into certain situations in the woods while hunting the wild turkey that you have never experienced in hunting any other animal. Not only is every hunt going to be a different experience, every single adult gobbler that you encounter in the woods is going to be different.

I have never seen two gobblers ever act the same. Turkeys are a lot like human beings in that regard -- each turkey has its own personality, its likes and dislikes. There are certain areas that some gobblers just will not venture in, and there are some areas that they like and where they will spend a great deal of time. But they are a lot like people in that every one has his or her own personality. Some of them are very vocal and boisterous, and will gobble a lot. There are some turkeys that will not gobble at all. Even among mature boss gobblers there are some that just will not say a word, while there are others that will gobble two and three hundred times to you in one morning or one afternoon. Some that will gobble every now and then. So, every turkey is different, and every experience you will ever have as a turkey hunter is going to be just a little different.

Now there is something you need to know about jake turkeys or juvenile gobblers, those juvenile male turkeys that are one year old or less. These turkeys have not had the experience of the old boss gobbler and they are not as call shy as some of the older gobblers. In many cases, it is very simple to call up and kill a jake turkey without a lot of problems. I have been hunting the wild turkey off and on all my life. I have a lot of experience with turkeys and I have called up a lot of turkeys. In my lifetime, I would estimate that I have called up probably five or six hundred jake turkeys, but to this day, in the spring, I have never killed a jake turkey and will never kill a jake turkey.

To me, the taking of a jake turkey just does not offer any challenge simply because these turkeys are inexperienced. They are not looking for female companionship in the sense that they are going to mate. They still have a herd mentality or a flock mentality about them and they are just looking for other turkeys. I urge every turkey hunter in this country to please not kill these jakes if you want to ever have mature, trophy size turkeys.

There are many other reasons why I would not kill a jake turkey. Number one, he is very small. A jake turkey is probably not going to weigh more than sixteen or seventeen pounds, the mature gobbler is going to weigh eighteen to twenty-two pounds and some are a little bit bigger than that. So, after you get that jake turkey skinned and dressed, you do not have much meat there.

In addition to that, you really have accomplished nothing because most anyone can call up a jake and it is really no challenge to take one. Jake turkeys have short beards. Every now and then you will find a jake turkey that has a four or five inch beard, but that is the exception not the rule for a first year turkey. Usually his beard is going to be two to three inches long, and it is going to stick straight out from that bird's chest so it is easy to tell a jake. He is not going to have a full set of waddles on his head, and he is not going to have nearly as much red on his head as an adult tom gobbler has. His head is not going to be as pretty and blue on the side, and he is not going to get that solid white crown on his head that just turns snow white when he is coming in to you. So a jake turkey is not near as pretty as a grown gobbler.

If you look at a jake turkey's legs, he will usually have little bumps where his spurs will eventually grow. So once you have killed him, you do not have a trophy, there is really nothing there that you can be proud of and there is just absolutely no need to kill him.

A year later, when that turkey is a two year old turkey, he is going to have a full fan. When he is a jake, his fan will not be full. Three feathers on both ends of his fan will be shorter than all the other feathers in the middle of his fan, so you will not even have a pretty fan when you kill him. If you wait and let that turkey mature and get a little older, by the time he is a two year old turkey he will have spurs about three quarters of an inch. Sometimes you may even find a two year old turkey with spurs longer than that. When he is a two year old turkey, he is going to have a seven or eight inch, or maybe a nine inch beard, something you can be proud of once you harvest that turkey. The fan on that turkey is going to be full. Every feather in his tail is going to be exactly the same length and when he fans it out there, it is going to be a beautiful sight to see. Plus he is going to have a full set of waddles on his neck, and right on the top of his head is going to be a beautiful, pretty snow white color. He is going to have a little more experience in that second year and he is going to be a little bit tougher for you to call up.

Many people say "Well I am going to go ahead and kill that jake because if I do not kill him, a coyote is going to catch him or a bobcat or something is going to catch him before next spring and I might as well go ahead and kill him." That is just not consistent with the facts. Once a jake turkey gets to be a year old, actually after he is about three or four months old, the probabilities of that turkey being caught by any kind of predator are very slim. Most of the time the jake turkey is going to survive his first year. If jakes were not hunted, about nine out of ten jakes would survive to be full grown gobblers and would not be caught by predators. The absolute worst enemy of a jake turkey is a human being. There are more jake turkeys killed each spring by humans than are taken the entire year by all other predators combined.

If you are one of those people who will kill a jake turkey and the next season you do not hear a turkey gobble all year long, then you can blame yourself for that. If you had not killed that jake turkey the year before, then that turkey would have probably been there the following year, and you could have hunted the full grown gobbler.

Another reason that I do not like to kill jake turkeys is because most jake turkeys, before they are a year old, cannot gobble. There are exceptions to that though, and I have heard jakes that will gobble just as big and just as loud as a full grown mature four year old tom turkey. However, the general rule is that jakes cannot gobble, and about ninety-eight percent of the jakes you see during the spring while you are calling to a turkey will come in to you often without saying a word.

I have heard most of the jakes I have called up in my lifetime yelping, or clucking off in the distance before they ever got to me, but I have also had a lot of jake turkeys come up to me without ever having said a word, just looking for companionship and looking for the bird that is making all the racket.

So, if you are a serious turkey hunter and you love to hear turkeys gobble in the spring and you like to call turkeys to you that are gobbling, then you should give serious consideration to whether or not you ever want to kill another jake. You just cannot have the kind of experience hunting in the woods and killing jake turkeys that you can have killing full grown turkey gobblers.

I am so serious about my commitment not to kill jakes that if I never kill another turkey in my entire life, I still would not ever kill a jake. So if you are serious about your turkey hunting and you love the wild turkey, then I urge you to make a commitment to yourself that you will not kill jake turkeys. Encourage your friends and companions and those that you know hunt, to let the jakes walk and you will be better off for it. You will have more long bearded gobblers in the future.

If I ever call jake turkeys up to me and I am hunting by myself, I will scare those turkeys simply because I do not want somebody else to be able to call that turkey up and kill him. If I can teach him a lesson by scaring him, letting him know that I am the thing that called him up there, I might save that jake turkey's life and prevent somebody else from killing him. That gives him a chance to mature and to mate with hens in his second year of life.

It may be a mistake for me to do that because it makes him a harder turkey to kill in the future. He will never forget that experience and he will be very cautious about how he approaches yelping hens in the future. He will be a great deal more aware of what is going on around him. At least he had a chance to live to his second year, and I then have the opportunity to go on his turf and in a fair chase situation, call that turkey in and harvest him in a manner that is consistent with the standards that I have set for myself as a turkey hunter.

I have had many conversations with turkey hunting friends of mine who have expressed opposition to my opinion with respect to taking jakes. It is their position that beginning turkey hunters, especially young people who are beginning to hunt the wild turkey, should not be discouraged from taking a jake. My response to that is that a dead jake is a dead jake -- no matter who pulled the trigger. To encourage beginning turkey hunters to pass jakes teaches them a valuable lesson about this magnificent resource, and instills in them the challenge that accompanies the hunting of the mature gobbler.

11

CALLING

Calling the wild turkey is just a part of hunting and killing the wild turkey. It is a very important part of the process and should not be overlooked. It is probably accurate to say that if you do not know how to call to a wild turkey, you are probably not going to consistently kill wild turkeys. However, if you do not know the terrain you are hunting and you do not know how to set-up on a wild turkey, it is just as accurate to say that you are not going to consistently kill wild turkeys.

There has already been a discussion on the vocabulary of the turkey and you should know how to make all of those calls and you should know when to make them. However, there are other sounds made by the turkey which human beings have yet to name, so I cannot describe them for you. The only way you can discover these unnamed sounds is to listen to turkeys and hear all of the sounds a turkey makes as it travels through the woods. Once you hear the sounds, then you need to learn to make them on a turkey call.

One of the ways to learn to distinguish the different turkey sounds is to go to calling contests. The contestants are asked to make the sounds that have been given a name.

A call that I hear very often is the call a turkey hen makes when she is going to a gobbler that is gobbling or to another

Liz Barthel is becoming an experienced turkey hunter.

hen that is calling. I have heard this call many times, but I have never heard a name given it nor to my knowledge has it every been used in a calling contest. I have also heard jake turkeys make this call, but I have never heard a mature tom make it. The call is very loud and can be heard for a distance of two to three hundred yards with no problem. It consists of a very loud cluck followed by three or four yelps with a pause and ended with a cluck. When I hear this call it tells me that the turkey making it is searching for the gobbler or other hens that are calling.

In calling to a gobbler, I will always use two calls in sequence: the "Tree Call" and the "Fly Down Cackle." The reason for making these two calls in sequence is that the first call a turkey hen will make when she wakes up in the morning is a very soft "tree call" and many times she will repeat that call several times before she flies down. The second call she is going to make is the "cackle" while she is in the air flying from the tree to the ground. Since these are the only two calls I know that a turkey hen consistently makes in sequence, they are the only two calls I consistently make in sequence.

The only time I ever use these calls in sequence is immediately after daylight, whether or not I hear a turkey gobbler. I will use these calls several times on the same morning to make a gobbler believe there are several hens flying down in the same area. In effect these calls become "locator calls" when the owl hoot or crow call has failed to get a response from a gobbler.

If a turkey gobbles to you when you owl to him and within a few minutes you do a tree call the gobbler knows the hen is still in the tree. If after you have done the tree call you do a fly down cackle, he knows the hen has left the tree and is on the ground. Hopefully this will make the gobbler leave the tree and come to you (the hen) before you (the hen) leave the area. It has worked for me many times, and on several occasions gobblers have flown straight out of the tree and landed right in front of me. When this happens the hunt is over within five to ten minutes.

It is a memorable and awesome sight to watch a gobbler come flying through the woods, land within twenty yards of you and immediately go into a full strut. This happened to me one morning just after daylight. There was a bright golden beam of sunlight coming through the trees all the way to the ground. The gobbler landed right in the spot where the sun beam struck the ground. When he went into a strut in that sunbeam, he turned solid gold. I could not believe my eyes and it was a sight I had never seen before and have never seen since. I hope I live to see this happen again and the next time, I hope I am sitting behind a video camera.

For those who have never hunted the wild turkey or you are just starting to hunt the turkey, you need to know that there is no magic call you can make. I have heard some of the so-called professional turkey hunters say if you will do this or if you will do that a turkey will come in every time. If you hear someone say that you need to know that person is shooting you a line of bull fertilizer. Do not pay that kind of talk any attention and forget you ever heard it. There is no one thing you can do when turkey hunting that is going to work for you 25% of the time, not to mention 100% of the time.

Once you have a turkey respond to you while that turkey is still in the tree, you then have to get as close to that turkey as you can get before he flies down. After the turkey flies down, you then must make him respond to you after he is on the ground. Simply because a turkey gobbled when you owled to him does not necessarily mean he is going to respond to you when he hits the ground. After the turkey is on the ground, you then may have to try a variety of things to make the turkey gobble to you. There are those occasions that nothing you do causes the turkey to gobble, but the fact that he is not gobbling does not mean he is not coming to you. There are turkeys out there, and I have encountered many of them, that will gobble in a tree but will not make a sound once they are on the ground. These silent gobblers will come to you just about as often as a turkey that gobbles all the way to you.

What does it take to make a turkey gobble to you? There is no single or simple answer to this question. In many cases, the turkey will respond to a short series of yelps and I would guess that most turkey hunters will start their calling with a short soft series of yelps after they are sure

Troy Ruiz who is one of the best wildlife videographers I have ever known called this turkey straight off the roost to him.

the turkey is on the ground. However, if you can see the turkey fly out of the tree and land 50 to 75 yards from you, just one soft cluck followed by a contented purr may be all you need to bring him to you.

Once you have a turkey on the ground, you have to make some decision about how you are going to call that turkey. Some of the questions you must answer are: am I going to be aggressive or passive in calling to this turkey, am I going to use a rasp or clear call; am I going to call loud or soft; and am I going to call to the turkey every time he gobbles? Other factors can come into play and you will have other questions to answer. For instance, what if when the turkey flies down he puts water between you and him. Are you going to try to make him fly the water or are you going to try to get on the same side of the water with him?

Calling

The most common circumstance is that the turkey will fly down out of your sight with no obstacle between you and him. The distance between you and that turkey has a lot to do with how you call to him. If the turkey flies down within two hundred yards of you I would recommend you begin calling with some soft to moderately soft yelps. If he responds to that call, I would continue to yelp to him and try to maintain about the same volume on any calls. If the turkey is very slow to come to you, I would start to add a cluck and purr at about the same volume as every yelp. If the turkey is gobbling back frequently, I will answer him nearly every time he gobbles, but there are times when it is a good practice to wait several minutes after he gobbles to answer him. If he gobbles to you on his own (without you calling to him) you may want to wait until he gobbles three or four times before you answer. This is especially true if he is getting closer and closer to you every time he gobbles and he continues to gobble on his own.

Once the turkey is in sight, it becomes more and more difficult to decide how often you should call to him. The tendency for inexperienced turkey hunters is to call more often when the turkey is in sight. This can be a very big mistake, but whatever you decide to do once the turkey gets in sight and you do call to him, you had better pay attention to how the turkey reacts to your calling. You need to read his body language. If he starts to strut, drum and spit, he is trying to make the hen see him and come to him.

If this happens, you need to be very careful about your calling because it could hang him up right where he is. At this point, he knows he is close enough for the hen to see him and he wants her to come to him. If this happens, he may not move another inch in your direction. Once you see the turkey, exercise some patience and see what he does before you call to him again. If you call to him after you see him and he stands straight up and looks in your direction, my opinion is that you should do absolutely nothing. If you call to a turkey standing straight up looking at you, and he cannot see a hen turkey standing in the spot where the sound is coming from, you are inviting him to leave the area. In addition, you run the risk that he will make you out in which case he will be gone.

If you call to a turkey when he is in sight of you and he begins to walk kind of fast and starts to move his head back and forth, you are in deep trouble. The turkey may not have spotted you, but he has not seen a hen either. That is sometimes enough to make him suspicious about what is going on.

When a turkey gets suspicious about anything, his next move is to leave. If the turkey is in an erect position walking in a hurried sort of way, at the same time looks in different directions and starts to cluck, you had better do something in a hurry or you are going to lose this turkey. The next thing you may hear and see is a series of putts and flapping wings. When a turkey has given me this kind of body language, I have been able to stop him from leaving by hammering him with some very hard cutting or cackling. This works now and then, and it is always worth a try. Timing has to be perfect when using this tactic, the cackling or cutting has to be done just at that moment before the turkey breaks into a run.

You will learn to read the turkeys' body language as you gain experience in hunting them. For instance, if a turkey gobbler lowers his head from the upright position to about half way to the ground and then fluffs his feathers into about a 1/4 strut and continues to move in your direction, you better get ready to give him a barrel because that turkey is about to run right up your gun barrel. The worst mistake you can make on a turkey in that situation is to call to him. He is coming in so let him come.

Throughout this book, the subject of calling a wild turkey continues to come up. When you encounter a gobbler, there are times he gobbles to you and comes to you no matter what kind of call you are using or how bad you are calling. At other times it does not make any difference how perfect you call, you can make the turkey gobble, but you cannot make him come in to you. I do not care what the so-called professionals say, there is no explanation for why this will sometimes happen.

As has already been pointed out, the many different sounds that turkeys make can be used to call a turkey. The basic dilemma of a turkey hunter is knowing which to use and how often. The fundamental rule is to use whatever sound the turkey is responding to. It is probably a good practice to mix up your calls some, but you should always return to, and rely most heavily on, the call or calls the turkey is responding to. Simply because you are able to do many different sounds on a turkey caller does not mean that you want to use all of those sounds on every turkey you encounter. There may be times when you have to use every sound you know to call a turkey up, but I can assure you that is a very rare situation.

When the turkey is on the ground coming to you, most of the time soft yelps will get the job done. Other times, you may have to mix your yelp with some clucking and purring. Most gobblers that are going to come to you will come to yelping and clucking and purring. However, there are those gobblers that prefer very loud excited calling. With these turkeys, you can usually keep them excited by calling loud, calling often and by cutting and cackling. Many times these kinds of turkeys will double and triple gobble when you cut or cackle to them.

When you are hunting the wild turkey, you are confronted with a variety of situations, all of which may demand a different approach or tactic. By the process of elimination, you adopt the tactic that causes the turkey to respond. There is no one solution to a particular problem you may encounter while calling to a wild turkey. In some instances, you will have to try many different things before the turkey will respond, and there are those instances when you are not going to get a gobbling turkey to come to you no matter what you do.

When you are confronted with a difficult situation with a particular turkey, you must determine what it is going to take to kill it. It may take a particular sound, such as cutting, or it may take a particular calling device such as a box call instead of a diaphragm call. There are those turkeys that you cannot kill no matter what sound you produce or what calling device you use.

There are so many problems you will encounter while hunting the wild turkey that no one can anticipate what those problems may be. There is absolutely nothing special you can do that will work for you every time you encounter a particular problem. You must keep experimenting with different things until you find something that works. You may not find anything that will work for you in which case the turkey you are hunting will survive.

The best advice I can give to become familiar with every sound the wild turkey makes and learn how to reproduce those sounds. In addition, become proficient on diaphragm and friction calls and learn how to reproduce all of the sounds of the wild turkey on as many different kinds of calls as you possibly can. You never know which sound or which caller is going to work for you under a given set of circumstances. Know how to make all of the sounds and how to use all of the callers.

12

AFTER THE SHOT

It has been said many times that all of the joy, thrill and fun of hunting the wild turkey comes to an abrupt end when you hear the report and feel the recoil of your shotgun. This is very true because, immediately after the shot, you will either see a turkey flopping around in front of you or see him running or flying off. In the latter instance, you have probably missed and you get this feeling of dismay and disgust knowing that you have worked hard for this turkey and failed.

When you see a turkey flopping in front of you, you had better get to that turkey as quickly as you can. More times than not when I was slow to get to a flopping turkey, I have watched him get on his feet, and then I would have to either shoot him again or run him down. When this happens, most often you have to run him down and also shoot him again.

Once you shoot your turkey and you run up to him whether he is flopping or not, the first thing you should do is put your foot on his neck. If he is not flopping, he will probably start when you touch him. If he is flopping, you should put your foot on his neck and hold it there until he quits. Doing this prevents the turkey from getting up and running off and also prevents the turkey from sticking you with his spurs.

Verona Inabinette, the absolute best woman wildlife videographer in the country today, called this turkey in and videoed the entire hunt.

When you get ready to pick your turkey up you should get both of his feet together and then pick him up by both legs. If you do this, the turkey cannot spur you. If you pick him up by the head, his legs are free and if there is any life left in him, one kick of his leg can drive a spur into you. I know this for a fact because I had a dead turkey drive a one inch spur into the palm of my hand.

When I pick up a turkey I stand on his neck until he stops flopping. With my foot still on his neck, I reach down and lay his legs side by side. I then pick the turkey up by both legs, and when I have his body off the ground, I give him a jerk to make sure he is dead. At that point, I take my foot off his neck and sling him over my should and return to the spot from which I was calling to gather up my equipment.

When I get ready to leave the woods, I put the turkey in a turkey tote such as a garbage bag and walk out.

13

SUB-SPECIES OF THE WILD TURKEY

As every turkey hunter in the country probably already knows, four major sub-species of the wild turkey populate the United States. There are a total of six sub-species of the wild turkey that populate the world. The four major sub-species in the U.S. are: the Eastern; the Osceola or Florida wild turkey; the Rio Grande turkey; and the Merriam.

A fifth sub-species of the wild turkey, the Gould, has a very small population in the United States, limited to only two states. The sixth sub-species, the Ocellated turkey, has no population in the United States and is located in the Yucatan region of Southern Mexico, Belize, and northern Guatemala. There have been reports that the Gould sub-species has a very small and very limited population in southwest New Mexico and southeast Arizona, but I have not been able to verify this as an accurate statement of the range of the Gould turkey (Kennamer 1-20).

I must point out that I have never attempted to hunt the Gould turkey or the Ocellated turkey, and know little or nothing about them. Therefore, this book will not cover either of these two turkeys. However, I have hunted the Eastern, the Osceola, the Rio Grande and the Merriam.

Species	Range
Osceola	Mid-Florida to South Florida (Dickson 18)
Eastern	Alabama, Arkansas, Connecticut, Delaware, Florida, Georgia, Illinois, Indiana, Iowa, Kansas, Kentucky, Louisiana, Maine, Maryland, Massachusetts, Michigan, Minnesota, Mississippi, Missouri, New Hampshire, New Jersey, New York, North Carolina, North Dakota, Ohio, Pennsylvania, Rhode Island, South Carolina, Tennessee, Texas, Vermont, Virginia and Wisconsin (Dickson 18)
Rio Grande	California, Colorado, Hawaii, Idaho, Nebraska Oklahoma, Oregon, Texas, Utah and Washington (Dickson 18)
Merriam	Arizona, California, Colorado, Idaho, Montana, New Mexico, Oregon, South Dakota, Utah, Washington and Wyoming (Dickson 18)
Gould	Mexico, southeastern Arizona, southwestern New Mexico (Kennamer 1-20)
Ocellated	Yucatan region of southern Mexico, Belize, and northern Guatemala (Dickson 19)

The Eastern turkey is by far the most popular and widely hunted turkey in the United States because it has the widest range. Due to the hunting pressure that has been put on the Eastern turkey throughout its range, it has been my experience that it is by far the most difficult turkey to hunt. It is much more reticent or reluctant to come to the calling of a hen turkey than are the other sub-species. This is especially true of the Eastern turkeys found in the southeastern U.S., where it has been hunted the most.

The Florida, or Osceola, turkey is unique to the State of Florida, and has no range outside the southern portion of Florida. The range of this turkey and the range of the Eastern turkey overlap, and to the untrained eye, there is very little distinction between the Osceola, or Florida, turkey and the Eastern turkey.

A person watching an Eastern turkey and an Osceola turkey strutting in the same field at the same time at a distance of thirty yards would not be able to distinguish one bird from the other. However, there are some very subtle, distinct differences that you will notice on a closer examination of the two turkeys. If you have an Osceola and an Eastern that you can stand side-by-side with one another and view them at close range, you will note that the stripes on the wing feathers of the Osceola are much narrower than those of the Eastern. The secondary feathers on the tail of the Osceola turkey do not have the clear, distinct, dark stripe that the secondary feathers on the tail of the Eastern bird has.

As far as size of the two turkeys, it is difficult to say which one would outweigh the other without some scientific studies. It has been my observation that both the Eastern and Osceola can weigh between 15 and 22 pounds. However, without a detailed comparison of a large number of turkeys, it is impossible to determine which of the two turkeys, on the average, is larger than the other.

The Rio Grande turkey is easy to distinguish from the Eastern and Osceola due to the light cream-colored tip of its tail feathers. The secondary feathers on the Rio Grande also have different iridescent colors and the tips of the feathers of the Rio Grande turkey are much lighter than those of the Florida, Osceola or Eastern turkeys. As far as the size of the Rio Grande as compared to the other turkeys, again, it has been my experience, that you will kill Rio Grandes that are just as large as Easterns or Osceolas, and on other occasions, you will kill Rio Grandes that are smaller than some Osceolas or Easterns. So, without a large sample of turkeys to compare, it is impossible to make a general statement that one of these turkeys will grow larger than another sub-specie of the turkey.

The Merriam turkey is very similar to the Rio Grande except that the Merriam has a much lighter color on the tips of its tail feathers. Its secondary feathers are much lighter in color than the secondary feathers on the Rio Grande which distinguishes it from the Osceola and the Eastern turkey. It is my opinion that the Merriam bird is by far the most beautiful of all the sub-species.

It is virtually impossible to fully describe all the differences between the Eastern wild turkey and the Osceola turkey and between the Merriam and the Rio Grande. The only way that to really tell the difference is to actually see and physically inspect the turkeys.

While the Osceola and Eastern turkeys are very similar in appearance, there is a great deal of difference between the appearance of these two turkeys and the Rio Grande and Merriam turkey. That probably has to do with the geographic range of the turkeys. The Eastern turkey and the Osceola turkey range primarily east of the Mississippi River, with the Osceola being totally confined to Florida. The Merriam and Rio Grande turkeys range west of the Mississippi River in hill or mountainous country, or along the rugged flat areas of west Texas, Oklahoma, and parts of New Mexico.

Troy Ruiz and the author double-teamed this turkey in Oklahoma.

The two charts in this chapter indicate some of the most obvious differences in the coloration of the turkeys and the difference in size, including body weight, beard length and spur length.

However, any written descriptions will be vague and ambiguous, and it is difficult to determine whether or not you could distinguish these turkeys without being able to actually physically inspect the turkeys. If you are a turkey hunter, you already know that some turkeys from the same sub-species will have some variations in color. So it is virtually impossible to make an accurate description of the various sub-species and have it be completely accurate. Since the sample sizes used in the chart above are so small, it is impossible to make a comparison of the body weights, beard lengths and spur lengths of these turkeys.

In addition, the chart does not reveal the geographic areas from which the sample birds were taken, nor does it reveal what the conditions were for these birds during the time period they were killed. Differences in weather conditions, food supply, and geographic area could determine the body weights, beard lengths and spur lengths of these turkeys. Charts that compare body size, beard length and spur length with such a small sample without knowing the geographic area from which the birds come make it virtually impossible to come to a conclusive determination about which birds will be heavier, which birds will have the longest beards and which will have the longest spurs.

As many of you already know because you are turkey hunters, you will kill turkeys of different body weights out of the same sub-species annually, and you will take turkeys that have different beard lengths and different spur lengths, even though some of the birds with the longer spurs will be lighter in weight than some of the birds with longer beards and longer spurs. There are times when there will be a mix of that. The turkey with the larger body weight will have the longest beard but the shortest spurs, or he will have the longest spurs with the shortest beard. So you can see the difficulty in making a determination about which of these birds are larger in body size, have longer beards and longer spurs. Large samples of the turkeys would have to be taken from each geographic area of their range. I am not saying that it is a factor, I am saying it may be a factor. The only way to determine whether or not it is a factor is to have a large sample of birds taken from various parts of the United States. The samples indicated in the chart above are so small that it is difficult to arrive at any conclusions when, for instance, you only have ten Osceola or Florida turkeys in the sample.

In order for a turkey hunter to claim that he has taken a grand slam of the wild turkey, he must have killed one of

Sub-Species	Body Appearance	Rectrix Tips	Covert Tips	Rump
Eastern	purplish to coppery bronze	cinnamon to dark chestnut	chestnut	coppery to greenish gold
Osceola (Florida)	coppery to greenish gold	cinnamon to light chestnut	chestnut	coppery to greenish gold
Rio Grande	coppery to greenish gold	cinnamon to buff	cinnamon or pinkish buff black	greenish gold to blueish
Merriam	purplish bronze	buff to pinkish white	buff to pinkish white	blueish black

(Dickson 20)

Weight, beard length and spur length differences in the four sub-species located in the United States.

Sub-Species	Sample Size	Mean Body Weight	Mean Beard Length	Mean Spur Length
Eastern	120 gobblers	21.2 lbs.	10.2 in.	1.1 in.
Osceola (Florida)	10 gobblers	18.7 lbs.	9.8 in.	1.3 in.
Rio Grande	30 gobblers	20.0 lbs.	9.6 in.	1.1 in.
Merriam	20 gobblers	20.7 lbs.	9.3 in.	.9 in.

(Dickson 21)

each of the four sub-species that are located in the United States: Eastern, Osceola or Florida turkey, Rio Grande turkey, and Merriam turkey. It is not necessary that he take each of those birds in the same year. He can kill each of those birds over a number of years, as long as he kills one of each of the four sub-species.

In order for a turkey hunter to claim a world slam, he must not only have killed each of the four sub-species located in the United States, he must also take a Gould and an Ocellated turkey. So if you are interested in taking a grand slam or a world slam, you are now familiar with what is required to do so.

I find there to be very little difference in the method used or the calling tactics you might use to hunt the four sub-species located in the United States. Of course, geographic territory differs, terrain differs and you have to employ different tactics to suit the terrain in which you are hunting.

For instance, when hunting the Eastern turkey, keep in mind that its range is primarily hardwood areas where the turkey can be hunted in fairly open woods and can be seen at a fairly long distance. Compare that to hunting the Osceola or Florida turkey, where there is not a great deal of hardwood. There is a lot of pine timber, some hardwoods, a lot of marsh and swampy areas and there is a lot of palmetto growth which makes it difficult to see the turkey or to set up on him when you are calling him to you.

I have hunted the Rio Grande primarily in west Texas, where there is a lot of mesquite and cactus bush, and small scrub bushes which make it difficult to set up on a turkey. Plus, you do not have a long field of vision to see the turkey coming from a long distance. However, in Texas there are creek bottoms which contain hardwood trees, and it is extremely easy to set up in those areas and see turkeys coming for a long distance. Some of the creek bottoms in west Texas are dry during the spring, and some have flowing water in them. These are also usually roosting areas for turkeys in west Texas because along the dried creek bottoms, or the creek bottoms with flowing water, stand the largest trees in west Texas. And, turkeys prefer to roost over water.

I have had the good fortune to hunt west Texas a number of times and one of the most exciting and thrilling moments of my turkey hunting life has been to stand along the edge of one of these creek bottoms, owl to wild turkeys and hear as many as one hundred and fifty to two hundred full grown mature turkey gobblers gobble at one time and then hear them continuously gobble for twenty to thirty minutes before they finally flew down. It is an awesome sound that has been heard by this person only in west Texas. If you have never heard two hundred turkey gobblers gobble on the roost at one time, I recommend that you take the trip to Texas, if not to hunt the turkey, just to listen to the sound that you will hear when that many mature turkey gobblers gobble at one time on the roost.

I have also had the opportunity to hunt the Rio Grande turkey in west Oklahoma. It has been my experience that hunting the Rio Grande in Texas and Oklahoma is very similar. These turkeys respond to the same calling that the Eastern, Osceola and Merriam respond to and will come to the same type of calling. The hunter must find that call and the sound which the turkeys will respond to and use that call and that sound. The Rio Grande turkey in Texas and Oklahoma is exactly like the other three sub-species in that every gobbler is different and you have to deal with every gobbler in an individual sort of way. Once you have been able to determine what the gobbler is interested in, then you want to emphasize that call or that sound in getting the gobbler to come to you. It has been my experience that the Rio Grande is much more predictable than any of the other sub-species. It is my personal view that this is because in west Texas and west Oklahoma, the number of roosting sites for the wild turkey is limited, and therefore, it is much easier to predict their behavior.

If you are able to find a roosting site of a Rio Grande turkey, you can almost predict that the turkeys will return to that roosting site every evening, or you can go to that roosting site in the morning and almost be assured that turkeys will be roosting in that area. This is not an absolute truth, but the Rio Grande is much more predictable with respect to where it is going to roost than the other three sub-species in the United States.

Once you have located a roosting site for the Rio Grande turkey, it is much easier to hunt those turkeys in the afternoon since you are almost assured that he will return in the late afternoon. You merely have to position yourself in a location where you can call to the turkeys as they begin to return to the roost and you are much more likely to call a Rio Grande turkey to you in the afternoon than you are any of the other three sub-species. It is also much simpler to hunt the turkeys in the morning, since you can position yourself in such a way that you can call the turkey to you as he flies off the roost.

In locating the Rio Grande on the roost, it is not always necessary to use a locator call because many of these turkeys will gobble on their own from the roost, and do that much more frequently than any of the other turkeys I have hunted. However, this does not mean that you are going to harvest a Rio Grande turkey every time. Because roosting sites are not as available to the Rio Grande as to the other sub-species, it is not unusual to see gobblers and hens roosting in the same tree.

Of course, this presents a problem for a turkey hunter because, in many instances, when the hens fly down off the roost, the gobbler can see the hens and he will fly right to them. Calling a Rio Grande gobbler away from hens is just as difficult as calling any other species of gobblers away from hens. It is much easier for the Rio Grande gobbler to

From left to right, Jim Jones, the author, Greg Gregory, and Kurt Kremke, in New Castle, Wyoming, and were with me when I took this Merriam bird, which was my very first Merriam.

find hens in the morning than it is for the other sub-species simply because he nearly always roosts close to the hens. In every instance where I have hunted the Rio Grande turkey, if I could entice the hens to fly down to me as they come off the roost, the gobbler would follow them.

On one occasion, I was actually able to get the gobbler to fly off the roost first, and then the hens followed the gobbler to the ground right out in front of me. If you can get the turkeys to pay attention to your calling while they are on the roost, and make them come to you when they fly down, it will certainly increase your chances of taking a gobbler. If the hens fly down first, and they do not fly down to you, then it is almost an absolute certainty that the gobbler is going to follow the hens that he saw fly out of the tree rather than fly to you. In hunting the Rio Grande, you have a distinct advantage knowing where the turkeys are roosting.

In all of my years in hunting the wild turkey, I have only had the privilege to hunt the Merriam turkey on two separate occasions. On the first occasion, I hunted the Merriam for five days. On that occasion, on the Tuesday before I arrived in South Dakota on Friday, fifteen inches of snow had fallen in the area where I was going to be hunting. By the time I arrived in South Dakota, the only snow that remained was that which was left along the side of the roads and small patches of snow that remained in the higher elevations.

The weather conditions had changed dramatically over a about ten days, from being unseasonably warm to a fifteen inch snow, and then sufficiently warming up to melt that much snow over a only three or four days. I bring this up to merely show that the conditions under which I hunted the Merriam the first time were far from perfect. On that occasion, I did have the good fortune to encounter three or four Merriam turkey gobblers, but was unable to call any of them to me.

On the second occasion, I had the opportunity to hunt the Merriam in Newcastle, Wyoming with three good friends of mine, Greg Gregory and Kurt Kremke who reside in Newcastle, and another friend of mine by the name of Jim Jones who is one of the owners of Indian Archery Outfitters and Video.

When Jim Jones and I arrived in Newcastle, the weather was cold, there was intermittent rain, sleet and snow, all of which led me to believe hunting the Merriam turkey was going to be extremely difficult. On the afternoon before we were supposed to go out for our first morning hunt, it quit raining and sleeting and the rain and sleet turned to snow and the temperature dropped from the mid to high 30's down to the mid to high 20's. When we reached the place we were going to hunt on the first morning, the temperature was probably 25 degrees and there was a light snow falling. It had snowed intermittently the night before and about two or three inches of snow had accumulated on the ground.

Since I had never hunted the wild turkey in the snow, and had never heard a wild turkey gobble in the snow, I felt that it was going to be one of those mornings where we would return empty-handed. When we arrived at the spot where we were going to leave the vehicle, we waited for about fifteen minutes for it to get light enough for us to start into the woods. After we got out of the truck and had all of our equipment ready to go including the video camera, we decided that we should probably owl and get a turkey to gobble. When we did owl, a turkey immediately answered from the top of a nearby mountain.

We started climbing the mountain and went to an elevation of somewhere between five and six thousand feet where we felt like we were finally close enough to set up on the turkey. At this particular spot, we were approximately four to five hundred yards from the turkey, which is much further than I would like to call to a turkey, but because of the terrain and the area we were hunting in, we picked a spot and set up on the turkey with him at that distance from us. I was designated as the hunter, and would be doing all of the calling. Jim Jones would be operating the video camera, Greg Gregory and Kurt Krempke were going to be spectators on this hunt.

We actually got set up on this turkey right at daylight, and the weather was so cold that it was freezing my diaphragms and making them extremely difficult to blow. Because this turkey was so far from us, I decided not to do a tree call or any soft calling, but to call to this turkey with extremely loud yelps. Upon completing my first series of yelps with a frozen turkey call, the gobbler answered. I could tell that there was a difference in the volume of the answer the turkey made to my call and the volume of the turkey's gobble when we owled to him, so I assumed that this turkey had already flown down and was on the ground. The turkey was responding to three different calls, the yelp, the cut, and the purr, so I limited my calling to these three calls.

As the turkey got closer, I reduced the volume of my calls. At one point, as the turkey started down into a canyon, it sounded like he was going away from me, so I increased the volume until I could tell that he was still headed in my direction. About forty-five minutes to an hour after we had set up on this turkey, I looked off to my front right, and I could see the tips of the turkey's fan as he came over a small rise in full strut, and headed straight for me. As soon as I got the signal from Jim Jones that he had the turkey in sight of the video camera, it was time for me to pull the trigger. I harvested my first Merriam bird, and completed my Grand Slam of the American wild turkey.

For the rest of the week that we were in Wyoming, I was the designated camera man as we attempted to call up another Merriam so that Jim Jones could complete his Grand Slam. We were unsuccessful in that effort, although on several occasions, we had gobblers within thirty to forty yards of us, but just could not get in a position to take one of the turkeys. My encounter with the Merriam absolutely convinces me that they respond to the same type calling as the Osceola, the Eastern and the Rio Grande. Calling tactics for the Merriam are identical to the calling tactics you would use in harvesting the other three sub-species of the American wild turkey, but terrain features make other tactics different in your approach to the Merriam turkeys.

The terrain in which you hunt the Merriam is different from the terrain in which you hunt the other birds, and that is true of each of these four sub-species. They all live in different terrains, so you have to adapt your hunting to suit the terrain features of the area you are hunting. For instance, in hunting the Merriam turkey, I was hunting at elevations anywhere from 1,500 feet to about 6,000 feet, and was hunting wooded areas with interspersed meadows located in those areas. Some of these meadows were very small and some were areas that I would classify as large fields, but would have as many as two and three hundred acres of open fields or meadows where there would be no trees. You could see turkeys feeding in these fields at great distances, but they were extremely difficult to call at those distances.

In hunting the Merriam, I do recommend two things that will help more than they seem to help with the other sub-species: you should always have a crow call and a box call with you. I noticed these turkeys responded more to a crow call up in the day than any of the other sub-species, and it was extremely handy in locating gobblers during the midday. In addition, the use of a box call was extremely helpful in locating turkeys at all times of the day. The volume of the box call carries over these mountainous areas and high hills further than the diaphragm. It was much easier to get a turkey to gobble to the box call than it was to get them to gobble to a diaphragm call. Once the turkeys were gobbling to the box call, you could mix up both calls and keep the turkey interested but I would highly recommend, if you intend to hunt the Merriam turkey, that you become proficient with the calls.

This chapter of this book is by no means intended to be, nor does it purport to be, an exhaustive treatment of the differences and similarities between the four sub-species of the wild turkey located within the United States. It is merely an effort to let you know there are various sub-species of the wild turkey, what their range is or where you can find them, and basically what you have to do to hunt the four sub-species. There are similarities and there are differences in the way you hunt the various sub-species of the turkey, simply because there are differences in the terrain in which the turkeys are located. The ultimate test for you as a hunter will be to put your feet on the ground within the range of each of these four sub-species and actually undertake to hunt them and by so doing gain the experience you need to become a proficient turkey hunter of each of these four sub-species of turkeys. You can read books until you go completely blind and still never really understand or know how to hunt the wild turkey. You have to get in the woods with the wild turkey and actually experience for yourself the challenges, the difficulties and the obstacles that are going to interfere with you becoming a successful turkey hunter.

14

THE NATIONAL WILD TURKEY FEDERATION*

So that there is no mistake about it, I want to be absolutely certain that my position with respect to the National Wild Turkey Federation is understood at the beginning of this chapter. I am a lifetime member of the NWTF and I believe it to be the most worthwhile organization to which I have ever belonged. I make no pretense about being objective in my attitude toward the NWTF. I personally believe if you are a turkey hunter, or if you desire to become a turkey hunter, you have an obligation to become a member of the NWTF, and should support it in every way possible, including whatever you can do financially, to support the organization and recruit new members to it. This includes attending all functions put on in your area by the NWTF. If you do not become a member, then you are not doing your part to support the conservation and preservation of the American wild turkey. You are allowing those who are

---

*Much of the information contained in this chapter was furnished to the author by Gary Tanner, Director of Development, NWTF, and Daniel Young, Advertising and Circulation Manager, Turkey Call magazine, and The Caller tabloid NWTF. Without the assistance of Gary and Danny, I could not have written this chapter.

members to protect for you the opportunity to enjoy the sport of hunting the wild turkey.

In the late 1950's, and throughout the 1960's, it had become obvious that something had to be done to begin the process of protecting the habitat and restocking of the American wild turkey; to restore the wild turkey to areas where it had been virtually eliminated; and to educate the turkey hunting public and the general public about the wild turkey. As one who had his first experience of hunting the wild turkey in the 1950's, I can tell you that you were just about as likely to see or hear a wild elephant in the woods of Mississippi as you were to see or hear a wild turkey during that time. Because of poor cutting practices of some of the paper and lumber companies, much of the turkey habitat had been destroyed. In addition, there had been an attitude of hunters that the turkey population would always be here, and as a result, there had been an overkill of turkeys and the population of turkeys was quickly disappearing in Mississippi and other states.

In the early 1970's, Thomas F. Rodgers of Fredericksburg, Virginia started exploring the possibility of forming a national organization to work for the conservation and restoration of the wild turkey. By 1973, Rodgers had put together a group of people and had appointed the first advisory board of the National Wild Turkey Federation. Soon after the advisory board was appointed, the NWTF opened its first office in Edgefield, South Carolina. In early 1974, the first State Chapter of the NWTF was organized in South Carolina. Before the end of 1974, Georgia and Kentucky also organized State Chapters of the NWTF. During its first year of existence, the NWTF had managed to recruit about 1,300 members and this was the beginning of the NWTF. From those beginnings, how far has the NWTF come and where is it going?

From a mere 1,300 members in 1973 and three state chapters in 1974, the NWTF has grown to over 120,000 members in 1995 with members in all fifty states and in eight foreign countries. In 1973, it was estimated that there were 1.3 million turkeys in the United States, and that there were 1.4 million turkey hunters in the United States. At that time, only 39 states had a turkey hunting season. Contrast the figures of 1973 with those of 1993, only twenty years later, when it was estimated that there were over 4 million turkeys in the United States, and 1.9 million turkey hunters. Forty-nine states now have turkey hunting seasons. In 1993, there were over 550,000 turkeys harvested as contrasted with only 128,000 turkeys harvested in 1973.

You can see from these figures that, as the NWTF has grown, the turkey population has grown and so has the number of people who hunt the wild turkey. It goes without saying that the efforts of the NWTF are a major contributing factor to the growth in the numbers of wild turkeys and turkey hunters. This organization has worked closely with the various state wildlife departments, many outdoor related corporations like paper and timber companies, various utilities, many conservation groups, universities and other organizations throughout the U. S. to assist in educating those in responsible positions about the importance of the wild turkey, providing information on habitat preservation and conservation.

The NWTF has also provided funds for research conducted by universities throughout the U. S. on mortality and reproduction of the wild turkey, assisting greatly in identifying needs of the turkey and contributing to the astronomical growth in the wild turkey population. In addition, the educational efforts on the part of the NWTF have been very helpful in informing those who hunt the wild turkey about the importance of hunting the turkey in an ethical manner and abiding state game laws, preventing an over harvest of wild turkeys. These educational efforts have contributed greatly to the increase in population of the wild turkey. In addition, the NWTF has been instrumental in generating interest in wild turkey hunting, which in turn generates funds in the form of license fees and taxes levied on long guns and ammunition sold to those who engage in the sport.

As part of the NWTF's efforts to conserve the wild turkey and perpetuate the sport of hunting the wild turkey, to date it has reached agreements with 48 state wildlife agencies; with the United States Forest Service; the United States Bureau of Land Management; 11 forest product companies; 9 utilities, and 3 coal mining associations, all of which have under their control millions of acres of land which is now more often used in a manner consistent with the needs of the wild turkey. Many of the old land practices utilized by these agencies and organizations have now been changed to maintain and preserve wild turkey habitat simply as a result of the conservation efforts and agreements that the NWTF has made with these various agencies and corporations.

It is my understanding that between 1973 and 1983, the NWTF depended primarily on the dues paid by its membership together with some contributions to perform the services it provided during that time. However, in 1983, the NWTF held its first fund-raising banquet in Atlanta, Georgia. That banquet netted about $5,000.00. Since that time, the number of banquets put on by the NWTF has increased, and in 1996 the NWTF, together with its local chapters, will sponsor over 700 of these fund-raising dinners and raise in excess of $6 million as a result. As has already been pointed out, in 1973 there were only three states with NWTF State Chapters. Now there are 48 State Chapters, and there are presently over 740 local chapters of the NWTF. The NWTF has set rather ambitious goals for itself: more than 1,100 local chapters and 250,000 members by the year 2,000.

Looking at the figures already mentioned, it is shameful that the turkey hunting population of this country has not done more to support the NWTF. It is estimated that there are approximately 1.9 million turkey hunters in the United States, and of that number only 120,000 belong to the NWTF. Translated, this means that only 1 out of about every 19 turkey hunters belong to the NWTF. For each one of us who is doing his share and making a contribution to the NWTF to preserve and protect the wild turkey, there are 18 who are doing absolutely nothing. As a turkey hunter, it is not only my responsibility, it is my obligation to be an active member of the NWTF and to recruit for the NWTF every single member that I can. The more members we recruit, the more we can help the various state and federal agencies conserve the wild turkey.

The NWTF, in its fund-raising efforts, depends primarily on individuals in the various states participating in NWTF state and local chapter events. The NWTF raises some funds from the collection of dues from its members. Other methods by which the NWTF raises money is through contributions from corporate and individual sources.

The primary method by which the NWTF raises funds for the projects it conducts is through the banquets put on by local chapters of the NWTF. The local chapter is given a kit of material from the NWTF to assist in the preparation and sponsorship of the local banquets. At these banquets, anyone attending pays an admission fee which includes a membership in the NWTF which entitles that member to certain benefits which includes the Turkey Call magazine, which is a publication put out by the NWTF on matters of interest to turkey hunters.

In addition, at each of these banquets, there is dinner served for those participating. During the course of the banquet, raffle tickets are sold on certain items which are then drawn and given to the winner of the raffle. The major event which takes place at the banquet is the auction. The auction is usually conducted by a professional auctioneer who sells items which have either been contributed to the local chapter or which have been provided to the local chapter by the NWTF. The NWTF each year provides a variety of wildlife art, with emphasis on the wild turkey. Additionally, there is a limited-edition gun provided to each banquet that is unique to the Federation's fund-raising efforts. It is built to NWTF specifications, and it's low edition size makes it very collectible.

Based on a formula worked out by the NWTF, a percentage of the proceeds of each of these local chapter benefits or dinners is given to the NWTF and a percentage is to go into the Super Fund of the NWTF to sponsor projects dealing with research and conservation of the wild turkey and preservation of the wild turkey habitat. A percentage of the proceeds of each of these banquets is then sent to the state chapter of the NWTF which is retained for the state Super Fund. This money is used primarily for local projects that are designated by the committee at the state for either research or conservation of the wild turkey. Some of the Super Fund money from both the NWTF and the state chapter is allocated to research at various universities on the wild turkey. Some of the Super Fund monies are used to purchase transport boxes for trapped wild turkeys which are then relocated either in the state by the state wildlife agency or relocated in areas of the U. S. where turkey populations are low.

It must be pointed out that individuals who do the work to put on the local chapter banquets do so with no pay as volunteers. Those who serve on the state board of directors of the NWTF and other officers in the state chapters serve with no pay and are strictly volunteers. They are people who have devoted a great deal of their time and money to the wild turkey, based on their interest in seeing the wild turkey population grow.

Another project undertaken by the NWTF is a program for young people 17 years old and under called the JAKES program. The word JAKES is an acronym for Juniors

Acquiring Knowledge, Ethics and Sportsmanship. Usually JAKES events are sponsored by NWTF local or state chapters and include seminars on hunting safety, especially as it relates to wild turkey hunting, although gun safety and other hunting safety is taught to these young people. At some JAKES events there are seminars put on about turkey biology - how it survives in the wild, what its predators are, what it looks like, and its food habits. These programs also teach young people how to look for turkey sign in the woods. [I have been to JAKES events where young people have been taught how to use various kinds of turkey calls and how to hunt turkeys.] These seminars usually introduce young people to basic and sometimes extremely complicated methods of hunting the wild turkey and how that is done. The young people are taught how to recognize the difference between gobbler and hen tracks, gobbler and hen droppings, and how to recognize other turkey sign. They are taught primarily how important wildlife is and what its place is in our environment and what should be done to protect habitat and the environment for wild animals. These young people are taught an appreciation not only for wildlife but also an appreciation for ethical methods of hunting the wild turkey and all other game animals.

The NWTF has two publications that go out to all of its members. One, referred to earlier, is a very well organized and well written magazine that contains many articles on what the NWTF is doing and articles on how to hunt the wild turkey and other matters of interest to the members of the NWTF, and this publication is called Turkey Call which comes out six times a year. The other publication, which is a quarterly tabloid newspaper, is called The Caller, and this publication is one of extreme interest to members because it normally gives an update on what each state organization is doing, and in many instances, will report what local chapters are doing in connection with state chapters and the NWTF with respect to relocation of turkeys and habitat enhancement and in JAKES events. This publication will usually have several stories relating turkey hunting experiences of different members of the NWTF and some articles that are contributed by nationally known outdoor writers. These two publications come to every member of the NWTF and are included in the cost of membership. In other words, once you become a member and you have paid your dues to the NWTF, you receive ten publications per year.

The NWTF also keeps records on turkeys that qualify as world record class gobblers. In order to register a turkey for the NWTF record book, the person submitting the turkey must be a member of the NWTF, and at least one of the witnesses to the recording of the data on the turkey must be a member of the NWTF. However, a person wishing to enter a turkey for the record book can join the NWTF at the time he submits the turkey for certification. The three factors that determine scoring and ranking are the weight of the turkey, the beard length of the turkey, and the spur length of the turkey. All weights of the turkey must be weighed on scales that have been certified as accurate and must be recorded to the nearest ounce. Beards and spurs must be measured on a device that is accurate to 1/16 of an inch. The formula for the overall score is the weight of the turkey in pounds and ounces, plus ten times the combined spur length of both the right and left spur, plus two times the beard length. When measuring the beard length, if the turkey has more than one beard, each beard must be measured. Such nontypical turkeys are in a separate category. The NWTF keeps these records on the overall size of turkeys' spur length and beard length, and then the records are broken down even further to establish records for each of the huntable sub-species, and then the records are broken down another time to establish records for turkey weights, spur length, and beard length by general classification and for each of the four sub-species in the

United States, and the Gould's and Ocellated turkey located outside the United States. The NWTF will publish the records annually in The Caller newsletter.

Earlier in this chapter, mention was made of the cooperative efforts between the NWTF and certain forest product industries in the United States. One of the forest product industries with which the NWTF has undertaken a cooperative effort is International Paper Company.

In Appendix C of this book, you can see for yourself how important these cooperative efforts are between the NWTF and the forest products industry such as International Paper Company by reading the publication put out by International Paper Company entitled THE WILD TURKEY. It is indeed gratifying to me to know that private conservation organizations such as the NWTF are working so closely with industries such as International Paper Company, which holds large tracts of land, for the purpose of conserving and preserving for future generations this royal bird, the American wild turkey. It is extremely rewarding and gratifying to me to know that industries such as International Paper Company have committed not only financial resources, but have also committed their personnel in management to these projects which can only be beneficial not only to the wild turkey but to all of us who love the sport of hunting the wild turkey. If every industry in this country would adopt the approach taken by International Paper Company and cooperate with organizations such as the NWTF, we would have much more wildlife to hunt in this country.

Another very important example of what the NWTF has done is one about which I have personal knowledge. Having served on the Board of Directors of the Mississippi Wild Turkey Federation. I know that funds that have been collected in Mississippi through banquets and other fund-raising efforts of the State Chapter of the NWTF have been contributed to Mississippi State University to be used by

Dr. George Hurst in research he is doing on the wild turkey in the state of Mississippi. In addition to that, I have been made aware of certain grants and funds that have been provided to Mississippi State University by the NWTF to be used in research being done by Dr. Hurst. As a result of these grants and funds being made available to Mississippi State, Dr. Hurst has been able to conduct research by trapping and releasing both hens and gobblers, some of which were juvenile turkeys, to be studied on a long term basis. The money provided by the NWTF has been used to purchase radio tracking equipment, tags, cannon nets and other devices used in this research. Some of the funds have also been used to employ undergraduate and graduate students at Mississippi State to assist in doing this important research undertaken by Dr. Hurst.

The long term benefits from this research is not just limited to the knowledge and information acquired by Dr. Hurst and the graduate and undergraduate students he has working for him on these research projects. Graduate students, in many cases, will go on to teach either at Mississippi State University, or some other university, and can share the knowledge and information they acquire by participating in these research projects with their students. Many of these graduate students, and undergraduate students, who participate in this research will go to work for state and federal agencies as wildlife biologists and can use the information obtained in this research to help in the management of land under the control of state and federal agencies. The most important part of this research and the participation in this research by graduate and undergraduate students is the impact it has on private industry and its management and treatment of wildlife habitat. Many of the students who participate in this research will go to work for the private sector and will carry the knowledge they have gained in these research projects to the various private industries for which they work. These students are then in a position to convince the management of these private industries to be more conscious of the way in which they manage their land for the wildlife. Appendix B to this book is an excellent example of a publication put out by a public university with the assistance of the financial support of the National Wild Turkey Federation. Appendix B is a publication done by Dr. George Hurst and a wildlife biologist named Dave Godwin encouraging turkey hunters to refrain from shooting jake turkeys.

Appendices B and C of this book clearly establish the importance of every turkey hunter in the United States becoming a member of the NWTF. Appendix B is a cooperative effort between the NWTF and a state-supported public university in the State of Mississippi doing research on the wild turkey; and Appendix C is a publication done by private industry, International Paper Company, done with the support of and encouragement of the NWTF. If every turkey hunter in the U. S. was a member of the NWTF, these type projects would become much more widespread to the benefit of all hunters and all wildlife.

I am proud of my membership in the NWTF and encourage all turkey hunters and others to join this organization. You too can become a proud member of the NWTF by writing to the following address or calling the following telephone number:

National Wild Turkey Federation
P. O. Box 530
Edgefield, SC   29824
Telephone: (803) 637-3106

15

CONCLUSION

If you have managed to read every page of this book to this point, you obviously know that a great deal of what has been said is strictly the opinion of the writer. The opinions that have been reached in this book are based on the forty-six years that this writer has spent roaming the woods of southeastern Mississippi and other parts of the United States. At the age of six years, I was given a Daisy Red Rider lever action BB gun and embarked upon my hunting career. With that BB gun, I managed to kill several small animals including snakes and different kinds of small birds, and honed my stalking and shooting ability with that Daisy Red Rider BB gun. At the age of twelve, for my twelfth Christmas, I was given a single barrel 16 gauge Stephen Savage Arms shotgun. With that shotgun, my real hunting experiences began.

To this day, I still own that shotgun, but it has been placed in retirement and will never be shot again. It would be virtually impossible for me to tell you how much wildlife has been placed on the dinner table simply with the use of that gun, because during the early years of my hunting life it was the only gun I had. You had to be extremely proficient with it, because about 90% of the time using a single barrel shotgun you are only going to get one shot.

But I have hunted practically every wild animal indigenous to South Mississippi with that gun including turkey, deer, hogs, squirrel, quail, rabbits, doves, ducks and anything else which had a season on it including even snipe birds. It would be impossible for me to tell you how many animals I killed with that single barrel 16 gauge shotgun not to mention the numbers I have taken with guns I have owned since.

The point I am attempting to make is that the opinions expressed in this book are based on vast amounts of experience in dealing with wildlife of all kinds and observing wildlife for almost my entire existence on the face of this earth. There are undoubtedly opinions expressed in this book with which you disagree, and based on your own experiences, you have come to certain conclusions and have opinions of your own which are just as valid as the opinions held by me, and are just as productive in hunting the wild turkey.

I offer my opinions for no other purpose than to assist you in your effort to become a better hunter. I would certainly like to know what your opinions are with respect to hunting the wild turkey because it is from listening to others who have encountered the wild turkey that each of us learn new tactics and tricks which makes us more successful and better hunters in every way -- including making us more ethical and humane in the way we treat these important natural resources available to us. As a matter of fact, it is through the cumulative knowledge and opinions of hunters and the contribution that hunters have made to wildlife that we now have the abundance of wildlife available to us today.

In hunting the wild turkey, there are many things that you must keep in mind and it is my opinion that the greatest virtue, and the thing that will give a turkey hunter the maximum advantage, is for that turkey hunter to exercise the greatest degree of patience he can possibly exercise.

The author with the Merriam which completed the author's Grand Slam of the American wild turkey. With the taking of this turkey, the author had successfully hunted the Osceola, the Eastern, the Rio Grande and the Merriam turkeys, completing the Grand Slam of the American wild turkey.

Patience in hunting the wild turkey is as important to the ultimate success of a turkey hunter as any other single factor involved with the sport. When you can half way call a turkey and you are set up in a place where it is likely a turkey will travel, if you have the patience to stay in that spot long enough, you will, in all probability, be a successful turkey hunter. This does not mean that you want to stay in the same place from daylight to dark in every instance. But there are times when remaining stationary from daylight to dark will lead to success for you as a turkey hunter. There are other times when that amount of patience will be detrimental to you. Only experience will teach you when it is to your advantage to remain patient or when it is to your advantage to move on a turkey.

When I use the word patient, I am generally trying to convey the thought that you should remain in one spot as long as you possibly can. However, patience can have other meanings. For instance, you may be hunting one turkey for several days. In some instances, I have hunted a turkey - a single turkey - for a three years. So, patience not only means what you are doing on the day you are actually hunting the turkey, it means how you hunt turkeys generally -- and you have to be extremely patient when hunting turkeys. The turkey I hunted for three years taxed my patience to its ultimate extent and the turkey was eventually killed by a friend of mine who was able to ambush him. But had that turkey not been killed by my friend, I would have eventually found a way to kill the turkey, because over the years of hunting, I have learned that if you are patient with a turkey and you continuously watch that turkey and observe his behavior, he will eventually make a mistake and you can kill him.

The way this turkey was finally killed was one morning my friend called to the turkey and the turkey gobbled to him on the roost. Just after daylight, the turkey flew off the roost in the opposite direction from which my friend was calling. When the turkey hit the ground, there were several crows in the area making a lot of noise and the turkey continued to gobble to the crows. My friend decided to make an end run around the turkey and wait him out. The result was that the turkey continued to give his position away by gobbling to the crows and my friend was able to maneuver to get in front of the turkey. When the turkey walked into view, my friend was able to conclude the hunt. I will never forget this turkey because on his left foot, his middle toe had been broken, and when it healed the end of that toe pointed straight up.

I do not believe there is a single turkey hunter in the United States who would disagree with the necessity of being patient when hunting the wild turkey. How many times has it happened to every turkey hunter, (and it is not a question of whether or not it has happened, it is a question of how many times it has happened) that when you start to change your position and you start moving around to change your position on a turkey, at that very moment a turkey putts or makes a series of clucks and putts and you hear the turkey running off or flying off. You lost that turkey because you failed to be patient enough to wait that extra five minutes or ten minutes that was needed to harvest the turkey.

In addition, there is the discipline of patience which you must use to wait on the turkey to get within gun shot range. You may be watching a turkey for a forty-five minutes to an hour, or even longer, while that turkey is in a full strut and gobbling and walking around, but will not come in to your gun shot range. There are times when you will have a turkey within sight of you and just out of gun range, and that turkey will never come any closer. Eventually he will walk away from you and you will not get a shot. It requires a great deal of patience to sit there and watch that turkey and wait for him to come within range before you finally decide to take the shot. This is all a part of being patient.

Not only remaining patient while waiting for the turkey to respond to you or come in to you, but after the turkey has responded and has come to you, then you must have the patience to wait until that turkey comes within gun shot range so that there can be a clean kill on the turkey.

But patience goes beyond that, as I have already said, to those turkeys you will hunt not just for a day or a week or a month, but that you will hunt for years before you are finally able to harvest them. Then there are those turkeys that, regardless of how much patience you have, how good you can call, or how good you are in the woods, you will never kill. There are just some turkeys out there that are destined to die of old age or as a result of a predator of some kind catching them rather than at the hands of a turkey hunter. It does not make any difference what you do, how good you call, how well you set up, how silently you can slip through the woods, or how much patience you have in dealing with that turkey, not you or anyone else will ever kill that turkey.

I have heard it said by many people that a turkey's eyesight and hearing are ten times better than that of any human being. I personally do not pay that kind of specific talk a great deal of attention because, based on my experience, it is my opinion that the eyesight and hearing of a turkey are so much better than that of a human being that it cannot be measured. So it is a good idea to always keep in mind that, if you can see the wild turkey, he can see you and if you can hear the wild turkey, he can hear you. If you will always keep that thought in the back of your mind it will help you a great deal in hunting turkeys.

You must always work under the assumption that if you are looking at a turkey, the very next move you make, that turkey will see you and be gone. Or, if you are listening to a turkey, that turkey is hearing every thing that you do, and at that point you cannot make any mistakes in anything that you do. What I mean by that is, if you are calling to a turkey and you are hearing the turkey gobble back to you, or if you hear a turkey gobble and you make a sound with your turkey call, that turkey is going to hear any sound that you make. It does not make any difference what the weather conditions are or which way the wind is blowing. Even if the wind is blowing your calling away from the turkey gobbler, if you can hear that turkey gobble he can hear you calling.

It has been said, and I believe it is true, that if you can hear a sound at thirty yards, a turkey can hear that sound at three hundred yards. That goes to prove the point that a turkey's hearing is ten times better than a human being's hearing. In addition to the rule just set out, that is if you can see him, he can see you and if you can hear him, he can hear you. You must always keep in mind that the only predictable thing about the wild turkey and hunting the wild turkey is that it is unpredictable.

I have heard some of these so-called "expert" turkey hunters try to convince people that they could predict what a turkey gobbler was going to do under certain circumstances, or under all circumstances. I am telling you that if anyone tells you that he can consistently predict what a turkey is going to do under all circumstances, that person is not telling you the truth. There is absolutely no human being on the face of this earth who can consistently predict what a wild turkey gobbler is going to do next. This is especially true during that time when the mating season is at its peak.

I have heard people make comments like "you cannot call a turkey uphill" or "you cannot call a turkey downhill" or "you cannot call a turkey across water" or "you cannot call a turkey away from hens". I have heard these kind of comments made as absolute truths about the predictability of a wild turkey gobbler, and I am just telling you that none of those things are absolutely true. I have seen turkeys called uphill and I have called turkeys uphill. I have seen turkeys called downhill and I have called turkeys downhill.

Conclusion 239

I have called turkeys away from hens and I have called turkeys across water. So when people tell you that you cannot do those things with turkeys, I am telling you that whoever says that knows absolutely nothing about turkey hunting.

Admittedly, it is much more difficult to call a turkey gobbler away from hens than it is to call a gobbler who is not "henned up" (a turkey that has hens with him). It is much easier to call a turkey to you if you are on the same side of the water the turkey is on than it is to call the turkey to you if he has to fly water. I personally have not noticed a great deal of difference in calling turkeys when I have had to call them uphill or downhill. I do not believe that has a great deal to do with whether or not a turkey will come to you. That is whether or not the turkey has to travel uphill or he has to travel downhill. But when I am calling to a turkey, I do like to be on about the same level that he is on. That is, if he is at the top of the hill, I like to be at the top of the hill so that he can come straight on in to me, or if he is on the side of the hill or at the bottom of the hill, I like to be at about the same level the turkey is on to call him, simply because that is just a personal preference that I have, not that it makes any difference in the degree of difficulty in calling the turkey.

Going up or downhill does not present to you the same problems that flying water or crossing a ravine or crossing a fence or some other terrain feature that might be between you and the turkey, whether it be man-made or natural. The slope of a hill has very little to do with the direction a turkey will travel. What is most important, in my opinion, is an observation made to me by a fellow by the name of Ronnie Jolley who stated something that I believe is an absolute truth with respect to calling a wild turkey and that is: it does not make any difference how good you can hunt the turkey or how good you can call the turkey, there is no one alive or no one who has ever lived, who could call a wild turkey to a place that turkey did not want to be.

I believe Ronnie's observation is absolutely true and it is one that you should always keep in mind in choosing a site to set up on a turkey. You must choose a site that a turkey would want to come to, instead of a site that a turkey would never come to. The way you know the difference is that you scout an area, you know where turkeys travel, you know where turkeys are seen often, and you know where all your turkey signs are located so that you know turkeys come to those areas that you are going to hunt. If you are in an area where you never see any turkey signs or turkeys, then you do not want to set up in those areas because those are places that turkeys, for some reason, do not like to travel. I believe the observation made by Ronnie Jolley is absolutely true and it is imperative that you set up in a place where turkeys will come to you. When you set up on a turkey, you should have confidence that you are in a spot that a turkey will come to and that you are not in a spot that a turkey just will not come to.

I have heard it said by many turkey hunters that they wish they knew how to call turkeys like some of these world champion callers who compete in calling contests. Please keep in mind that a calling contest is a controlled situation where a person stands on a stage, and 99% of the time that person is using a diaphragm turkey call that has been specially built for him for the purpose of competing. That person is on a stage with four or five or six or eight or however many judges sitting there. All of the judges of this contest are human beings who have listened to wild turkey hens in the past or have listened to competitive turkey callers in the past, and those human beings give a score to the person making the call. Once those scores are added up, it is then determined who the winner of that calling contest might be. Nowhere in the contest is the wild turkey involved in any way. The ultimate judge of anyone's ability to call the wild turkey is not six people or eight people sitting with their back to someone using a turkey call and writing a score down on a piece of paper. The ultimate judge of your ability to call a wild turkey is a wild turkey gobbler, and only a wild turkey gobbler. There is a vast difference between winning a turkey calling contest and hunting and calling up a wild turkey gobbler in the woods. Just because you do not believe you can win a turkey calling contest, does not mean that you cannot call up a wild turkey. It certainly does not mean that you cannot become as good a turkey hunter as any competition caller in this country.

The very best turkey hunter I have ever known just happened to be the person who taught me how to hunt the wild turkey and that is my uncle, Charles Rodney McMichael. At the time my Uncle Rodney was hunting wild turkeys, there were very few wild turkeys to hunt; very few people owned anything other than a single barrel shotgun; there were no four wheel drive vehicles to get you in and out of the woods; there were certainly no four wheelers or ATVs to get you in and out of the woods; there was no such thing as aerosol insect repellant and the only thing that was available was DDT sprayed from a spray gun onto your clothes to keep ticks and mosquitoes off. Shotgun shells were made of paper and could not get wet, otherwise they could not go in your gun. If they were wet and you shot them, you could not get the spent hull out of your gun. To my knowledge, there were no diaphragm calls on the market; the primary method of calling turkeys was the use of a box call that you either made yourself, or had someone make for you. The one that was most frequently used, was a snuff can with half the lid cut out and the piece of prophylactic rubber stretched across the cut out portion of the snuff can. The wing bone was sometimes used to call a turkey. In addition to the box call and snuff can, some people would use leaves to make the sound of a turkey hen.

There was absolutely no camouflage on the market at all; I do not ever remember seeing a commercially made crow call or owl hooter in my Uncle's hand, and I certainly never had access to one during those early days. No one had access to any cassettes to listen to, learn how to hunt the turkey, nor was there any such thing as commercially produced videos to assist in learning how to hunt the wild turkey.

There is absolutely no comparison between the turkey hunter of today and the turkey hunter of the past. The woodsmanship skill and ability of the turkey hunter of the past was far greater than those of turkey hunters today. Now there are an abundance of turkeys today, as compared to early days, and the equipment one has today is so far superior to the equipment turkey hunters of the 1950s had available to them.

During the 1950s, the way you learned to turkey hunt was to find someone like Charles Rodney McMichael who would take the time to teach you. After you had been taught the basics, you were then sent in the woods on your own to learn from your mistakes. In those days, hunting was a sport, but it was also a very important means of furnishing food for families. Hunting was a much more serious pursuit in the 50s than it is today; therefore, the people who engaged in the sport in the 1950s were much better at it than the hunter of today.

Be that as it may, one's ability to call should not be underestimated. There is absolutely no doubt that if you have mastered the diaphragm and some of these friction calls and can make sounds that resemble or are identical to the sound of a wild turkey hen, then you will eventually call a turkey gobbler to you, and you will eventually kill a turkey gobbler regardless of how well you know how to hunt the wild turkey. So calling is a very important aspect of hunting the wild turkey, but it is not the only factor that one must consider in preparing to hunt the wild turkey. All of those things mentioned in this book dealing with equipment, ethics, scouting, safety and the biology of the wild turkey go into making up the total turkey hunter. You will from time to time be able to go into the woods, sit down by a tree, take your turkey call out, yelp a few times and kill a turkey. It just happens that way sometimes, but you are not going to be a consistent turkey hunter unless you know some of the things that have been brought out in this book and know how to use the ideas put forward in this book.

The only way that you are going to be able to use what has been given to you here is to go into the woods and practice. Hunting the wild turkey is like anything else in the sense that, the more you do it, the better you become at it because you begin to understand the wild turkey and what it takes to hunt him. This does not mean that you will be able to take every turkey you call to, because that is just not the case. There are some turkeys that no hunter can call and there are other turkeys that every hunter can call in and kill. But then there are the turkeys in between that will come sometimes and sometimes they will not come and those are the turkeys that you really want to know how to hunt.

I mentioned there are some turkeys that no one can kill. Those are the old, hermit turkeys that have a great deal of experience at survival and just will not come to any turkey calling -- whether it be a real turkey or a human being making turkey sounds. I have run into some of these old hermit turkeys in my lifetime, and the way you can really tell one of these turkeys is that he will always be alone. That is he will not associate with other turkeys and he very rarely says anything. You will always know when you are dealing with an old hermit gobbler because when you call to him, he will come to a full alert position, he will throw his head straight up in the air like a giant periscope and cock his head from one side to the other to try to determine the direction of the calling. Once he determines the direction of the calling, he will then turn and run in the opposite direction as if he had been shot from a canon. A turkey like this will never be killed in a fair chase hunt because he is just too smart; too old; and too experienced to be fooled by a human being.

I am convinced there are turkeys who will play games with you, make you believe you are going to kill them, and then deliberately outmaneuver you so that you cannot kill them, but this is not the old hermit gobbler. The old hermit gobbler will not play any games but is deadly serious about staying alive. He will not gobble to you, he will not come anywhere close to your calling; you might happen upon him in a field or you might be sitting in the woods calling and see him at a distance but you will never see him with other turkeys and he will not get close enough to you for you to ever get a shot at him. At some point, when he hears your calling he is going to go in the other direction. The turkeys that will play games with you are killable turkeys and it is just a matter of you employing the right tactic to get to those turkeys.

In hunting the wild turkey, you must always keep in mind that to you this is a sport that you partake in for enjoyment, pleasure, amusement, recreation, exercise, and an opportunity to exhibit your hunting skills, your woodsmanship and your calling ability. If you go into the woods to hunt the wild turkey and you lose the battle with the wild turkey, you have lost absolutely nothing. You walk out of the woods without a turkey. But on the other hand, from the turkey's perspective, this is a deadly game. It is a life and death struggle with the turkey. He must constantly be alert to protect himself if it is his desire to live and I have seen turkeys that I thought were ready to commit suicide when called to by some hunters.

You must remember that a turkey knows that his life depends on every move he makes in the woods. You will never see a turkey carelessly walking around without stopping occasionally to determine what is around him by listening for strange sounds and looking for movement. Since the wild turkey perceives everything around him as a potential enemy and lives his daily life with the prospect that there is some predator or human being out there that is going to kill him, he is extremely cautious and very difficult to kill. One of the things that will make you a better turkey hunter is for you to adopt the view that the turkey has adopted. That is, you approach turkey hunting from the perspective that it is a life or death struggle for you and you will then become a much, much better turkey hunter. Just pretend that your life depends on your ability to sit still, be patient, know the wild turkey, and call him to you. If your life depended on you developing those skills, you would become very proficient at turkey hunting. The life of the turkey depends on him being able to determine what is a real turkey hen and what is not a real turkey hen; for him to determine where it is safe to travel and where it is unsafe for him to travel; for him to determine that the movement he sees is dangerous or benign; and for him to determine that once he gets in range of the sound of a turkey hen and he is unable to spot that turkey hen should he hang around or should he leave?

Turkeys have a very strong instinct to live and if you are going to be a successful turkey hunter then you must acquire all of the skill, ability, and knowledge you can about the wild turkey and how to hunt him or otherwise you will never kill a wild turkey. Remember, when you call a wild turkey gobbler to you, you are reversing nature. The wild turkey gobbler gobbles to attract hens to him. When you take into account the wild turkey gobbler's ability to see; his ability to hear; and his constant vigil for danger; together with the fact that you are reversing nature when you call a turkey gobbler to you, you get a better understanding of how difficult it is to hunt the wild turkey and what a great sport turkey hunting is.

APPENDICES

Appendix A - Glossary of Terms

Appendix B - References

Appendix C - Don't Take a Jake

Appendix D - The Wild Turkey

Appendix A

GLOSSARY OF TERMS

Ambush: The process of hiding from a turkey gobbler and killing him as he passes by. Shooting turkeys off the roost or over bait is considered ambushing.

Beard: A type of feather that projects from an area between the base of the neck and breast of a turkey gobbler. Some hen turkeys will grow a beard but this is unusual.

Boss Gobbler: The gobbler within a geographic area or within a flock of turkeys that has established himself as the dominant gobbler. The dominance of one gobbler over another is determined by fights between gobblers and the pecking order is established.

Boss Hen: The hen within a geographic area or flock of turkeys that has established herself as the dominant hen. The dominance of one hen over another is determined by fights between hens and the pecking order is established.

Call Shy: A turkey gobbler that refuses to come to a turkey call for no apparent reason. This turkey does not have hens with him and is not hung up on a terrain feature. He just simply refuses to come to a call. He may have been shot at or scared by a hunter in the past.

Closed Mouth Gobbler: (1) A turkey gobbler that comes to calling without ever having gobbled or made any other sound. (2) A turkey gobbler that initially gobbles but then stops gobbling but comes to the hunter without making any other sounds.

Clutch of Eggs: A nest of eggs laid by a turkey hen. Usually refers to a complete nest of eggs.

Droppings: Polite term used to describe defecation.

Drum: A low humming sound a turkey gobbler makes while he is in a strut. This sound is usually made while he is in a full strut and he will walk very fast for a short distance. The humming sound is usually followed by a spitting sound.

Dry Calling: Calling to a turkey not knowing whether or not there is a turkey in the area. Done when a hunter has been unable to get a turkey to respond to him.

Dusting: The process whereby turkeys of either sex roll around in dust to rid themselves of insects. They usually do this in sandy areas or in an area where there is loose soil.

Fan: The tail of a turkey gobbler spread out in a 1/2 to 3/4 circle. On a mature gobbler all the feathers in the fan are of the same length and make an even fan. On a jake, the three feathers on each end of the fan are shorter than the middle feathers and the fan is uneven.

Fired Up: A turkey gobbler that will gobble every time the hunter calls to him. Sometimes a "fired up" gobbler will double gobble or triple gobble.

Flock of Turkeys: A congregation of turkeys into a group: Some flocks consist of adult hens and juvenile turkeys of both sexes. Some flocks consist of adult gobblers only which is also referred to as a group of gobblers. Flocks may also consist of a mix of the sexes.

Fly-Down: (1) This term describes the process of a turkey leaving the roost by actually flapping its wings and flying to the ground as opposed to pitching down. (2) It sometimes describes the time that a turkey leaves the roost, i.e. "we need to be in the woods before fly-down."

Fly-Up: (1) A term that describes a turkey going to roost. (2) It also refers to the time that turkeys go to roost.

Fuzzed Up: A term used to describe a turkey gobbler in full strut.

Gobbler Fever: A condition that comes over a turkey hunter which prevents a hunter from taking a shot at a turkey gobbler or causes the hunter to take a shot while the turkey is out of range of his gun.

Henned Up: Applies to gobblers when the gobbler has one or more hens with him.

Hermit Gobbler: Usually an old turkey gobbler which no longer associates with other turkeys. These old turkeys will never come to the calling of another turkey.

Hot Gobbler: (see fired up) A turkey gobbler that will gobble every time the hunter calls to him. Sometimes a "hot gobbler" will double or triple gobble.

Hung Up: A turkey gobbler that will not come to calling because he has reached some terrain feature or other obstruction which the turkey will not cross. The turkey will not come beyond a given point in the woods.

Incubate: The process whereby a turkey hen stays on a clutch of eggs until the eggs hatch. The process usually takes about 28 days.

Jake: A young turkey gobbler between the age of one day and about eighteen months of age.

Jenny: A young turkey hen between the age of one day and about eighteen months of age.

Juvenile: A young turkey between the age of four weeks and one year of age.

Limb or Limbing: A hunter shoots a turkey off the limb before the turkey flies off the roost.

Limb Hanger: A harvested turkey gobbler that has spurs of sufficient length to support the turkey gobbler when hung over the limb of a tree by the spurs.

Locator Call: A piece of equipment used to make a turkey gobble so the hunter can locate the position of the gobbler.

Molting: The process whereby turkeys shed feathers and grow new feathers.

Ornament: The fiery red fatty tissue around the head and neck of the turkey gobbler, sometimes referred to as waddles.

Pecking Order: The dominance of turkeys in the order of dominance. Each turkey in a geographic area or flock will have its own place in the "pecking order." Gobblers have their own "pecking order" that is separate from the "pecking order" of hens. Juvenile turkeys are always at the bottom of the "pecking order."

Pitch Down: This term describes one method a turkey uses to leave a tree and come to the ground. To pitch down a turkey does not flap its wings, but merely spreads its wings and sails to the ground.

Poult: A young turkey between the age of one day and four weeks of age.

Predator: Any animal that preys on the turkey itself or turkey eggs.

Roost: (1) A place where turkeys spend the night. Turkeys usually roost in trees over water. (2) This term also applies to a hunter going in the woods to determine where turkeys spend the night usually on the day before the hunter is going to hunt the area.

Running Turkey: A turkey that will continue to move away from you as you move closer to him.

Scratching: Turkeys move leaves, bushes and other ground litter around while feeding in order to find insects, grubs, worms, small snakes, acorns and other food.

Set: The process of incubating a nest of eggs by a turkey hen. The process usually takes about 28 days.

Set Up: (1) The place where a turkey hunter positions himself or herself to call to a turkey. (2) Also used to describe the method used by a hunter to prepare to call to a turkey.

Snood: Fatty tissue located at the base of a turkey's beak. When the turkey is sexually excited, this tissue will become fiery red and hang over the beak or along side of the turkey's face or neck.

Spit: A sound the turkey gobbler makes while he is strutting and drumming. The sound is similar to the sound a human being makes when spitting.

Spooked: This refers to a turkey that has been alerted or scared by some animal, such as a predator or deer, or a human being.

Spur: A projection growing from the back side of a turkey gobbler's leg. The spur is a weapon the gobbler uses in fighting other gobblers.

Strut: Mating posture assumed by a turkey gobbler. The gobbler will have all of his feathers puffed out; his tail will be in a full fan; the top of his head will be solid white; his waddle or ornament will be fire red; his snood will be long and over or by his beak; and his head will be pulled in close to his body. He will drum and spit while strutting.

Tom Gobbler: A mature turkey gobbler. Usually will have a full fan; will have a 7 inch or longer beard; will have spurs at least 3/4 inch long; can gobble; and will have a full set of ornaments or waddles.

Turkey Tote: A bag or strap used to carry a turkey out of the woods after he has been harvested.

Turkey Vocabulary: Different sounds or calls that can be used to call a turkey gobbler:

1. Yelp
2. Purr
3. Cackle
4. Tree Call
5. Cluck
6. Lost Call
7. Assembly Call
8. Gobble
9. Kee Kee
10. Kee Kee Run
11. Cutting

Alarm Call of Wild Turkey: 1. Putt

Waddle: The fiery red fatty tissue around the neck and head of the turkey gobbler - sometimes referred to as ornaments.

Appendix B

REFERENCES

Dickson, James G. **The Wild Turkey Biology & Management**. Stackpole, 1992.

Hurst, George, and Dave Godwin. **Don't Take A Jake.** Mississippi State University, Department of Wildlife Fisheries, 1993.

Kennamer, Mary C., Ronnie E. Brennaman, and James Earl Kennamer. **Guide To The American Wild Turkey.** National Wild Turkey Federation, Inc., Edgefield, SC, 1992.

The Wild Turkey. Ed. Walter Dennis, International Paper Co., Natchez, MS.

Appendix C

Don't Take a Jake

Reprinted with permission from the authors

Don't Take A Jake
by
George Hurst and Dave Godwin

Give 'em a break, let 'em become gobblers before you take 'em. You get the theme of this article? Deer managers are advocating "Don't shoot yearling bucks — let 'em walk". Obviously, if you harvest most bucks as yearlings, you will not have many mature bucks to hunt the next season. If you harvest most of the jakes, there will not be many older, larger, and wiser gobblers the next year. We are advocating a self-restraint practice for turkey hunters.

A jake is a juvenile male wild turkey. The origin of the term "jake" is not known, and consultation with several dictionaries failed to give a definition of "jake" as we understand the word. However, one dictionary explained that jake was an adjective, used as slang, and meant fine, suitable, or all right. We agree; they are fine. When you see a flock of jakes, we want you to think — all right — future gobblers! Given another year to mature, jakes will be a suitable challenge.

Jakes hatched from April to June are less than a year old when the next spring hunting season begins. By then, they have learned a lot from their hen, including some critters to be wary of; then she ran their obnoxious butts off. However, jakes have not had any experience with mating season behavior. These "rookies" inherently know that something (courting, mating) is going on and would like to take part. But should they get interested, try some gobbler-stuff, and meet real gobblers, they will ultimately get their young bodies whipped. Some can mate and fertilize eggs; most are on-lookers. For the majority, the message is wait until next year!

Experienced turkey hunters generally agree jakes present less of a challenge than mature gobblers. They do foolish jake things and pay a high price. Too many of them sometimes even a flock, will run to the first yelping "hen". They have not learned to identify and avoid diaphragm, slate, box, or mouth calls. A finely tuned wing-bone sounds too good to resist!

Jakes can usually be identified by the knowledgeable turkey hunter. They are smaller, weigh less, and have a leaner body than mature gobblers. They have short (3-4 inch) beards and their spurs are short bumps. Many do not gobble, and even if they do it rarely sounds like an adult gobbler. A strutting jake is readily identified by the uneven contour of his tail feathers (see illustration). The central four feathers of a jake's tail are longer than the adjacent feathers.

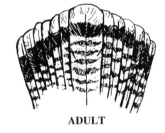

ADULT

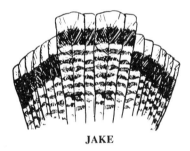

JAKE

This article does not advocate legislation that prohibits the taking of jakes. Some jakes really act like gobblers; they "do it all" and present a real challenge. There are cases or scenarios where taking a jake is fine, such as a hunter's first ever wild turkey! This article does advocate self-restraint for the more knowledgeable and experienced hunter.

There are all kinds of turkey hunters, and there is "room" for many opinions. Some "ole timey" hunters believe it is bad to shoot jakes. Another hunter's philosophy might be "A jake eats better than an old gobbler." Yet another hunter might live by the creed "pass 'em up!" Many hunting clubs do not permit the killing of jakes and others use peer pressure to discourage a hunter from taking a jake.

Hunters should always consider the reasons for hunting. Many hunters go turkey hunting to hear 'em holler, or listen to real gobbling. Others go to see 'em strut their stuff. Some go to be among 'em, in the wild, and all that goes with a beautiful spring morning. Still, others go hunting just to go. Jakes certainly can add to or provide some very interesting hunts, but maybe they could be saved for another year.

One general belief is that if one hunter doesn't take a jake, someone or something else will. Well, that is partly true, depending on where you hunt. On public hunting areas, jakes are fair game. First opportunity — boom, dead jake. On heavily hunted areas, jakes often make up 25-40% of the harvest. There would be some unhappy hunters if they were not allowed to harvest jakes. The no-jake rule is not for everywhere or everyone.

What about natural (predation, disease) mortality? If a jake is <u>not</u> harvested by a hunter, the odds are very good he will be there next year. Research conducted on Tallahala Wildlife Management Area, Bienville National Forest in central Mississippi conclusively found jakes have a high survival rate (excluding getting shot). This long-term, comprehensive study of a turkey population is being supported by the Mississippi Department of Wildlife, Fisheries and Parks, National Wild Turkey Federation (NWTF), Mississippi and local chapters NWTF, U. S. Forest Service (Mississippi), and Mississippi State University.

Dave Godwin and Randy Kelley intensively studied gobbler habitat use, home range, movements, and survival rates for several successive years. They and their co-workers captured and radio-equipped 130 gobblers from 1986-1990. Each gobbler was wing-tagged for visual information, (i.e., Red 33-wing tag color and number), and a numbered band secured to each leg. The gobblers were monitored at regular intervals using radio telemetry equipment. As Tallahala is a public hunting area, all gobblers harvested must be checked at headquarters.

IMMATURE

Before continuing with this article, an explanation of a couple of terms used by wildlife managers is in order. Annual survival rate is the rate at which gobblers survive over a 12-month period (January-December). The rate is expressed as a number (0.0 - 1.00) or as a percent. If you started with 100 gobblers and they all survived the entire year, the survival rate would be 1.00 (or 100%). However, if half (50) died during the year, the survival rate would be 0.5 (or 50%). The annual survival rate for Tallahala gobblers ranged from 0.39 to 0.54. Survival rates for jakes and gobblers did not differ. So, if you started with 100 gobblers you would expect 39 to 54 to survive the entire year.

The next term to discuss is seasonal survival rate. For this study, the twelve months of a year were divided into eight periods of about the same number of weeks. Therefore, survival rates for one particular period, 15 March - 01 May, (gobbler hunting season) could be compared to non-hunting periods during summer, fall and winter.

During the hunting period, gobbler survival rates varied from 0.42 - 0.63, and were significantly lower (all years) than during the other periods. Survival rates during these other periods (late spring, summer, fall, winter) ranged from 0.93 - 1.00! This means that 93 - 100% of the jakes or gobblers survived during the other periods. Bottomline — if a jake makes it through his first spring hunting season, he has a very good chance of living until next hunting season...don't take a jake.

What were the causes of gobbler mortality during the study? Of the known 81 mortalities, 74 (91%) occurred during the six-week hunting period. Some causes of death were listed as unknown. Several were attributed to crippling loss. Personnel at the MSU College of Veterinary Medicine x-rayed the carcasses and performed necropsies. If gun shot pellets were present, crippling loss was suspected.

What about predation? It was a very minor factor. In fact, not only during the 1986-1990 period, but for the entire study period, 1983-1992, predation on male turkeys has been a non-factor. Not many critters mess with gobblers. Hens? — another story? A few of our gobblers "died" during the squirrel/deer season.

One special gobbler was known as Blue 24. He was originally captured in February, 1984, and was believed to be three years old at the time. We did not see or know anything about him until he was captured in February 1989 — five years later! Can you imagine handling an eight year old (minimum) gobbler and then turning him loose? Maybe someone passed him up as a jake and he became a boss gobbler.

One expert turkey hunter recently expressed a very important point. By not taking jakes, you are "banking" some birds for the lean years. Turkey populations fluctuate widely according to good or poor hatches. If turkey reproduction is poor for several years in a row, few jakes are added to the population and fewer gobblers are present each successive year. For example, much of Mississippi experienced four consecutive poor hatches from 1988 - 1991. The turkey population declined markedly. The male portion of the population became mostly older, wiser gobblers. Veteran turkey hunters liked these conditions — real challenges, but other hunters quit hunting.

The hatch of 1992 was good to excellent throughout Mississippi, and poor to fair in 1993, and the turkey population is well on the road to recovery. This presents a grand opportunity to recruit many gobblers from the jake crop of 1992 and 1993. As Stan Priest, the current graduate student on Tallahala WMA noted, "Our two year old gobblers do most of the gobbling and if they are spared (as jakes) in the spring of 1994, imagine how the woods will be echoing with their hollerin' in the spring of 95." Ya' gotta like jakes, leave 'em for another year!

ADULT

Appendix D

The Wild Turkey

Reprinted with permission from International Paper Company

A Letter From the Editor

INTERNATIONAL PAPER

LAND AND TIMBER GROUP

Dear Sportsman:

Management practices for wildlife, including the Eastern Wild Turkey, are one of the stewardship goals of International Paper Company's sustainable forestry programs.

For almost 30 years, International Paper has provided numerous turkey trapping sites, continued assistance in relocation and propagation programs and provided funds and donations of turkey transport boxes, educational materials, and related items to enhance the future of the wild turkey.

In addition, International Paper has funded and provided a land base for selected wild turkey research projects at various universities, including Auburn and LSU. International Paper has funded various projects of local and state chapters' of the National Wild Turkey Federation. In 1992 International Paper was among the first major corporate landowners to sign a memorandum of understanding with the NWTF to maintain and increase wild turkey populations for the best interest of the people of the United States. In 1993 International Paper became the first recipient of the Federations' turkey stewardship award.

We encourage all sportsmen that use International Paper properties to incorporate principles of safe conduct and ethical sportsmanship and to participate in turkey management programs' of State Wildlife Agencies and the NWTF.

This publication has been developed to provide information to answer the rapidly growing number of questions and concerns sportsmen have on enhancing wild turkey populations across the South. Information in this publication supplements many turkey related articles periodically published in the International Paper South Central Region's magazine Woods-N-Wildlife, which is available to any interested sportsman.

There are thousands of acres of suitable productive turkey range on International Paper lands in the South, particularly in Alabama, Louisiana and Mississippi. Over 1,500 hunting clubs, 20 extensive state public or International Paper permit hunting areas, and 2 commercial hunting lodges currently operate on company lands in this three state area providing varied alternatives to the hunter.

Questions for professional advise and assistance on wild turkey management may be directed to your local state agency district biologist or to an IP certified wildlife biologist. We hope this information is useful to you and that your trips afield are safe, productive, and enjoyable.

Walter B. Dennis
Manager - Forest Ecology

WBD/sch SOUTH CENTRAL REGION • BOX 999 • NATCHEZ MISSISSIPPI 39120

Wild Turkey In The Gulf States .... 4 - 8
- Geographic Range 5
- Appearance 5
- Behavior 5
- Flocks 6
- Hen & Tom Characteristics 6-8

Wildlife Management Memorandum Signed 8

IP Publication Features Turkey Management 8

Habitats Used By Wild Turkeys .... 9 - 15
- Wild Turkey Diet/Foods 9
- Turkeys & Water 10
- Reproduction 10
- Nest/Egg Losses 11
- Brood Rearing 12
- Predators/Predation 13
- Parasites & Diseases 13
- Survival Rates 14-15
- Hunting the Wild Turkey 15

Barnyard Chickens & The Wild Turkey 15

Turkey Hunting Ethics 16-17

Management of the Wild Turkey .... 18 -20
- People Management 18
- Habitat Management 18
- Forest Management 18,19
- Field Management 19
- Predator Management 20

Turkey Harvest Data Form 21

Turkey Stewardship Award 22

IP & Turkey Transport Boxes 22

Code of Conduct 23

THE
WILD TURKEY
IN THE GULF STATES

T he wild turkey was originally found in the Americas and was first domesticated by the Aztecs. During their conquest of this continent the Spaniards took it back to Europe, and in the 1600's the white settlers reintroduced this domestic strain into New England. Early settlers found wild turkey in all the forested areas in the southeastern states. Turkey populations probably remained fairly constant until the coming of the lumber industry from 1880 to 1920 when the wild turkeys were almost wiped out because of the destruction of their habitat.

We can usually learn from history, so we will not make the same mistakes. Wild turkeys were abundant in the Louisiana/Mississippi/Alabama region according to observations made by early explorers. Native Americans used the turkey for food, implements (feathers, quills), and ceremonial apparel. They did not seriously impact turkey populations and habitats.

The first pioneers or settlers enjoyed a bounty of wildlife, including the wild turkey. Our numbers swelled and the killing of turkeys greatly increased due to no restrictions on the killing, it occurred year-around. Some hunters were really good at killing turkeys, and subsistence hunting turned into **market hunting**. Turkeys were killed in large numbers and sold to feed an ever increasing number of people.

If the rampant killing was not bad enough, we began large-scale clear-cutting of most mature forests at the turn of the 20th century. The good ole days of "cut-out and get-out" destroyed most turkey habitats. Most of Mississippi's forests were felled between 1900-1925 and the wild turkey was nearly gone from Louisiana and Mississippi. Imagine, there may have been 1 million turkeys in each state before white man arrived, and when we finished the killing and cutting by 1940, there were perhaps 2,000 in Louisiana and 3,500 in Mississippi. The Father of Game Management, Aldo Leopold, visited Mississippi in 1929 and said that the wild turkey is 90% cleaned out as to potential area and 99% cleaned out as to potential abundance. The big "hunt" and "cut" left little. The return of this beautiful bird began with the establishment of Game and Fish Departments in the early 1900s in Louisiana and later (1932) in Mississippi. Early restrictions or regulations were not effective, but closed hunting seasons helped. Protection by landowners and game wardens was critical to save the few wild birds, while public support was building to save the turkey.

Both states tried to restore the wild turkey by raising or buying pen-raised turkeys. We wasted a lot of time, money, and effort by releasing stupid half-breed turkeys, farm-raised turkeys, Purina birds, and expecting them to become **WILD** turkeys. It did not work and will never work. Only wild turkeys can beget **wild** turkeys. Tough laws have been established to prohibit the release of semi-wild turkeys. Please do not even think about using pen-raised birds to restore a wild turkey population.

The single most important tool for restoring the wild turkey was the discovery that wild birds could be baited to an area, and a cannon net could be shot over them. The captured wild turkeys were then moved to suitable habitats and given protection, thus populations "exploded."

Forest industry moved to the region and began restoring and protecting the forests. Cut-over areas were planted and turkey

The Wild Turkey • 4

habitats began to appear. One of the great successes of modern Game Management is the restoration of the wild turkey to not only the Gulf States, but to all of the U.S. Imagine, Mississippi went from a few thousand turkeys in the 1940s to nearly 400,000 in 1988, and the turkey in Louisiana numbered about 40,000 in 1990. There is still much to do in the Sportsman's Paradise, but the future looks bright. We owe a great **Thanks** to those who sat in blinds for weeks during the last several decades to capture turkeys and relocate them so we can once again enjoy this big, black, beautiful bird. Today turkey populations exist in every state except Alaska. Turkey hunting is now the fastest growing shooting sport in the United States.

GEOGRAPHIC RANGE

The eastern wild turkey (<u>Meleagris</u> <u>gallopavo</u> <u>silvestris</u>) inhabits most of the area east of Big Muddy, including our region; other subspecies occur in Florida, and the southwest (Rio Grande, Merriams, Gould's). Due to restocking, hybrids now occur in northcentral and western states. We have stocked wild turkeys beyond their original geographic range (e.g., California, Oregon).

APPEARANCE

Domestic or part-wild turkeys can be distinguished from <u>wild</u> turkeys by having white tips on their tail feathers; whereas, tips of tail feathers are brown or chestnut colored on wild turkeys. In addition, domestic turkeys have short/stubby legs, "fat" feet, huge breasts (bred for), and shorter necks. Domestic turkeys weigh much more than wild turkeys and can be pure white, bronze, or mixed colors. You are unable to see it, but domestic turkeys have much smaller brains than wild turkeys; therefore, they are <u>stupid</u>. Wild turkeys are slender, sleek, and long legged—the end product of millions of years of natural selection.

In addition to the usual basically black color, there are two color phases of the wild turkey. The most frequently observed is the smokey gray phase, often thought (wrongly) to be domestic or part domestic. "Smokes" produce both normal and smokey poults, and should <u>not</u> be shot to preserve the wild turkey. Some people also mistake this color phase for an albino, but albinos are rare. The red phase of the wild turkey (see photo) is quite beautiful, some call it the "roan" phase, and it occurs mostly in south Mississippi. There also is a black (melanistic) phase which is solid black, no other colors. This phase is seldom seen.

Depending on the light, wild turkeys can reflect many beautiful colors—on their basic black background. Copper, green, purple, orange, bronze, brown,

gold, etc. can be detected depending upon the light. Head colors go from bright red, to dull blue, gray, and whitish —depending on turkey's state of mind. Turkey advocates think this bird is most beautiful, but some say, after seeing its head up close, it is ugly.

BEHAVIOR

The wild turkey is spooky, edgy, nervous, scary and always alert. You would also be nervous if from the day you were in an egg until the day you die you were hunted by some critter. Only the very wary survive. Turkeys can fly at slightly over 55 mph, run at about 12 mph, and walk at 3-4 mph. Daily movements of gobblers in central Mississippi averaged over 1 mile in the morning and afternoon. We call them wary wanderers! Annual home ranges of gobblers averaged nearly 5 square miles (sq. mile = 640 acres) in this same area, and were larger in an area dominated by loblolly pine plantations. Hen annual home ranges averaged about 1,100 acres in an area that contained mixed habitat types.

Turkeys have a rigidly structured social order, a peck-order, which is established soon after hatching. By intimidation, bluffing, and fighting, every turkey has its place in the social order. Stay in your place or get reprimanded —pecked. Do you want to change your status? Then you must challenge and "whip" the bird above you. Young gobblers can only hope the big, bad tom gets killed, so they can move up. Each turkey knows all other turkeys in the general area.

The first pioneers or settlers enjoyed a bounty of wildlife, including the wild turkey.

FLOCKS

Turkeys occur most of the time in flocks, and they are strict segregationists. There are hen flocks and gobbler flocks. Hen flocks, from 3 / 15/flock, contain all ages of hens. Hen flocks begin to break-up in March as individuals begin their search for nest sites and lay eggs. Gradually, the hen flock decreases in size. When you see individual hens, you know the reproductive period is in full-swing.

Hens that successfully hatch their eggs and have poults (age 1 - 4 weeks) are referred to as brood hens. Brood hens usually remain alone with their poults for 2 - 3 weeks, and then often join other successful hens to form multiple brood flocks. You have probably seen 3 hens with 14 juveniles. We have a special term for this flock — Creche. Turkeys gain safety in numbers by forming a creche. These flocks contain <u>only</u> successful hens and their juveniles.

Hens that have their eggs or poults killed (eaten) form another type of flock, called Female Failure Flocks. Unsuccessful hens are not allowed with the creches. These flocks remain intact during the summer/fall, but in winter, membership in flocks can change.

A CRECHE

Gobbler flocks segregate by age class. Usually, there are flocks that contain only jakes; males less than a year old (young of the year). Jake flocks contain from 3 / 18 or more have been observed. Sometimes, jakes hang-around flocks of older birds. Gobbler flocks contain toms of various ages, and flock composition does change during the year. Some gobbler flocks contain 9 / 10 birds in the fall/winter, but breakup into smaller flocks during the breeding season. Individual gobblers with a hen flock in March might be boss gobblers. Also, some gobblers remain in flocks during the breeding season. Some gobblers use the same area for gobbling and strutting, while others are constantly on the move with a hen flock, or searching for hens.

HEN AND TOM CHARACTERISTICS

Weight

In our region, mature gobblers or toms weigh 18-20 pounds. Juveniles or jakes weigh from 9 -13 pounds, with 2-year-old birds weighing about 16 pounds. Mature hens weigh about 9 pounds, with juvenile hens (jennys) weighing about 6 pounds. Obviously, weight will vary according to availability of food resources and date of hatch and death. Toms are taller than hens because they have longer legs and necks.

Other Characteristics

Males are blacker than hens, because the tips of the breast and midback feathers on toms are black; whereas, the feathers on hens are brown-tipped. Gobblers are far more iridescent than hens. A hens neck and back of head are feathered, while toms have more bare skin. Hen heads are bluish-gray, but tom heads are pink to red. The crown of a gobbler head can be white, but a hen crown is not white. An obvious difference is the presence of red, bulbous caruncles (small sacks) at the base of the neck on toms. Toms also have a snood, which elongates when they are sexually aroused. You will not see a

The Wild Turkey • 6

snood on hens. The dewlap, a flap of skin on the throat, is much larger and redder on toms than on hens.

Toms have a horny, bone structure on the lower leg—the spur; hens do not have this feature. Some gobblers do not have spurs, or they have only one spur. Gobblers have a beard, but so do some (<2%) hens. A beard on a hen is usually quite thin and can be as long as 9 inches. Multiple beards on a tom are not uncommon. Gobblers strut and drum. Believe it or not, a few hens have been seen strutting.

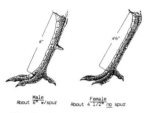

Vocalizations

Gobblers gobble, putt, cluck, yelp; whereas, a hen does not gobble. They do cluck, putt, purr, yelp, cackle, cut, etc. Hens have a vocabulary that deals with hatching and raising poults. Communication between a hen and her young begins even before hatching. The wild turkey is vocal, using a variety of calls to maintain contact, give warnings, indicate a source of food, find each other, etc. Hearing is acutely good. The birds seem to hear at a lower frequency and at a greater distance than humans.

Tracks and Droppings

Tracks made by gobblers are broader and have a wider spread. Also, the length of the middle toe, from tip of the claw to the back of the heel pad is much longer. A gobbler track is over 4 inches long. The stride of a gobbler is much longer than that of a hen.

Turkeys have two kinds of droppings, one a blackish/green mess, pancake shaped-splash, called a cecal dropping, which comes from the cecal pouches. Regular droppings are white on the top (urinary waste) and male droppings are larger, wider, straighter, and longer then hens. Male droppings are usually J-shaped, whereas hen droppings are, bulbous, or spiral (like soft ice cream from a machine).

How To Age Turkeys

There are methods to determine the age of embryos, those still in the egg and and poults or juveniles. However, only those conducting research need these methods.

Jennys, or young females, can be differentiated from adult hens by having an unequal contour tail (see sketch), the four central tail feathers are longer than those on either side. Also, primary feathers (large flight feathers) number 10 and maybe 9 will be pointed, and will not have white bars all the way to the tip of the feather (see sketch). These feathers are more rounded and have white barring to the tip of the feather on adult hens. If you had several hens, weight could probably be used to separate adults from jennys. Currently, there is no method to distinguish 2 year old hens from 5 year old hens, etc.

Now to toms. The tail feather and primary 10 and maybe 9

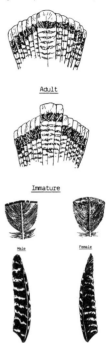

characteristics hold true for separating young males called jakes from the adults. Weight can separate jakes from adults. Jakes usually do not have a full, strong gobble (but some do). The beard on a jake usually is 3 - 4 inches long, whereas that on a 2-year-old is 6 - 8 inches long. Older toms might have beards from 6 - 10 inches (few reach 11 or 12 inches). The beard grows continuously, but is worn off by contact with the ground. Beards of adult gobblers are normally black and the longest eastern wild beard on record is 16.9 inches.

What about spur length, pointedness, and curvature? We know the spur increases in length, curves upward, and becomes sharp pointed as the gobbler matures. However, there are no full proof characteristics we can measure to determine the exact age by spur conditions. You have seen graphs where you measure spur length and plot it on the axis, which will then tell you the gobbler was 5 years old. Well, this method is quite inaccurate. Simply put, we can not age a gobbler just on spur length. A new aging technique was devised in Mississippi, but you have to X-ray the spur and measure the length of the spur cap apex (see photo). This method will very accurately separate jakes from 2-year-old gobs, and 2-year-olds from 3-year-old gobblers. However, even this method can not separate 3 year olds from older gobblers. We are unable to age a 5 or 7+ gobbler. We "know" some gobblers are older than 3+ years, but do not know exactly how old one might be.

You can estimate a gobblers age by spur conditions. The spur on a jake is about a 1/4 inch (certainly less than 1/2 inch) and is rounded. Jakes are easy to age based on several other characteristics. Spurs on 2-year-old gobblers usually are about 1/2 to 3/4 inch long, and are straight and have a blunt point. Three-year-old or older toms have spurs that are 1-1 1/4 inch long, and are curved and pointed. What about 4-year-old toms? I do not guess at their spur conditions. Let's agree that long, curved, and pointed spurs are impressive and are probably on a gobbler 3 + years old. Exceptions do occur to all the above spur/age class conditions, so it is estimating, not scientifically proving.

As impressive as length, is the diameter of the spur at its base – "beam" diameter! Remember, some gobblers do not have spurs, others only have one spur, and frequently spur conditions are different on the same tom. Spurs do provide topics for hunting camp tales and arguments, so they are important. ∎

Wildlife Management Memorandum Signed

International Paper has signed a long term MOU with the National Wild Turkey Federation under which both parties agree that wild turkey habitats need to be properly managed to insure viable populations of the species.

The memorandum of understanding is intended to provide a continuing foundation for cooperative development of management strategies and projects needed to maintain and increase wild turkey populations. The document applies to those International Paper Company lands located in the northeast and southeast U.S.

The MOU represents International Paper's ongoing commitment to manage its land for multiple use. IP has long demonstrated that forest management objectives are compatible with wild turkeys and their habitats. International Paper Forest Resources is the managing general partner of IP Timberlands, Ltd., a limited partnership which owns or leases virtually all of the 6.3 million acres of forests controlled by IP.

IP's lands in Alabama, Louisiana, and Mississippi are a viable productive part of this project and provide habitat for many turkey flocks.

The National Wild Turkey Federation is a non-profit conservation corporation that has responsibilities to foster management of wild turkey resources throughout the U.S. ∎

The Wild Turkey • 8

IP PUBLICATION FEATURES TURKEY MANAGEMENT

Additional detailed information pertaining to various wildlife management practices will be featured in a series of publications made available by International Paper Company. One of the more recent publications entitled "Wild Turkeys and Industrial Forest Management" is now available. Wild turkey populations can be established and maintained on southern lands being managed for pine and hardwood. Stable winter food supplies, brood habitat, predation, protection from illegal kill, and excessive legal harvest are critical criteria for developing turkey populations.

Copies of this publication may be obtained by requesting them from the editor at the address given on the back of this publication. ∎

Habitats Used by Wild Turkeys

Turkeys live in a variety of habitats, including all of our major forest types such as longleaf, loblolly, shortleaf, and slash pine; bottomland and upland hardwoods, and mixtures of all these forest types. Turkeys use many types of fields, such as row crops (corn, soybeans), pastures (native and improved grasses/forbs), hayfields, and old fields (abandoned fields). Combinations of different types of forests and fields probably are the best for turkeys. As with other species, those areas with "rich" or highly fertile soils are better turkey range than areas with poor, nutrient deficient soils. However, other factors, such as amount of protection given the flocks from greedy man, are important.

We are fortunate in that the wild turkey is a **generalist**, a species that can thrive under a variety of habitat conditions. Turkeys do not require a narrow set of living conditions, but rather accept many different living conditions. When the restored wild turkey population peaked in 1987 in Mississippi, you could observe turkeys in the city limits of many towns and communities, feeding on interstate highway right-of-ways, in people's backyards, destroying gardens, and even living in fence rows and woodlots. Many people were surprised to see turkeys in such non-traditional habitat types or in areas with no large forested tracts. When abundant, turkeys live **everywhere**.

Some thought that with the conversion of hardwood or pine-hardwood forests to pine plantations, the wild turkey was doomed. They thought the turkey had to have old forests, and these forests had to be mostly oak. Well, the turkey has proved those folk wrong. Turkeys are doing quite well in pine "thickets." We do want hardwood corridors, streamside management zones, or other hardwood areas left along creeks or rivers for many wildlife species. See the management section.

Wild Turkey Diet/Foods

Knowing that the wild turkey inhabits a variety of habitat types, you could guess that it is an Opportunistic Omnivore. If a food item is found, it is eaten. About 87% of an adult turkeys diet consists of plant matter, with the remainder being animal matter. Turkeys eat all parts of plants including: seeds, fruits, leaves, stems, flowers, and buds. Seeds of all kinds of plants (forbs, grasses, sedges, vines, woody plants) are eaten. Turkeys eat hard mast such as acorns and wild pecans, and eat all types of soft mast such as dogwood, black gum, muscadine, honeysuckle, huckleberry, and blackberry fruits. Pine seeds are a favorite turkey food. Turkeys even eat some ferns, mushrooms, and galls. Most everything produced in a forest is a potential turkey food. They do not eat many hickory nuts, but feast on white oak and red oak acorns <u>when</u> available.

Turkeys graze like cattle on grasses and sedges, and even dig up tubers (e.g., chufa, spring beauty). Turkeys have favorite foods, such as white oak acorns, but will scrounge around and find other foods as necessary. They can subsist on green foliage when choice items are not present. In fact, new-growth plant materials are essential for vitamins in late winter and early spring.

When timberlands are flooded, turkeys stay up in the trees and subsist on buds, leaves, and flowers from several tree species. They might also find some insects among the fast growing canopy. A management plan would include a diversity of habitat types to provide food options—hard and soft mast, green foliage, seeds from many species, etc.

Turkeys begin their life as predators. Upon hatching and up to age 4 weeks, poults consume mostly animal matter, chiefly insects! Particularly during the first 2 weeks, almost 80% of the poult diet consists of grasshoppers, beetles, bugs, etc. Poults are forced to find their own food, because hens do not feed them. Insects

The Wild Turkey • 9

are high in protein and compounds essential for fast growth of bones, muscles, and feathers. Brood habitats must provide plenty of protective cover and insects. As the poults mature, and become juveniles at age 4 weeks, their diet is mostly seeds, berries, some greens, and insects.

Adult turkeys eat a great variety of animal matter including: insects, pupal stages of moths and butterflies, spiders, sow bugs, worms, small snakes, frogs, lizards (anoles), crawfish, and snails. Hens eat many snails in the early spring, apparently seeking calcium to be used in their egg shells. We have seen adult gobblers eat drugged sparrows at a bait site! If a turkey finds it, it is eaten!

Turkeys like many agricultural crops, such as soybeans, corn, millets, sorghum, and cool season grasses such as ryegrass and wheat, and clovers. Turkeys find food in many ways, such as scratching through the forest litter, flying-up into trees, walking long distances, and seeing the tiniest seeds. They are alert to all sources of food; they are an adept scrounger. Our climate is mild, so there is little winter stress, but drought in the summer/fall is a problem because it affects mast and green forage food production. A total mast (e.g., acorns) would disadvantage turkeys because a ready energy source would not be available.

Turkeys and Water

Turkeys of all ages will drink water when it is available, such as from pools, ditches, creeks, ponds, and even skidder ruts. However, water is not a limiting factor. In fact, hens with broods do fine in hot, very dry slash and loblolly pine plantations where there is seldom any standing water. Turkeys can obtain water from dew and high moisture content insects and berries.

Water is a major limiting factor when it causes major flooding along rivers, creeks and in the Delta region. Some years, reproduction in the Louisiana and Mississippi Delta region is nearly zero due to longterm flooding. Hens that nest in floodplains are at risk. In addition, precipitation operates in conjunction with predation. It appears that many nests are predated by raccoons and other egg-eaters during or following spring rains. We are studying the wet hen theory—wet hens are more easily detected by predators. Wet springs generally mean low hatch rates.

Turkeys dislike heat, and in the summer, generally avoid feeding in areas until shade is present. Cool, bottomland hardwood forests are excellent places to avoid the heat of summer.

Reproduction

The success or failure of the reproductive period is the dominant factor affecting turkey density or population size. Several good hatches in a row translate into a population "explosion" and range extension. Several poor hatches mean the population makedly declines. So it is up to the hens to produce poults. I stressed hens, because gobblers do little—mate with hens and take the rest of the year off. Hens are responsible for choosing a nest site, laying and incubating the eggs, and raising the poults. <u>SHE</u> is the future of a turkey population.

Gobbling can be heard in February and increases as the day length increases—hormones at work. Mature gobblers probably "start" the reproductive period by gobbling and seeking-out hen flocks. Social strive or peck order problems will increase as the breeding period commences. Serious disputes, such as a 1/2 hour fight between dominant gobblers are something to observe, and even jakes get into the fighting mode. Some jakes do it all, gobble real good, and act like mature gobblers. Some jakes can even successfully breed hens, if they can get near them. Other jakes appear to know nothing about reproduction, but wait'til next year.

Some gobblers establish a mating area and do their thing (i.e., gobble, strut, drum) there each day. Openings with little and low vegetation in forests or fields serve as mating areas. One turkey hunter watched a tom mate with 10 hens on a sand bar on a creek. Other toms seem to be free-floaters, searching everywhere for hens. Some gobblers (1-3) are seen accompanying hen flocks in late

February. By early March, the breeding season is in full swing. Hen flocks usually remain intact during the early breeding period. Hunters tend to complain at this time, because the gobblers are with hens and are not responsive to their phoney calls.

One mating of a hen is sufficient for up to 50 days because the hen retains the sperm in her oviduct. However, hens are mated several times, and can usually find a tom still in breeding condition later in the season if renesting is attempted. Home ranges of toms average 4-5 square miles, and overlap hen ranges, so seldom is a lack of gobblers a factor.

Gradually, a hen flock disintegrates as individual or

small groups of hens leave to search for nest sites. When many hens begin incubation, gobbling tends to increase. Most hens are incubating by the third week of April. The hen is on her own—good luck!

Habitats used for nesting are variable and include old fields, wheat fields, young pine plantations, cut-overs, briar patches, mature pine forests, rights-of-ways, etc. Usually brush/vines are present at the nest site, but with open areas near the nest site. Generally, there is some over-head cover, and most nests occur near some type of edge (e.g., road, trail). When hens select the nest site, there is not much new-growth, but as the vegetation rapidly grows, visibility of the nest is diminished. Some hens nest in virtually wide-open places, like against the butt of a tree, but most are pretty well hidden.

Turkeys nest on the ground, and they suffer high nest losses because of this behavior. The hen may scratch out an area about 12 inches in diameter and about 1 inch deep. Litter, such as pine needles or leaves gradually increases in the scooped-out nest site. A hen lays one egg per day, maybe skipping a day. The eggs are not much larger than average chicken eggs and weigh just over 2 ounces. Eggs vary in shape and color, but a single hen's eggs are very similar. The eggs are a light buff (i.e., tan, light brown) or even light purple with brownish spots. The average clutch size is 11, but varies. If a hen's first nest is destroyed, she might renest, and generally, the number of eggs in the second clutch is fewer than the first.

The hen usually leaves her nest/eggs once a day, usually around mid-day to feed, drink, and defecate. Hens do **not** defecate at or near the nest. Droppings from incubating hens are huge. The hen generally walks to and from the nest. Incubation is continuous; some hens stay on the nest for several days. Incubation lasts around 28 days. The hen will use her bill to turn the eggs to promote even growth of the embryos. The poults (embryos) begin vocalizing to the hen and fellow poults while still in the egg. The hen/poult bond is taking shape.

Hatching begins by the poult chipping (pipping) a hole in the egg shell. Gradually a line of broken shell emanates from the pip hole all-around the egg at the large end. Once the "cut" is made, the poult pushes up and finally pops the "lid" off and emerges, wet and tired. Turkeys have synchronous hatching, since incubation only begins when all eggs have been laid. In a period of 24-36 hours, all poults have hatched, dried off, and are ready to leave the nest. Peak hatching in our region occurs around the third week of May.

If weather conditions permit, the hen talks to her brood and walks off, poults follow because they have imprinted on the first living/moving thing they see—their hen. She has been communicating with them for sometime with special hen/poult "talk." The hen and brood do <u>not</u> return to the nest, the brood depends on the hen for warmth, protection, and the hen must keep them dry. She must also take them to suitable brood rearing habitat—lots of cover and insects. She is the the poults guardian and educator!

Nest/Egg Losses

Many, or most turkey nests are unsuccessful. Most ground nesting species are fortunate if 50% of the nests

The Wild Turkey • 11

are successful—hatch. During poor hatch years, less than 20% of the hens hatch their eggs. A very good hatch occurred in Mississippi in the spring of 1992—58% of the hens on research areas hatched their eggs. Fertility is about 97% and is not the problem, it is predation of eggs and hens. There are many critters that eat turkey eggs and/or hens.

We have studied survival rates of hens living in pine plantations and mixed forests. Their annual (12 months) survival rate was 68% (range 50-81%) over a 5-year period. On a seasonal basis, we found that outside the reproductive period, in the summer, fall, and winter, the survival rate was 94%. Reproduction is costly for hens, for the survival rate dropped to 81% during the reproductive period.

When hens strike off on their own, they are more vulnerable to predation by the great-horned owl, gray fox, bobcat, coyote, and domestic dog. Most (95%) hen mortality was caused by PREDATION, and most (69%) of the mortalities occurred during the breeding period. Others die to disease, poaching, vehicular collision, and mechanical accidents (e.g., high-speed mowers). It is dangerous to visit the same nest site and lay eggs (about 2 weeks), take short breaks by yourself (only 2 eyes watching for trouble), and remain on the eggs all day for 4 weeks.

The main turkey egg eaters are raccoon and opossum, and to a lesser degree the striped skunk, snakes, crow, and domestic dog. Armadillos and fire ants have not eaten turkey eggs to our knowledge. Flooding does cause loss of eggs, as does burning in late March-April. Modern hay cutting with a disk mower/conditioner is a new problem. One rancher killed six (6) incubating hens in one field. Another rancher killed three (3) incubating hens in one small field. Plowing fields, combining wheat, and timber harvesting during the nesting period (March-June) can destroy many nests. Other disturbances by man and his pets also cause nest losses.

Despite the general belief, most hens do not renest. Many hens lose their eggs to predation and simply go into a nonreproductive phase—wait'til next year. Renesters suffer the same fate as first nesters. That is their eggs, poults or themselves are eaten. In one long-term (12 years) study, only one renester successfully hatched her eggs; she raised 3 poults. That does not say much for renesting. You had better get a good hatch from the first try if you want a large population.

What about juvenile hens? Do they contribute much to the population? Answer. NO. Some juvenile hens do not even lay eggs. In our long-term studies, juveniles have contributed very little to the population. To hope to increase a turkey population when the conditions are right, we must protect the hens, let'em mature and hope they learn how to raise poults. Hens keep trying to hatch their eggs and raise poults through the years. One adult hen (age unknown) was captured in February 1989. She failed to raise poults that year and the next 2 years (1990, 1991), but raised 4 poults in 1992, none in 1993, and 7 in 1994. We need those old hens around to keep trying and add turkeys to population. Sav'em hens.

Brood Rearing

It does not get much better for hens that hatch their eggs. Brood hens are "tied" to their brood and often pay the price—they are killed and eaten by bobcat, great-horned owl, gray fox, domestic dog, and infrequently the coyote. The hen broods the poults under her at night for about 14 days—good luck. Something is going to find the hen and her poults.

The mortality rate for poults is high, ranging from 65-95% in several studies. If the hen is killed while the poults are young, they all die. Poults are preyed upon by many critters. A recent study in Florida found that the raccoon killed more poults than any other critter which includes: hawks, snakes, crows, owls, domestic dog, and others. Some might die due to exposure—get wet and die, or flooding. A prolonged rainey period means the poults can not get about and feed, creating real problems.

Mortality rates decrease once the poults can fly up to lower limbs to roost—maybe at age 14 days. Mortality rates for juveniles, age 4 weeks plus, appear to be quite low, but little research has been conducted. Observations of broods with marked hens at bait sites in pine plantations for 5 years has shown virtually no loss of juveniles from July - August. The hen is "making" real wild turkeys.

Brood hens take their newly hatched poults to brood habitat. The hen "knows" what poults need, mainly cover and food—insects. Brood habitats vary, including mature bottomland hardwood forest, to edges of forest/fields, to dense pine plantations. The common theme is herbaceous vegetation (forbs, grasses) and brush in a forest. The brood home range is small at first, perhaps only 20 acres, but increases in size as the poults grow and can travel. Many brood ranges are less than 100 acres by poult age 2-3 weeks. By age 4+ weeks, the brood travels much farther. Many successful hens join with other successful brood hens when the poults are about 3 weeks old. This multiple brood flock remains intact into the winter and deserves special protection, because it is the next generation, and it contains hens who "know how" to hatch eggs and raise poults!

Our information strongly indicates that adult hens are far more successful at rearing a brood then juvenile (jenny) hens. Some hens appear to either be lucky or know how to avoid predators when with a brood. Many brood hens are killed trying to protect their broods. This loss is particularly bad because the hens hatched their eggs—a major accomplishment.

Predators/Predation

Predation of eggs, poults, and reproductively active hens is a major factor affecting wild turkey population size. Predation is a complex process involving the number of turkeys, habitat/vegetation conditions, types and numbers of predators, affects of man on the habitats and all populations (i.e., hunt, trap), food abundance/availability, and weather conditions. The main predator of turkey eggs, and perhaps poults is the raccoon. When fur prices were relatively high and many people ate raccoon meat, this species was harvested in large numbers, which probably controlled the raccoon population. Due to low fur prices, animal rights activities, and anti-trapping sentiment, the harvest of raccoons and other predators by hunters and trappers has greatly declined. In fact,

most predators, formerly called furbearers by some, are thriving in our area.

Restocked turkey populations "exploded" in many areas during the past three decades, but control (a density dependent factor) by predation and pathogens (i.e., diseases) began operating. As the density of any species increases, the "take" by predators increases. Predator populations face some of the same problems. Canine distemper is a major killer of raccoons, skunks, and gray foxes. This disease swept through much of Mississippi in 1990-1993 and significantly reduced populations of the three species. Parasites, such as lung worms, could also act as regulators of some predators. Rabies, a deadly disease that would kill many raccoons, skunks, coyotes, and foxes has not been found in Mississippi, but occurs in Alabama and occasionally in Louisiana.

Parasites and Diseases of the Wild Turkey

Turkeys are susceptible to many diseases and parasites, particularly in the South. Several external parasites have been found on turkeys: lice, mites, mosquitoes, ticks, and a lousefly. Generally, external parasites are not major problems to wild turkeys. Some midges and blackflies also feed on turkey blood. While these arthropods and mosquitoes may only seem to be a nuisance, they transmit diseases such as malaria (Plasmodium) in poults in Florida, avian poxvirus, and several blood parasites (live in turkey blood)—Leucocytozoon and Haemoproteus. The latter blood parasites are common in most young turkeys, but their effect(s) are not known.

Adult turkeys usually have an assortment of internal parasites, including tape worms, round worms, flukes (flatworms), and other "worms." These parasites occur in many organs; roundworms usually are present in the intestines. Most of these parasites are not a major problem to wild turkeys. However, one round worm, Heterakis gallinarum, which is a cecal worm that lives in the blind pouches, or caecae, off the intestine, is a problem because it carries the protozoan parasite Histomonas meleagridis that causes blackhead (histomoniasis).

The main disease affecting wild turkeys in Mississippi over the past 10 years is avian pox, an infectious, contagious viral disease. Mosquitoes are vectors of this disease. Many cases have been reported or diagnosed by the College of Veterinary Medicine at Mississippi State University. Infected turkeys usually have a terrible looking head because of the many sores (lesions). They may be blind and can not breathe due to lesions in the mouth. Predators will generally remove sick or near death turkeys. You can help by always capturing sick turkeys and getting them to a conservation officer or other wildlife official who will transport the sick turkey to a vet school or state diagnostic lab.

None of the diseases or parasites can be controlled. However, you can help by **NOT** releasing pen-raised turkeys that might carry parasites or diseases to the wild birds. Put all pen-raised turkeys in their place—the freezer.

SURVIVAL RATES OF WILD TURKEY HENS

In the last issue of Woods-N-Wildlife, we discussed survival rates of gobblers. Now, let's talk about the important SEX – hens, and their survival rates. Hens do all the "work," and are really responsible for keeping the population going.

A paper published in the Journal of Wildlife Management presents information (i.e., data) on the survival rate of 111 hens (95 adults, 16 subadults) from a study area near Scooba, Kemper County, Mississippi. The dominant habitat type was loblolly pine plantations. Hens were captured by connon-netting in either January-March or July-August, 1987-1990.

Each hen was fitted with a transmitter and numbered wing tags (cattle ear tags) and was released at the bait/capture site. Then, the graduate students monitored the hen's activities on a regular, intensive basis throughout the year. How do they know where a hen is? Telemetry and triangulation. The students have a receiver which "picks up" the signal transmitted by the transmitter. Each transmitter has a different frequency, such as 151.089. So, you dial in the frequency and, then by use of an antenna attached to the receiver, find the loudest (i.e., peak) signal. Then, use a compass to get the bearing of the loudest signal. Quickly, drive to another telemetry station and repeat the process. The hen is located where the two compass bearings cross. We try to get as close to a 90 degree angle as possible.

Each transmitter has a motion (i.e., movement) or mortality switch in it. Thus, we can tell if a hen is moving (alive). If a hen does not move (i.e., is dead, or incubating) for three hours, the mortality switch is activated – changes from a slow beep, beep, to a constant, fast beeeee (much like the code blue on TV).

Remember, survival rate is the rate at which an individual or a group (hens) survives for a given period. The annual (12 months) survival rate for this sample of hens over the four years averaged 0.66 or 66% and ranged from 0.50 to 0.81. That is, on average 66 of 100 hens survived the entire year, or the mortality rate averaged 34%. We had some ole-timers. Two hens (number 10 and 11) were captured in February 1986 and were still alive in August 1991 (No. 10) and August 1992 (No. 11). Both hens were adults in 1986!

Seasonal survival rates were calculated for the winter (1 Jan. - 31 Mar.), spring (1 Apr. - 30 Jun.), summer (1 Jul. - 31 Sep.), and fall (1 Oct. - 31 Dec.). Survival rates were high in winter (92%), summer (97%), fall (94%), but were comparatively low (81%) in the spring.

What happened during the spring that caused a significant decrease in hen survival rate? You know the answer! Hen flocks break up and hens try to reproduce – a very dangerous period. On their own, hens lose the protection of the flock – many eyes, ears, etc. Individual hens are much easier prey for the host of turkey predators.

Start with searching for a good nest site, then laying an egg a day. Remember, turkeys nest on the ground, where many predators HUNT! After laying from 9-11 eggs, the hen begins the long (28 days) incubation period. Upon hatching, the poults are the sole responsibility of the hen. Poults roost on the ground beneath the hen for 10-14 days – a very dangerous time. Finally, the poults fly up to low limbs and roost under the hen's wings for the next week or so. At last they are off the ground for the night.

The reproductive period is very costly for hens. The nutrition demand to produce eggs (albumin, yolk, shell) and incubate them is high. Danger is present all day and night. Many (i.e., most) hens do not successfully lay, incubate eggs, or raise poults. In most years, only 22% of the hens hatched their eggs and even fewer raised poults to beyond age 14 days. In the spring of 1992, 57% of the hens raised poults – a banner year.

Most (92%) hen mortality was caused by predation, and most (69%) mortalities (i.e., deaths) occurred during the nesting and brood-rearing period. Often, it was not clear what predator killed a hen. Sign was mixed or was not readily apparent. Nesting (on or off nest) hens were killed by great-horned owls, gray fox, bobcat, feral dog, and raccoon. Two hens died of fowl pox and one was poached-slob hunter.

It was interesting to find that the raccoon was the number one turkey egg eater, and actually killed several hens on their nests. A recent study in Florida found that poult mortality averaged over 90% (! !) during the five-year period, and the raccoon was a major poult killer. Some good coon hunters might help our turkeys.

So, turkey hens have high (over 90% chance) survival rates during the non-reproductive periods. Hens, the egg layers, incubators, and brood raisers are treasures! Only a wild turkey hen can "make" us more wild turkeys. We need every hen we have so maybe some will be successful. Turkeys ain't deer.

BARNYARD CHICKENS AND THE WILD TURKEY:

People frequently ask if there is any problem with having free-ranging chickens, tame turkeys, or peafowl on areas used by wild turkeys. YES, is the answer. Do not allow barnyard birds into or on your forests or fields. Keep the domestic stock in pens! What is the problem? Chickens are carriers of histomoniasis (blackhead). Most barnyard chickens have the worm (Heterakis gallinarum) that carries the protozoan (Histomoniasis meleagridis) that causes blackhead, a deadly disease in wild turkeys. Keep chickens, domestic turkeys and other fowl off wild turkey range!

HUNTING THE WILD TURKEY

No, we are not going to discuss methods or equipment to use hunting the wild turkey. You can find that information in many places. We prefer to discuss wild turkey hunting ETHICS—turkey hunter behavior, which is very important for the future of turkeys and hunting.

HUNTING ETHICS
AND THE FUTURE OF THE TURKEY RESOURCE

Most people enjoy seeing and hearing wild turkeys, because just knowing that turkeys inhabit your area is a source of great satisfaction and pride. We are pleased that this species is thriving. Land owners and turkey hunters are thrilled to have turkeys on their property or know where turkeys can be found.

Several southern states have large turkey populations, Louisiana is still in the restoration phase, but is making great strides. With the increased turkey population, an "army" of turkey hunters has appeared. In 1988, there was an estimated 65,000 turkey hunters in Mississippi. Turkey hunters are a small percent of the total population of people—we are a minority and how we behave makes a big difference.

Since we live and hunt in the deep South, we (hunters) are still thought of as pretty good people. Most citizens think hunters and hunting is OK. However, the number of people who dislike hunting, and the number of organizations dedicated to outlawing hunting are increasing. There are only 17-18 million hunters in the entire U. S. So how we act, talk, behave, and conduct our hunting is very important.

Hunting is a large economic factor for many small towns and counties/parishes. In addition, many turkey hunting items are manufactured in the South, so protect hunting and the associated jobs. To do this, we must convince the average person that we are not all outlaws, bums, slobs, trespassers, or poachers. Our behavior is constantly being watched.

We are not going to try to tell you how to hunt to get a boss gobbler. First, we are not qualified or experienced enough. Second, few hunters are expert on calling or setting-up. You can read a dozen articles, attend seminars,

and buy video tapes to improve your hunting skills.

We are going to discuss hunting ethics/behavior—a more important subject to most people such as non-hunters, anti-hunters, land owners, and John-Q-Public! We like to think that most turkey hunters are good sportsmen. Sportsmanship relates to the qualities and conduct of a sportsman. A sportsman is one who participates—hunts turkeys in this case, and abides by the regulations and rules. Sportsmanship relates to the qualities and conduct of a sportsman. We frequently use the word ethics, a principle of <u>right</u> or <u>good</u> conduct. Do what is <u>right</u>! As a group, turkey hunters have always rated high as regards to ethical behavior, sportsmanship, fair chase, and obeying all regulations and rules of the sport.

Regulations are statutory laws, such as seasons, limits, guns, etc. Rules are just as important and are self-imposed by turkey hunters via tradition and general behavior while hunting.

You know that not all turkey hunters are good sportsmen. Seems like some wear black hats, and they give us all a bad name. We are judged to be as bad as the lawbreakers and turkey shooters.

Real turkey hunters "love" and respect turkeys and the sport of turkey hunting. Sportsmen will **NOT** do anything to degrade either the bird or the sport. You must respect yourself, the wild turkey, and turkey hunting. Sportsmen do not run rough-shod over land owners or fellow hunters. If you just need to kill a turkey, find a farmer that has barnyard turkeys, buy one, and shoot it. Then go brag on how big a gobbler ya got.

Turkey hunters will **not** be judged on how many long beards they harvest, but on the way they got the gobblers! Did you follow all the regulations? These regulations include: a valid license, the season was open, it was during the legal hours, you had permission to hunt on private land,

The Wild Turkey • 16

you used a legal gun, you did not shoot from a public road, bait was not involved, etc.

Too often we hear stories of turkey hunters exceeding the limit of gobblers in the spring season. Do you stop at the legal limit? If you get your legal limit and must continue to hunt, take a kid, a friend, your boss, etc. to attempt the harvest. To shoot a gobbler called-in by someone else is only part of turkey hunting, but you increase the interest in the sport by taking a rookie. The shooter must learn to do it alone the next time.

We must work with the next generation of hunters. We want young kids, or new hunters, to be introduced to the this wonderful sport. However, make sure the trainers/educators are ethical—sportsmen. We should be improving the behavior of current hunters and setting good examples for future hunters. Please train our youth to do it right. We spend too much time instructing them on how to kill a turkey, and not enough time on sportsmanship and rules of the sport. Our mandatory hunter education courses will have to put more stress on ethics, sportsmanship, and responsibility. You must work to improve the image of turkey hunters.

As important as regulations are, there is another set of RULES you must follow. Turkey hunting is much more than shooting a stupid jake off of a limb. This behavior is not illegal, but it sure isn't turkey hunting. Bushwhacking or ambushing a turkey from a blind in a green patch is not turkey hunting. So you killed a turkey, but have you turkey hunted? Turkey <u>shooters</u> get a gobbler then they have to dream-up a story. Turkey hunting is usually a one-on-one basis, only you know if you did it right. Let's hope your hunting stories are true and they could be told to everyone.

Sportsmen know that hens are not legal in the spring season. I know of a rookie hunter who shot a turkey, ran-up to it, and then identified it as a hen. He threw it in a briar patch, but a real nearby hunter persuaded the shooter to leave the woods and not return—take up golf. You should also know that a hen with a beard is **not** legal in Mississippi in the spring hunt. The law is specific—gobblers only. Outlaws shoot hens and use the beard as an excuse. Bearded hens lay eggs and raise wild turkey poults.

Sportsmen put something back into the sport. They join and work with conservation organizations, attend educational seminars, and work for improved turkey habitats. The National Wild Turkey Federation and its State Chapters are working hard to help the wild turkey-join'em today. The do-nothing guys just take and take not being concerned for the future.

Do you take chances when you shoot at a gobbler? Some hunters think they can kill a gobbler at 80 paces, and through thick brush. Too often I hear, "I didn't hit him, or I didn't hurt him." New bullets, improved barrels, super guns are not suppose to take the place of hunting skills and ethical behavior. You are suppose to out-wit the gobbler, bring him in-close, then take a killing head shot. Think of all the wounded or crippled gobblers that are "wasted" by people just shooting at turkeys. Sportsmen do not take chances.

Turkey hunters usually mature from "gotta get one," to going turkey hunting to enjoy the total experience: friendship with fellow hunters, owls hooting, first light, nature awakening, redbirds singing, dogwoods flowering, naps, cool spring mornings, gobbling, hens calling, and watching a gobbler do his thing. Being among'em is fantastic. A gobbler will not be taken unless he comes to you—you made him respond and seek you.

There are many other rules of the sport: don't shoot at turkeys as they fly overhead, roost on a limb, feed in a field, run away or flush when they discover you. It is legal to harvest a jake but many turkey hunters do <u>not</u> kill juvenile gobblers—JAKES. They pass-up jakes and save'em for another year. Let'em walk so they can become gobblers—a real challenge. Some jakes do it all, but just think what they would do if they were 2 or 4 years old!

Part of ethical turkey hunting is being absolutely safe. Do not take chances. No gobbler is worth shooting a person. We must not make mistakes when guns are involved. Be sure—be safe. Do not put pressure on young people or fellow hunters to bag a gobbler, this leads to wrong decision making. There is much more to turkey hunting than killing a turkey.

Ethical turkey hunters respect their fellow hunters. They do <u>not</u> go-in on a hunter already in an area. You find a truck parked—go somewhere else. Ethical hunters do not sneak in to "cut-off" a gobbler being worked by someone else. Do not ruin a hunt and create an unsafe and confrontational situation. Abide by the rules!

Turkey hunters must police their own ranks. Peer pressure is more powerful than law enforcement. You must convince your hunting buddies to do it right. Adopt strong hunting club rules regarding turkey hunting. You must report illegal activities and help our Wildlife Conservation Officers. Some yahoo kills three jakes with one shot—report him and <u>talk</u> to him. You can help save turkey hunting. Your conduct is important—sportsmanship must prevail.

MANAGEMENT OF THE WILD TURKEY

People Management

Turkey management involves people, such as land owners, the general public, public and private agencies, and turkey hunters. If you own or manage large acreage, you can manage turkey habitat. Many turkey enthusiasts do not own much land, but you still can help. We must manage man, the problem in many situations. Man directly impacts turkeys by hunting them (legal and illegal). Private land owners and state and federal conservation officers protect the turkey. You, the average citizen must also help "patrol" turkey woods and fields to protect turkeys from poachers. As a member of a hunting club, you can see to it that violators are apprehended and convicted. Do not tolerate unethical behavior by members of your club or your buddies.

You can help wildlife law enforcement by insisting that violators be given stiff sentences. Impress upon your local officials (e.g., supervisors, JPs, etc.) that you think wildlife laws are important—not to be dismissed or treated as trivia. Elect officials that believe it is important to uphold wildlife laws. Report all violations of wildlife laws to the proper authorities.

Land owners must know who is on their land and what they are doing. Don't assume Joe Blue is a good guy, find out all you can about him before permitting access to your property. You should gate/lock all your roads to limit access. Gates help keep road shooters from plundering your flocks. If you lease your lands for hunting, insist that all state laws and hunting rules be obeyed. Having ethical sportsmen on your property is a real asset. If the hunters do not obey all laws and rules, cancel the lease (have an option in your lease agreement). People (farm lease, logging, etc.) working on your property must not be allowed to carry firearms.

Land owners can help by not allowing free-ranging (wild, feral) dogs on their property. These dogs kill nesting and brood rearing hens, and ruin turkey hunts. Also, do not release game farm or pen-raised turkeys on your property. Keep all game farm birds (e.g., quail) off your property since pen-raised stock could "carry" disease to wild turkeys. All domestic birds must be in pens away from wild turkey range.

You can help the wild turkey by learning all you can about the species. Read books, magazines, and attend seminars to gain information. You should join the National Wild Turkey Federation and its state chapter to help the wild turkey. Get involved to ensure the future of this grand bird.

Turkeys tolerate disturbance, such as logging, but try to minimize disturbance during the nesting and brood rearing periods (March - June). If possible, delay mowing or bush-hogging fields until late June or even later—mid August. The new, fast and silent disk mower/conditioner is killing many incubating hens in hay fields.

Habitat Management

Man, through his land use practices (e.g., forestry, farming) dictates quantity and quality of wild turkey habitats. We dictate if turkeys have a place to live. We have altered or destroyed many acres of habitat—it is now man habitat (e.g., cities, towns, airports, malls, fields, roads, etc.). You can help by voting for conservation measures. You can save turkey habitats by your decisions on land uses. We can provide turkey habitats for future generations by providing more public lands: national forests, national and state wildlife refuges, parks, preserves, etc.

Forest Management

Turkeys inhabit all of our forest types (e.g., pine, hardwood), and eat a variety of seeds and fruits produced by trees, vines, and bushes. Turkeys and trees are a perfect match. Forest management practices affect turkey habitats.

Pine Forests

You can provide mature stands for a longer time for turkeys by increasing the rotation to yield more $$ from large sawlogs and poles. Mature pine forests should be control burned in the winter season, and about every 2 - 3 years. Complete all burning before onset of the nesting period—late February to early March. You can

obtain information and assistance on controlled burning from your county forester. Depending on your ownership size and location, it is best to burn some mature pine each year so you will have a variety of age/burned blocks.

Frequently, pine stands have too many trees or too high a basal area. Under these conditions, little sunlight can reach the forest floor, which means few seed or fruit producing plants can grow. Commercial ($) thinning will increase forage/food for turkeys.

If you harvest (e.g., clearcut) mature pine stands, regeneration can be obtained by artificial (i.e., plant seedlings) or natural (i.e., seed tree) methods. Contact your county forester or forest consultant before harvesting timber. When harvesting timber, make sure you abide by all Best Management Practices. For turkeys, leave strips of hardwood forest (i.e., streamside management zones) along all creeks, rivers, and other sensitive areas. You should have a forest management PLAN.

Pine Plantations

Some people thought that turkeys would not live in or use pine plantations (pine thickets, monocultures, biological deserts). However, turkeys do quite well in managed pine plantations. Young plantations are used for feeding (seeds, green forage, fruits), and hens nest in them. As ground vegetation density increases, and the pines take over (canopy closure), turkeys avoid plantations for several years. When the pines are about 9-years-old, and shade out much of the under story vegetation, turkeys begin to use plantations. Use by turkeys will increase as the pines age.

To improve plantations for turkeys, deer, etc., commercially thin and control burn them as soon as possible. You may want to fertilize and/or prune your plantations. Seek professional assistance! Remember, pine seeds are excellent turkey food, and managed pine will produce more seed.

Hardwood Forests

Both upland and bottomland hardwood forests are good turkey habitats, particularly as winter habitat because they have the potential to produce hard mast (e.g., acorns, pecans) and soft mast (berries). Plan to grow your hardwoods for at least 80 years and retain mature hardwoods wherever possible. Avoid conversion of hardwood forests (on hardwood sites) to pine. In managing for pine or hardwood, you should leave hardwood leave strips (e.g., SMZs) or hardwood corridors to connect mature forests or fields. Make sure turkeys can traverse your area and have some mast producing forests. Quality hardwood sawlogs are valuable but many of our hardwood stands have been ruined by hi-grading, or repeated diameter limit cuts—taking the best stems and leaving the worst. Many of our hardwood stands are in pitiful condition and need to be regenerated to provide better wood and mast for the future. Hardwood manage is not as easy as pine, but it can be done. Get help from hardwood managers.

Timber stand improvement practices (i.e., injection, sales) can be used to favor more valuable oaks—acorns. Young hardwood regeneration areas will have the same problems (i.e., too thick) as pine. Eventually, stem density will decrease and turkeys will be able to forage in the young forests. You should consider precommercial thinning, select species (oaks) and good stems to be in the new forest.

Field Management

Fields, such as pastures, hayfields, and old fields (abandoned fields) are good turkey habitats. In fact, a mixture of forests and fields is the best arrangement for turkeys. Turkeys eat most of our crops, such as soybeans, corn, millets, wheat, clovers, and rye grass. So farmers and ranchers provide food for turkeys. Please Thank your farmer/rancher friends for providing turkey habitats.

Many (3/4 million acres in Mississippi) highly erodible areas were put in the Conservation Reserve Program (CRP). Good, but wildlife lost some fine food plots. Most CRP fields were planted to pine or were annually mowed, thus, they provided little for turkeys. Some were used for nesting. In a few years the vegetation became too dense, and worse, they became rat and rabbit "factories"—good for predators of turkeys. Hope we can thin and harvest them soon.

Turkeys use fields for feeding (i.e., green forage, seeds, fruits, insects). If mast is limited in forests, turkeys move to fields in late winter. Turkeys use fields for courtship and mating in the spring. Brood hens or multiple brood flocks use fields from late spring through early fall to feed on insects, berries, green forage, and seeds. Turkeys use fields as drying-off areas after rains. Save'em fields.

Old fields usually get too rank for turkeys. You can control burn them (disk around the field), and/or you can disk the fields to stimulate new growth and decrease plant density. Do not work in the fields during the nest period.

Special Areas

You can manage spur roads and rights-of-ways (e.g., gas lines, power lines) to provide linear strips of native weeds, grasses, and vines—food and nesting places for turkeys. Burning or mowing can do the job. You should day-light your roads—remove trees at edge of the road to allow sunlight to reach the ground. This promotes growth of

forbs and grasses, and thus seeds and insects. It also improves road conditions and cut costs of road maintenance. If the roadsides are not highly erodible, you could plant clovers or bahia grass for turkeys.

You can have managed access ponds to provide food and water. You may have to control beavers to save a special swamp area for roosting and foraging by turkeys.

Following timber harvest you can plant woods roads and deck/loading sites to food plants (bahia grass, wheat, etc.) for turkeys. Make sure all roads are closed, dirt mounds do a good job. Never plant where feeding turkeys can be seen from highways.

Food Plots

Food plots are a mixed "bag" for turkeys. They can provide supplemental food, and they can be dangerous—diseases, poachers, predators, etc. Do not let food plots become killing fields. Routinely move food plots to new ground. No doubt, turkeys love a hand-out. They eat plants (rye grass, wheat, oats, clovers) usually planted for deer. They also like chufa, a sedge that produces nutlets (like peanuts) in the soil. Chufa requires more attention then most supplemental food plants. **You can obtain information on how to plant all these plants from International Paper Company or your wildlife agency, county agent, SCS, or selected qualified consultants.**

Turkeys like cracked or whole corn, but be careful. Not only is baiting illegal, it is dangerous to turkeys. We have found several turkeys that were dying of Aspergillus, a fungus that grows on corn. You have probably seen moldy corn, well it can kill turkeys. Do not pile corn out on the ground thinking you are doing turkeys a favor. In that regard, please move your food plots to "new" ground every few years. Do not have deer and turkeys feeding from the same plot, decade after decade. Parasites and pathogens can become a real problem. Burn the plot and then disk or plow it a couple of times during the growing season. Expose the parasite eggs and "germs" to the sun and fire. A number of smaller, scattered plots or openings is preferable to a few larger ones.

Some people advocate planting sawtooth oak or fruit-bearing bushes for turkeys. I would rather manage our native oaks for increased acorn production. Sawtooth oaks will produce acorns at a relatively young (7-9 years old) age, if cared for, and growing on a really good site. Trouble is there acorns drop in early fall and are all gone when turkeys need food. If you plant sawtooth, also plant wheat/clover under the trees to provide turkeys with some food for the winter. Remember openings or plots can be maintained by moving and/or burning native vegetation. However don't mow during nest and brood seasons.

Predator Management?

Predation is the major factor affecting turkey populations. Can we manage predators? We can hope that fur prices increase so trappers/hunters will increase their efforts to take raccoons, opossums, etc. Fur coats and trapping have become "bad" because of publicity and emotional attacks. We must retain trapping as a wildlife management tool. Some land owners have an Adopt a Trapper program to decrease the number of coons, opossums, etc. on their lands. The trapper takes these critters during legal seasons, prior to the turkey nesting period. Hunting clubs or land owners can help defray trappers costs.

Weather conditions during the nesting period impact the turkey hatch. We are studying the "wet hen" theory. There is a relationship between rainfall during the spring, wet hens, and predation of eggs. We can not manage weather, but might affect predator populations.

Record Keeping

As with deer management programs, you and your hunting club should keep turkey harvest records. Each gobbler taken should be weighed, and beard and spur measurements taken. Have a log book to record harvest data—who, when, where, and what. A sample data form we developed is included in this publication for your use and guidance. Call to get assistance.

Contact your Wildlife Agency (wildlife biologist) for help with a management plan. Most forest industry companies have biologists, call them. Private landowners should consider the Forest Stewardship Program, call your state's Forestry Commission Office. Get Help. Other turkey information is available from International Paper by writing to the editor.

TURKEY STEWARDSHIP AWARD

Recently, the National Wild Turkey Federation (NWTF) awarded International Paper its Industrial Forest Stewardship Award at the Federations 1994 annual meeting in Memphis. This was the first year the NWTF has presented this award. It recognized IP for its efforts to preserve wildlife and wildlife habitat on company-owned lands.

International Paper was the first forest products company to formally agree to manage its forests in ways to benefit the wild turkey and other species. IP has worked cooperatively with state wildlife agencies to restock turkeys in many southeastern states. IP was instrumental in developing and making cardboard boxes used to transport wild turkeys in restocking efforts. International Paper's plant in Springhill, Louisiana produces these special boxes.

IP and Turkeys – Transport Boxes
TALKING TURKEY

The wild turkey has made a remarkable "comeback" due to state wildlife restoration programs. Much time, money and effort was wasted trying to make tame (pen-raised) turkeys wild turkeys. The only way to have wild turkeys is to capture genetically pure, wild raised (by wild turkey hen), wild turkeys and move them to suitable habitat – then give them protection from poachers.

> To safely move the turkeys, special turkey transport boxes were designed . . .

The company recently continued a long range cooperative management agreement with Louisiana Department of Wildlife and Fisheries for propagation and management of the Eastern Wild Turkey on its land holdings in four parishes along the Mississippi River. Hens and gobblers have been trapped and released in numerous areas in the State and cooperative research work has been carried out with various organizations and State Universities. To safely move the turkeys, special turkey transport boxes were designed by National Wild Turkey Federation (NWTF) personnel in cooperation with IP people at the Springhill plant. The paraffin-coated boxes meet strict requirements for transport of wild turkeys. IP paid for the construction of the boxes.

Transport boxes are distributed through the NWTF by Dr. James Earl Kennamer, Director of Research and Management, Edgefield, SC. Boxes have been shipped to nearly all the state wildlife agencies and to several universities conducting research of the wild turkey. A nominal fee is charged to offset transportation costs. Usually, state chapters of the NWTF will pay the charges. The cooperative effort has helped the wild turkey!

The Wild Turkey • 22